Giovanni Paclo Maranɜ, William Bradshaw, Robert Midgley

Letters Written by a Turkish Spy

Vol. 3

Giovanni Paolo Marana, William Bradshaw, Robert Midgley

Letters Written by a Turkish Spy
Vol. 3

ISBN/EAN: 9783337294243

Printed in Europe, USA, Canada, Australia, Japan

Cover: Foto ©Thomas Meinert / pixelio.de

More available books at **www.hansebooks.com**

LETTERS

WRIT BY

A TURKISH SPY,

WHO LIVED

FIVE AND FORTY YEARS

UNDISCOVERED AT

PARIS:

GIVING

An Impartial Account to the Divan at Conſtantinople, of the moſt remarkable Tranſactions
of Europe : And diſcovering ſeveral Intrigues
and Secrets of the Chriſtian Courts (eſpecially
of that of France). Continued from the Year
1645, to the Year 1682.

Written originally in Arabick, tranſlated into Italian, and from thence into English, by the
Tranſlator of the Firſt Volume.

VOLUME III.

THE TWENTY-SIXTH EDITION.

LONDON:

Printed for A. Wilde, J. Brotherton and Sewell,
C. Bathurst, E. Ballard. W. Strahan, J. and
F. Rivington, W. Johnston, S. Crowder,
E. and C. Dilly, J. Wilkie, C. Corbett,
S. Bladon, W. Harris, B. Collins,
and W. Flexney.

MDCCLXX.

TO THE

READER.

OUR Arabian, having met with so kind entertainment in this Nation, since he put on the English dress, is resolved to continue his garb, and visit you as often as convenience will permit.

He brings along with him many foreign commodities, to gratify the various expectations of people. His Cargo consisting of jewels, and other rarities, which are the genuine product of the East; and some kinds of merchandise, which he has purchased here in the West, during his residence at Paris.

It will be pity to affront this honest Stranger, by raising scandals on him, as if he were a counterfeit, and I know not what. This

will

will appear inhofpitable, and unworthy of the Englifh candour and generofity.

To fpeak without an Allegory, in this Third Volume of Letters, as in the former Two, you'll find an exact continuation of modern Hiftory, acquainting you with all the memorable fieges, battles, and campaigns, that were in Europe, from the Year 1645, to 1649. As alfo, with all the remarkable Negotiations and Tranfactions of State, Embaffies, Leagues, and Overtures of Princes; the Policies and Intrigues of public Minifters, efpecially thofe of Cardinal Mazarini; the great and ftupendous Revolutions and Civil Wars in England, China, Naples, Turkey, and Paris; the prodigious Rife of a poor young beardlefs Fifherman, to the height of fovereign Power; the difmal Tragedies of an Englifh King, and Chinefe Emperor; with the Murder of a Turkifh Sultan. And all thefe intermix'd with proper and ufeful remarks, pleafant and agreeable ftories; couch'd in a ftyle, which being peculiar to the

Ara-

Arabians, cannot be match'd in any other Writings that are extant.

If his Philofophy will not bear the teft of our learned Virtuofi, yet it may pafs mufter in a Mahometan; fince it is taken for granted, That the Men of that Faith rarely apply themfelves to fuch ftudies; or, at leaft, not in the method ufed in Chriftian Schools. They may have the fame Ideas of natural things as we; but they exprefs themfelves in a different manner.

As for his Morals, they are folid and grave, and fuch as could not be reprehended even in a Chriftian Writer, if we reduce what he fays to Univerfals. For, abftracting from the particular obligations he had to his native Religion, and to the Grand Signior, whofe Slave he was, there will be found little difference between his Ethics and ours. He every where recommends loyalty, juftice, fortitude, temperance, prudence, and all thofe other virtues which are requifite to fill up the Character of a Hero, or a Saint.

And who will not bear with him;

for.

for patronizing the Religion and Interest in which he was bred? It being natural for all men, to adhere to the Notions they have suck'd in with their Mother's Milk. In this also he shews great moderation, and a more unbyafs'd temper than one would expect from a Turk; which may, in part, be ascribed to his studying in the Christian Academies, his conversation with the learned'st men in Paris, and some of the most accomplish'd persons in the world. Hence it was, that he was accus'd by his Superiors at the Ottoman Port, of inclining to Christianity or Atheism; as he takes notice, in his Apology to a religious Dignitary, in the First Letter, of the Third Book of this Volume, Page 182, to which the Reader is referred for farther satisfaction.

In his most familiar Letters, such as this last mention'd, and others to his intimate friends, you will find some expressions, discovering a certain fineness and strength of thought, which is not very common in Christian Writers. Which is an argument that the
Maho-

To the R E A D E R.

Mahometans are not all such block-heads as we take them for.

And though his Picture, which we have affix'd to our Translation, since we had the Italian Tomes, represents no extraordinary person, yet you know Juvenal's remark; " Fronti nulla " Fides." And it has been a common observation in one of the greatest Philosophers in this age, " That by his " outward aspect, no man would guess " what an illustrious soul lodged with- " in."

If you would know how the Italian came by this Picture, (for, in his Preface, he asserts it to be the true Effigies of this Arabian) he says, That being acquainted with the Secretary of Cardinal Mazarini, and frequenting his house, he saw a Picture hang in his Closet, with this Inscription at the bottom, " TITUS DE MOL- " DAVIA, CLERICUS. Ætatis suæ " LXXII." He asked the Gentleman who this Titus was, who informed him, That he was a great Traveller, and understood many Languages, especially the Sclavonian, Greek, and

Arabic;

To the R E A D E R.

Arabic; on which account Cardinal Richlieu, and his fucceffor Mazarini, had made great ufe of him; and that the latter had caufed that Picture of the Moldavian to be drawn and hung up in his Clofet, from whence he had it. Our Italian being fatisfy'd, after fome difcourfe about him, that this Stranger was the very Arabian, whofe Writings he had fo happily found, got leave of the Gentleman to have a draught of the Picture taken, by a fkilful Limner, which he afterwards placed in the Front of his Tranflation.

There is one of thefe Letters, Page 220, wants a Beginning in the Italian copy. Which the Author of that Tranflation takes notice of in his Preface, faying, That by fome accident or other, the Arabic paper had been torn afunder, and one part was miffing.

There needs no more to be faid, but to acquaint the Reader, that we are going forward with the Englifh Tranflation of thefe Letters, as faft as we can. So that in all probability, you

To the READER.

you may expect a Fourth Volume before Chriſtmas. Wherein you will
find more particular remarks on our
Engliſh affairs, with political diſ-
courſes on the original and diſſolution of governments. As alſo many
curious Paſſages during the Wars of
Paris, which have not hitherto come
to public view. In fine, you will
there be inform'd of all the remarkable Events that happen'd at that time,
either in Peace or War, on the whole
Globe.

Adieu.

A. T. A.

A

TABLE

OF THE

LETTERS AND MATTERS,

CONTAINED

IN THIS VOLUME.

BOOK I.

LETTER I.

He

Of

BOOK II.

LETTER I.

Of

The TABLE.

He

The TABLE.

BOOK

BOOK III.

LETTER I.

LETTERS

WRIT BY

A SPY AT PARIS.

BOOK I.

LETTER I.

Mahmut, an Arabian at Paris, to Nathan
Ben Saddi, a Jew at Vienna.

I Believe the news of my imprifonment might
fill thee with doubts of thy own liberty, and
make thee careful to avoid at Vienna, fuch
a misfortune as befel me at Paris. Yet if thou
wert much furprized at this accident, it is an
argument that thou art but a novice in the world,
and art yet to learn the firft rudiments of ufeful
wifdom, which teach us, That there is no Sted-
faftnefs in human affairs.

'There has nothing happen'd to me in this,
which I was not before provided for; neither
did the fuddennefs of the event make me
change countenance. I fmiled at the fulfilling
my own prefages, and went to prifon as uncon-
cern'd, as I would have gone home to my lodging. Not that I would have thee think, I was infenfible of a lofs fo afflicting as that of liberty;
but my chains did not appear fo very formidable,
having made them familiar to my thoughts long
before.

When I firſt came to Paris, I look'd on my-ſelf but as a priſoner at large, owing the freedom I had to walk about, only to the careleſsneſs of the State, and the favour of Deſtiny. So that when that indulgence was retrench'd, no new things happen'd to me. What I had expected for ſeven years together, could not ſeem ſtrange when it came to paſs.

By what I have ſaid, thou may'ſt learn to pre-pare thyſelf for the worſt events, which com-monly ſteal upon the ſecure and unthinking, be-ing wrapp'd up in greater darkneſs and ſilence, than the moments which bring them to light. Theſe ſlide away without our advertiſement, un-ſeen, unheard: Neither can our watches or di-als inform us any thing of them, 'till they are paſs'd. So there is no Index to point out to us the hidden Decrees of Fate, 'till they are accom-pliſh'd; no Ephemeris of Deſtiny, but our own experience.

Thou, and all thy nation, are ſuſpected by the Chriſtians: They eſteem you enemies of their Intereſt as well as of your Law. They deſpiſe and vilify you, calling you, The Accurſed of God. Yet they admit you as members of their com-monwealth. They receive you to the prote-ction of their laws, and entruſt you with their ſecrets, that they may ſerve themſelves of your money. Thus are you become bankers for your ſworn enemies: And while you profeſs an eternal obedience to the injunctions of Moſes, you make underhand leagues with the Diſciples of Jeſus. I do not accuſe your commerce with theſe Infidels: But, I ſay, you have reaſon to be upon your guard, when you are environed with ſo many millions of enemies. They are not ignorant of the intimacies between the Mi-niſters of the Sublime Porte, and thoſe of thy na-tion: It is common in the mouths of the French, That the Jews are the Turks Intelligencers. Thou oughteſt therefore to have a ſpecial regard to

thy

thy conduct, that no imprudent actions may expose thee to the jealousy of the State where thou resideft. That Court is full of Eyes; and thou haft need of a ftricter veil, than what thou weareft in the Synagogue. The very walls of the houfe will betray thee, and thy domeftics may prove thy greateft enemies: Yet fufpect none more than thyfelf. This will not feem harfh counfel, if thou reflecteft twice on it, there being nothing more certain, than that it is not fo eafy to defend ones felf from him in whom we confide, as from one we are jealous of. And every man is apt to put too much truft in himfelf. I believe thou art faithful, and abhorreft treachery; yet at the fame time, thou may'ft be remifs and weak: What could not be extorted from thee by an open enemy, may be difcovered by the infinuations of a pretended friend. Thy own good nature may cajole thee; and therefore it will be no fmall point of wifdom To beware of thyfelf. As for contingencies, I advife thee not to be perplexed about them, or be uneafy. Thou canft not avoid the inevitable appointments of Heaven. Only be ready for the worft that may happen, fince thou canft never be certain of any thing.

Thy predeceffor Carcoa was a man of exquifite forecaft, always on the watch, prying into the dark orb of futurities; yet an accident furprized him once, of which his ftricteft caution never gave him warning. I read it in one of his letters to the Kaimacham, which thou fenteft me from Vienna. The ftory is this: As he was one day writing Difpatches to the Port, a certain tame bird which he kept for his divertifment, fnatches from the table the paper on which he was writing to the Tefterdar: And the window being open flies with it out into the ftreet. The paper was dropped in the garden of the Auguftin Friars, the very moment when the Spanifh Ambaffador was walking there with the General of that Order. 'Tis

true, the letter was unfinifh'd, no name fubfcribed, and fo Carcoa efcaped an imminent hazard of his life.   But the fecrets therein contain'd
gave a vaft fufpicion to the Imperial Court, it being foon carried to the Principal Secretary of State,
and by him communicated to the Emperor and
Divan.   Strict inquifition was made throughout
the city for the author of that letter.   A reward
of a thoufand Rix-Dollars promis'd to any
that would difcover him.   The bird was feen by
many to fly along with a paper in her bill, but
from whence fhe came, none knew.   Nor had any
curious eye attended her uncertain motion back:
No man divining, that that paper was defign'd to
tranfmit to the ever happy Port, the moft important counfels of the German Empire.   Neither was
Carcoa's hand taken notice of, having lived very
privately, and ufed another character in his common dealings.   But how near he was to a difcovery, when he fays himfelf in his letter, That he
wanted but five words to the conclufion, where
he would have fubfcribed his name!   From hence
thou may'ft learn, That a Mariner in a tempeft,
amongft rocks and fands, runs not greater hazards, than he who acts in thy Station.

However, thou may'ft now continue thy ad-
vices to Paris, but obferve the directions of Eliachim, who brings thee this letter.   He will inform thee of whatfoever is neceffary for thee to
know, taking this journey on purpofe to prevent
the wakeful jealoufy, and active inquifition of
Cardinal Mazarini, from whom nothing can be
hid that's trufted to the Pofts.   Receive him with
fingular honour; he is an incorruptible friend of
the Ottoman Port.   From him thou fhalt learn the
fafeft method of our future correfpondence.   He
is the Apollo of thy nation; and his wifdom and
fidelity will be recorded in the Regifter of that
Empire, which fhall know no earlier period than
the Moon, whofe Crefcent is her Arms, and the
happy Omen of her encreafing Luftre.

When

When thou beholdeſt that noble Enſign of Mahomet on the top of the chief Temple of Jeſus in Vienna, let it augment thy veneration of our Law, and convince thee, that all nations muſt ſubmit to the Meſſenger of God, and Seal of the Prophets. Be faithful and wiſe, and thou canſt not miſs of happineſs.

Paris, 28th of the 7th Moon, of the Year 1645, according to the Chriſtian ſtyle.

LETTER II.

To the Kaimacham.

SINCE my releaſe, I have informed myſelf of ſome paſſages, to which I was a ſtranger during my reſtraint. The Tranſylvanian Agent continues ſtill at this Court; and his Negotiation is not now a Secret. Monſieur Croiſſy is gone Ambaſſador Extraordinary to Prince Ragotſki, on the ſame errand from this Crown. The ſubject matter of both their Embaſſies, is a League. Cardinal Mazarini ſuſpected tergiverſation in that Prince, and that he would privately treat with the Emperor, if the Grand Signior ſhould withdraw his aſſiſtance and protection from him ; or if he himſelf ſhould grow weary of the war. Wherefore Monſieur Croiſſy, according to the Cardinal's inſtructions would not ſign the League, till Ragotſki had called home his Ambaſſadors, who were treating with the Imperialiſts at Tyrne, and ſent away the German Envoy from his camp.

The League being concluded ; he inſiſted on the neceſſity the Prince lay under, of marching his army nearer to Torſtenfon the Swediſh General, that ſo they might ſupport one another againſt the German forces.

This

This was the pretence; but in reality it was defigned to engage the Tranfylvanians beyond the power of a retreat, and to poft them under the eye of the Swedifh General, who foon after poffeffed himfelf of Tyrne, the place appointed for treaty between the Imperialifts and Prince Ragotfki.

It is a town in the Lower Hungary, not far from Prefburgh. The Swedes enter'd this place the 17th of the 5th Moon, but left a garrifon in it of feven hundred Hungarian horfe, and three hundred foot, according to their Articles with the befieged.

Thefe were foon forc'd to quit the town by Count Forgatfch, an Imperialift, the Swedes and Tranfylvanians being march'd a great diftance off: And 'tis faid, this Hungarian garrifon yielded not unwillingly to the Imperial arms.

'Tis certain, General Torftenfon puts but fmall confidence in the Hungarian foldiers: For above fix hundred of the common fort deferted him, the 29th of the 5th Moon, and the reft raifed fuch frequent tumults and mutinies, that their commander ftood in more fear of them, than of their enemies. It's reported likewife, That there has been lately no good underftanding between Ragotfki and Torftenfon, about the defigned fiege of Prefburgh: The former feeming too much to favour the Hungarians, and being rather inclined to carry his arms into the Emperor's hereditary countries. Yet he would not confent, that Prefburgh fhould be in the hands of the Swedes.

The French fay, that the Prince is humorous, and wavering, yet of a fair intention, but that the greateft part of his officers are corrupted by the Emperor: And that therefore both they and the common foldiers were for peace; only his wife, his fon, and fome few of his counfellors perfuaded him to adhere to the Swedes.

They add, that the young Prince, being inftructed by his mother, one day in a full affembly of the

the chief commanders, made the following oration, Ragotſki himſelf being alſo preſent.

" PErmit me, moſt ſerene and illuſtrious
" Prince, my Royal Father, to perform the
" part of a dutiful ſon, a faithful counſellor,
" and a loyal ſubject. The Law of Nature and
" of Nations entitles you to my Obedience ; and
" the particular honour you have done me, in ad-
" mitting me to your cabinet, obliges me to ex-
" emplify it, in an humble remonſtrance of my
" ſentiments, at a time when the intereſt of
" Tranſylvania calls for freedom of advice.
" It is with no ſmall complacency that I now
" behold you encompaſſed with a circle of Heroes,
" whoſe valour and fidelity may give ſuch a lu-
" ſtre to your victorious arms, as ſhall eclipſe the
" glory of the Roman and Grecian conquerors.
" The Alexanders, Cæſars, Scipios, and Hannibals,
" ſhall no longer draw the world into an admi-
" ration of their obſolete atchievements. The
" Regiſter of your Deeds ſhall foil their antiquated
" Hiſtories; whilſt Plutarch, Tacitus, and Livy,
" muſt veil to modern Pens, the Recorders of your
" matchleſs Actions.
" Let not the crafty inſinuations of the Ger-
" man Court, warp your reſolutions, and cajole
" you with the deceitful umbrages to peace, only
" to gain time, that they may more ſucceſsfully
" carry on the war. Neither ſuffer yourſelves,
" already in part victorious, to be amus'd with
" feign'd treaties and overtures, which you can-
" not but ſuſpect. We are now in a condition
" to give the law, and ſhall fortune turn the
" ſcale, it will ſtill be in our power to make
" our own terms of compoſition. The Alliance
" of Sweden and France has rais'd us to a ca-
" pacity of braving all Europe ; whilſt the one
" with a potent army on the Rhine, the other on
" the Danube, keep the Imperialiſts in ſuch perpe-
B 4 " tual

" tual actions, that it will be impoffible for them
" to barrier Germany from our conquering arms.
" Now is the time to raife Tranfylvania above
" the title of a Tributary Province, and reftore
" this Kingdom to her ancient renown. If we
" mifs this opportunity, we muft for ever be
" Slaves to the Turks or Germans. Let us not
" feek any longer protection, but from the juftice
" of our caufe, and the dint of our fwords.
" Let not France and Sweden boaft of their Tu-
" renne, their Torftenfon, as if no other Nations
" could furnifh the world with famous Generals!
" Whilft Prince Ragotfki lives, and lives at the
" head of fuch an army, your fidelity and cou-
" rage fhall render his name more terrible than
" that of Tamerlane, and his attempts more pro-
" fperous than thofe of Scanderbeg. And our
" pofterity fhall be obliged to raife Pyramids to
" your honour ; and from your prefent atchieve-
" ments to date a new Epocha, the eternal Memoir
" of Tranfylvania's Redemption. „

'Tis faid, that Ragotfki was not very well
pleafed with his fon's fpeech, fufpecting that he
held fome private correfpondence with Torftenfon, for whom he had no great affection. Laft
Moon he infifted earneftly on the money and men
promifed him by Rebenftock. But General Torftenfon thought it fufficient, that he himfelf was fo
near him with his forces. Yet left he fhould
take an occafion of difcontent, he fent him a
fupply of money ; though he was not without
fome apprehenfions that the Prince, having received it, would under-hand treat with the Emperor.

'Tis faid here, that a Chiaus was arrived in the
Tranfylvanian camp, exprefly forbidding Ragotfki
to enter into the Hereditary Provinces of the
Emperor. But that he, trufting to the ftrength of
his army, (which confifts of five and twenty
thoufand Germans, Tranfylvanians, Hungarians,

and

and Walachians) was refolved to purfue his firft
refolution.

Thou knoweft what reafons the Port had to
fend him this prohibition. The French fay, 'twas
out of fear that he would join with the Emperor's
forces.

By this thou mayeft know what opinion the
Infidels entertain of the meafures taken by the Sovereign Divan. They defcant at liberty, whilft
I fend up Vows to Heaven for the exaltation of
the Ottoman Empire.

Paris, 4th of the 8th Moon,
  of the Year 1645.

LETTER III.

To the Inftructed in all Knowledge; the Venerable Mufti.

HAIL, Holy Interpreter of the Sacred Law;
  may the Divine Light guide thee beyond
the errors of Human Frailty. I am amongft Jn-
fidels, enemies to the truth; who yet feem as
certain of being in the right, as thou art fure they
are in the wrong.. They hate us with an inevitable hatred. I muft diffemble my refentments;
whilft, with the loweft proftrations to the Unity,
I celebrate his glorious mercy, who has fent us
fuch a Star to guide our Feet into the Way of
Peace.

The Chriftians fcoff at the Faithful People, as divided into feveral Sects. Would my death could
wipe out thofe reproaches, and vindicate the
honour of the Holy Profeffion. I could retort,
that error fhews itfelf infinite in them; but I muft
hold my peace, and reftrain myfelf, left my zeal
tranfport me beyond difcretion; remembring I am
not fent here to difpute, but to act fecretly for my

B 5   Great

Great Mafter, whofe Empire be extended over all the habitable World.

These poor wretches boaft much of their Traditions, their Sacred Synods and Fathers, as if we ever wanted Holy Men, working Wonders, and penetrating into the profoundeft Myfteries, but only wiping their Eyes with the Duft of their Feet.

They talk much of Faith and Reafon ; at which I fmile, as knowing it to be only Education. Yet, as the worft of people have fomething that is good, fo thefe are not wholly deftitute of Devotion. They pray often, but not fo often as the True Believers ; it being, as thou knoweft, a juft exception againft a witnefs amongft us, That he prays not fix times a day. They pray to men and women deceafed, whereas thou knoweft, there is no Deity but one. They faft often, but not fo ftrictly as the affifted with the virtue of the Supreme Difpenfer of Graces. They are charitable, but this hinders them not from excluding all from the bleft Abodes, who are not of their Belief: Whereas thou affirmeft (who art the Refolver of all the Problems of Faith) that it will go well at the laft day with all honeft people, feeing thefe have all the fame Objects of Worfhip ; and their different Religions are but as fo many different Ways, which lead a man to the fame Place of Reft, like various Roads to the fame City.

Thefe Chriftians whip themfelves often with fmall cords ; which humour, fay they, was fet on foot by an Hermit's preaching and example. Not many countries diftant from that where I am, there happen'd fuch an odd inftance of this extravagant zeal (which was to be heighten'd, it feems, with the fumes of wine) as plainly juftifies our Prophet's wifdom, in charging the Faithful to avoid it. It was particularly the cuftom of feveral people in this place, in their Proceffions, to whip themfelves, till the blood ftreamed down their frocks, which were fo made, as to cover their faces, and leave only their backs bare. One

of

of these Zealots, distrusting the firmness of his constitution, had taken such large draughts of this intoxicating liquor, that reeling up and down with his whip in his hand, and his head against the walls, he was follow'd by all the boys of the town hooting after him, which so lessened the repute of this sottish Religion, as made them abstain for the future from this pompous usage of it. What low thoughts have these people of the Almighty Lord of All; when, allowing him to be Omnipotent, yet represent him to themselves and others, as delighting in cruelty; whereas, thou knowest, this passion is only to be found among the weak and miserable.

That the Divine Preserver of men may continue thee long for the edification of his Elect, are the passionate wishes of the meanest of thy servants, Mahmut.

Paris, 4th of the 8th Moon,
   of the Year 1645.

LETTER IV.

To Muftapha Berber Aga.

WOULD to GOD I could converse with thee face to face in the Seraglio, as in former times. I vent my passionate wishes to Conftantinople, that happy residence of my best friends, the nursery of my childhood, the school of my youth, and, I hope, the future repository of my old age. When I think of that city, 'tis with a passion hardly second to that which I cherish for the place of my nativity. In Arabia, 'tis true, I firft saw the light of the Sun, but 'twas in Greece I received the more friendly Illumination of the Moon, the Splendors of the True Faith; which, though they disclose not to us so clear a prospect of the Earth and all its gaieties;

B 6

ties; yet they prefent us with an unveiled difcovery of the Heavens and Stars; fhewing us Paradife, with its glittering inhabitants, the pur-
pled Colonies of True Believers, Champions and
Martyrs of the Eternal Unity. In the Defart
I left my father, or rather he left me, before
I found myfelf, being but an infant when he
died, but in the city I found friends, which is
not a lefs endearing title. He gave me but my
birth, whereby I entered on the ftage of miferies; with which he foon after left me to ftruggle,
before I could diftinguifh mifery from happinefs. But they gave me education, which taught
me how to fhun thofe evils, which are the natural
confequences of our birth. So that in the main,
I am more indebted to them than to him. Let
it be how it will, I cannot ceafe to love them,
and often wifh myfelf with them. This is a
fecond nature. And becaufe I cannot have my
defires fulfill'd in that, I gratify myfelf by often
writing to them. Should I make comparifons,
thou wilt fay, I am a flatterer. Suffice it to tell
thee, that thou art one of the number, whofe
remembrance affects me with fenfible complacency. Yet I cannot write to thee, nor any
of my friends, fo often as I would, without en-
trenching on the obligations I have to the other
Minifters of the Sublime Porte. I fend Difpatches
to all by turns, facrificing my private regards
to the Expectations of the State, and the Pleafure
of my Superiors.

Had I been at liberty, I could have fent thee
the earlieft news, of the flaughter which the Germans made three Moons ago in the French army
at Margentheim. 'Tis not too late now to fay
fomething of it. The Imperalifts owe that triumph to the candour of Turenne, and the degenerate craft of the Duke of Bavaria; who, to lull
the French in a fatal fecurity, fent an Agent into
France to negotiate a Peace, with deceitful overtures and umbrages; commanding alfo, that none

of

of his foldiers fhould dare to call the French their enemies. Yet fome lay the blame of this over-throw to the Swedes, whofe unfeafonable fufpi-cion of a private Treaty between the French and Germans, hinder'd Torftenfon from joining with the former; and expos'd Turenne, with his raw and unexperienc'd forces, to the numerous army of veteran Imperialifts.

'Twas a fatal engagement, and the French loft many brave men; befides an hundred and fifty commanders taken prifoners, fifteen hundred of the common foldiers, fifty enfigns, with many waggons, and four mules laden with money.

It is reported, that whilft Turenne, in the gene-ral retreat and flights of his army, betook him-felf to Margentheim, as he lay on his bed the firft night, one of his officers was coming to alarm him with the news of the Germans approach to that town, but unfortunately ftumbled at his chamber door, with the noife of which Turenne awaked; and fearing fome attempt on his life, leaping off his bed with his drawn fword, and making toward the door, juft as the officer open'd it, he run him into the heart. By which miftake he himfelf, and the troops that were in the town with him, had like to have fallen into the hands of the Bavarians. But receiving notice of their approach accidentally by fome other means, he withdrew his troops out of the town by a contrary road, and efcaped the pur-fuit of his enemies.

This victory has given new courage to the Im-perialifts, and has not much difpirited the French, who are by this lofs enflamed with greater ardors, me-ditating a fpeedy revenge. The Genius of this Court feems to be undaunted, breathing nothing but war.

I fhall not fail to fend thee fuch intelligence, as will demonftrate, that Mahmut paffes not away his time in vain.

I pray the Sovereign of as many Empires as there be Worlds, to diftinguifh thee by fome particular

mark

mark of his favour, from the crowd of those
he makes happy.

Paris, 4th of the 8th Moon,
of the Year 1645.

LETTER V.
To Shahim Iftham, a Black Eunuch.

AT length thou haft condefcended to beg my
pardon, for the calumnies thy tongue has
loaded me with. I am not ill pleafed with thy
letter. It abounds with elegant expreffions of
thy forrow, for an offence to which thou hadft
no provocation. Thy fubmiffion, though late,
abates my refentment ; and, if thou performeft
thy promife, 'tis banifhed. The firft crime fo
ingenuoufly acknowledg'd, claims a title to for-
givenefs. Let eternal oblivion feal it. I am not
by nature revengeful. I rather blufh for fhame,
than grow pale with anger at him that injures
me. Yet felf-prefervation will rouze our choler,
which is the moft active humour, and precipi-
tates many to violent courfes. The effect it has
on me, is to put me on my guard, left he who
has wronged me, without any figns of repen-
tance, fhould continue his malice to my deftruction. But thou haft difperfed all my fufpi-
cions by thy feafonable addrefs ; and if I cannot
pronounce thee innocent, I will believe thou art
not incorrigible. The beft advice I can give
thee is, henceforwards to attend to thy own affairs, and refrain from thofe of others ; remembring the Arabian proverb, He that peeps in at
his Neighbour's Window, may chance to lofe his
Eyes. There is a great deal of wifdom couch'd
in thefe fhort fentences. They are not the product of one man's experience, nor of a few;
but they are the refult of univerfal obfervation.
And our country has been happy above others

in

in the choice of her Proverbs. This that I mention'd, is peculiar to the Eaſt, yet I can produce an inſtance, whereby 'twas lately verified in the Weſt.

There is hardly a night paſſes in this populous city, wherein ſome murder is not committed in the ſtreet. Two nights ago a man was found dead on the ground : whereupon a tumult was gather'd about his bleeding carcaſe. Amongſt the reſt, a fellow came crowding in, inquiſitive what ſhould be the matter. Thoſe who ſtood by beholding his cloaths bloody, which he was not ſenſible of himſelf, ſeized on him as the murderer. His wild looks encreaſed their jealouſy, and the incoherent words with which he endeavour'd to excuſe himſelf, render'd him guilty in the judgment of the rabble. They carried him before a Cadi, by whom he was ſtrictly examin'd : He ſtoutly denied the fact; and no proof could be brought againſt him, but his ſtained cloaths. 'Tis the cuſtom here, to put to the torture perſons ſuſpected of capital crimes, in order to draw a confeſſion of the truth. This they did to this poor wretch ; and in the extremity of his pains, he acknowledged, he had killed his wife that evening, but was altogether innocent of this poor man's death, who was murder'd in the ſtreet. All the torments they inflicted, could force no other confeſſion from him, ſave that which his real guilt prompted him to make. For which he was condemn'd to death, according to the laws. Thou ſeeſt by this, that had he gone about his buſineſs, without prying into other men's matters, he might have eſcap'd a diſcovery. But that meddling itch of the impudent betray'd him (not without the particular direction of Fate) to a death, which indeed he merited, but not on the ſcore of the murder'd man, whom he went out of his way to ſee.

Thou wilt ſay, this ſtory is not applicable to thy caſe, ſince thou haſt never yet embru'd thy hands

hands in any man's blood. I tell thee, what I have faid, was not defigned as a reflection on thy paft offence (let it be forgotten) ; but as a caution for the future, not to engage thyfelf in matters out of thy fphere. For a bufy body is never without troubles.

Above all, I counfel thee to practife the government of the tongue, which is a great virtue, efpecially in the Courts of Princes. The Arabians fay, That the wife man's foul repofes at the Root of his Tongue ; but a fool's is ever dancing on the Tip.

Thou haft no reafon to take in ill part the freedom with which I advife thee for thy good; unlefs thou thinkeft thyfeif too old to learn. But, I have a better opinion of thee, than to rank thee among Pythagoras's affes.

I have faid enough for a friend ; too much for an enemy. It is in thy own choice to make me which thou pleafeft. Adieu.

Paris, 4th of the 8th Moon,
of the Year 1645.

LETTER VI.

To Zelim of Rhodes, Captain of a Galley.

THOU haft never vouchfafed to acknowledge the advice I fent thee fome years ago, of a Chriftian's defign againft thy life. Perhaps he wanted an opportunity, to put his revenge in execution that way ; and therefore the caution I gave thee look'd like a falfe alarm. Thou trufteft in thy courage, the ftrength of thy veffel, the multitude and fidelity of thy Slaves, and thinkeft thyfelf invulnerable. But let me tell thee, That neither thy courage, nor thy veffel, can defend thee from the Stroke of Deftiny ;

ftiny; and thou haft no greater enemies than thofe who eat thy bread. Whether it be the continuance of thy cruelty, or the natural regret of fervitude has render'd them fo, I know not; but if what I am informed of be true, thou art the miferableft man in the world. Wert thou only in danger to lofe thy life by a ftab, a bullet, or the fwift effects of poifon, it would be a happinefs, in comparifon of the method that is now taken to deftroy thee. And the invifible death which thou wert formerly to receive from a Prayer-Book, would have been foft as the ftroke of Cupid's arrow, in refpect of the tragical and unheard of fate, which is now preparing for thee. Think not I go about to amufe or affright thee with Chimæra's and Tales, fuch as nurfes ufe to awe their children into compliance and good manners. What I tell thee is matter of fact, and confirmed by many letters from Italy, to feveral eminent Merchants in Paris : I have feen fome of them, and hear that the reft agree in the fame relation.

They give an account, That at Naples, on the fecond of the laft Moon, three Witches were feized, and accufed of practifing Diabolical Arts; of enchanting feveral perfons; of doing great mifchief; and, in fine, of having private commerce with the Devil. They ftoutly denied all at firft, and made very fubtle and plaufible apologies. Infomuch, as the Inquifitors were almoft perfuaded of their innocence; till it was fuggefted, that their houfes fhould be fearch'd. Officers were fent accordingly; who, after a narrow fcrutiny, found fome Magical books, feveral vials of ftrange liquors, pots of ointment; with an Image of Wax, refembling a man, but partly melted. There were imprinted on the breaft of the Image feveral unknown characters, figures and Magical fymbols: And on the forehead was to be read Z E L E M E B E N   S A G R A N. All thefe were brought, and expofed before the Inquifitors; (of whofe Office

fice thou art not ignorant) great deliberation was
had about this unuſual emergency. The Imaums
and Cheiks were ſent for and conſulted. The
Witches were examined apart, and put to the
torture, as is the cuſtom in capital crimes:
Admirable was their conſtancy for a conſiderable
time; but at length, overcome by the continuance and ſharpneſs of their pains, they confeſſed they had for ſome years practis'd Magic
Arts, convers'd with familiar Spirits, raiſed tem-
peſts, earthquakes, and done other wicked feats.
Being examin'd about the Image of Wax, they
declared, That it was the Image of a Turkiſh
Captain of a Galley whoſe name was written on
the forehead: And that they were hired by certain
Italians, who had been ſlaves in the Galley of the
ſaid Captain, to bewitch him to death, in the
moſt lingring method they could invent; that in
order to this, they had made this Image; that
every night they met together, with a fourth
of their gang (who was not to be found) and
made a fire of the Bones of dead Men, which they
ſtole from the Graves and Charnel Houſes. That
they laid this Image down at a convenient diſtance before this fire, repeating certain Magical
Words and Charms; and as this Image gradually
melted, ſo the body of the ſaid Turkiſh Captain
did inſenſibly waſte and decay. And, to add to his
lingring death an intolerable torment, they ba-
ſted the melted Image with the oils, and other
liquors which were contained in the vials and
pots: That by this means he was perpetually
racked with moſt pungent and acute pains in
his bowels, head, and all parts of his body,
raging under moſt violent fevers, inſatiable thirſt,
and want of ſleep. Finally, That this lingring
kind of death would continue, as long as they
pleas'd to protract the diſſolution of the Waxen
Image.

This Confeſſion, tho' extorted from the Witches
in the midſt of inſufferable torments, yet was deliver'd

liver'd without any inconfiftencies, and with all
the demonftrations of a real Penitence. And being feconded with the teftimonies of many cre-
dible witneffes, who had overfeen them in fome
of their nocturnal Ceremonies ; the Inquifitors
moved with a juft horror of fo nefandous abominations, fentenc'd them To be burnt, and their
afhes to be fcatter'd into the fea. Which was accordingly executed on the fixth of the laft Moon,
in the prefence of infinite fpectators.

The news of this extraordinary event is frefh
in the mouths of almoft all the inhabitants of this
city ; yet no man, I dare fay, hears it with that
concern for the Turkifh Captain, as I do. Even
thofe among the Chriftians who abhor witchcraft,
would neverthelefs rejoice, if not only thou, but
all the Muffulmans were deftroyed with Enchantments ; fince they can never hope it will come to
pafs by fuccefs of their arms.

I am not credulous of every ftory, that is related of Witches, being fatisfied, That Superftition
and Ignorance has lifted many in that infernal
number, who were innocent, and never deferv'd
it ; fome having been forced by racks and tortures to confefs themfelves guilty of practifing Enchantments, when, after their execution, there
have appear'd evident proofs to the contrary. Yet
I cannot be fure, but that there have been fome
in all ages and nations, who have entered into
leagues and affociations with Devils, and have
been enabled thereby to perform things above
the power of Nature. However, I have a particular defire to hear from thee, and to be informed,
whether thou haft experienc'd the effect of their
Enchantments. If thou haft not, blefs thy ftars
that thou wert born and bred a Muffulman, againft
whom the Magic of the Infidels cannot prevail ;
and that thou haft fwallowed the Impreffion of Mahomet's Seal, which is of force to diffolve and
make invalid, all the Charms of Men and Devils.
But if thou haft felt the force of their Enchantments,
and

and pineſt away with unaccountable pains and lan-
guors, then think with thyſelf, that thou art defective in keeping ſome Point of our Holy Law ;
that Mahomet is angry with thee, withdraws his
protection, and expoſes thee to the malice of evil
Spirits. Neither perſuade thyſelf, That becauſe
the Three Witches are put to death, thou ſhalt
preſently recover thy former health and eaſe again:
For ſo long as there is a Fourth living, and out of
the reach of Juſtice, thou art not ſafe. Nay, if
ſhe were taken and executed too, ſo long as thy
enemies are yet alive, who firſt employed theſe
Hags, thou art ſtill at their mercy. They will
ſearch every corner of Italy, and of all Europe,
but they will find inſtruments of their revenge.
They will rummage Hell itſelf, to gratify their
fury. The beſt counſel I can give thee in this
caſe is, to pacify thine enemies, by extraordinary acts of civility to the Chriſtians, where-ever
thou meeteſt them ; by uſing thy Slaves mildly,
and giving them their freedom, after a limited
time of ſervice, without exacting a ranſom,
which neither they nor their relations and friends
can ever be able to pay. This will abate the ran-
cour of the Infidels, and turn their revenge into
kindneſs and love. Thou wilt every where be
free from dangers ; and thoſe very perſons, who
now ſtudy all means to take away thy life,
will then hazard their own, to preſerve thee from
death.

Think not that I go about to perſuade thee to
change temper with thy Slaves, and from the
reſolution and bravery of a true Muſſulman, to
ſink into the abject timorouſneſs of a Chriſtian.
Be fearful only of thyſelf, and ſtand in awe of
none more than of thy own Conſcience. There is
a Cato in every man, a ſevere Cenſor of his manners ; and he that reverences this Judge, will ſeldom do any thing he need to repent of. Let not
the Authority of any Station tempt thee to be cruel
and unjuſt ; but, in all things, Do as thou wouldſt
be

be done unto. This is a Precept engraven on every
man's heart; and he whofe actions write after this
copy, will always be at eafe here, and tranfcen-
dently happy hereafter. Follow this Rule, and
thou wilt experience the Effect. Adieu.

Paris, 1ft of the 9th Moon,
    of the Year 1645.

LETTER VII.

To the Invincible Vizir Azem.

IF one may judge of future events, by applying
to them the fymptoms of things paft; and if
a man may compare one kingdom with another,
I fhould think that France will in time extend the
Limits of her Empire, as far as any of the four
great Monarchies, that have been recorded in Hiftories for the univerfal fway. I will not fay, as far
as the wide-ftretch'd Empire of the ever-victorious
Ofmans. Yet the Genius of this nation feems
in fome manner to infpire the French with as ar-
dent a thirft of glory and conqueft, as that,
which has in all ages appear'd to be the infepa-
rable Virtue of the Muffulmans. They prefs forward to the mark for which they take up arms ;
that is, to fubdue all before them, and lay kingdoms, provinces and cities, at the feet of their
Sovereign. They are not difcouraged at difficulties
and loffes. The checks and oppofitions they
meet with, do but animate them with new and frefh
vigours. So that it is become a fure prognoftic
of fome great fuccefs to that nation, when at any
time they receive ill news from their armies. In
this, their courage feems to be of the quality of
Naptha, which by pouring on of water takes fire,
although, thou knoweft, thefe two Elements be
contrary to each other. So this warlike people,
                                          inftead

inſtead of being dejected, or made timorous by any defeat given to their armies, are rather inflamed with more active and valiant reſolutions, as will appear by the repulſe given them by the Duke of Bavaria, not many Moons ago.

As ſoon as that news arrived in this city, one would have expected to have ſeen ſome tokens of fear in the people, but it wrought a contrary effect. No tears of women and children, no compaſſionate ſighs for their ſlain huſbands, fathers, or other relations ; no down-caſt looks, or ominous ſhaking of heads ; no melancholy whiſpers or portentous ſtories were murmured in the ears of the multitude : But all things appeared lively and proſperous : The very women exciting the young men to liſt themſelves ſoldiers, and the boys in the ſtreets making all their paſtimes conſiſt in imitating the Men of Arms, and learning the Diſcipline of War. There was no need to force men to the field. No ſooner was the King's intentions to raiſe new forces divulged in the Provinces, but thouſands came voluntarily, and took up arms, chuſing rather to ſeek honourable deaths in the toils and hazards of war, than to lead inglorious lives at home, in the ſoft enjoyments of peace.

Theſe things appeared to me as certain preſages of the riſing greatneſs of this Monarchy, and an evident ſign that the French nation in this age, ſhall out-do their Anceſtors in warlike Deeds.

The ſtage of that bloody combat, between the forces of the Duke of Bavaria, and thoſe under the command of Mareſchal Turenne, was Mergentheim. Since which there has been a more fierce encounter between the French and Imperialiſts at Allerſheim. Wherein the former have recovered the honour they ſeemed to have loſt in the ſpring, owing much to the bravery of the Landgrave of Heſſe-Caſſel, who, with his regiments, had a conſiderable ſhare in the actions of this

day ;

day ; and therefore he has been prefented with magnificent gifts by the Queen Regent. The Bavarians loft in this battle above two thoufand common foldiers, befides many officers of note. On the French fide, the Duke of Enguien, (who had newly joined his forces to thofe of Turenne) was wounded in the arm, with two other commanders. Monfieur Grammond was taken prifoner, but honourably treated, and fent away with prefents by the Duke of Bavaria, together with inftructions about a neutrality, who is exchanged for a German of equal quality. The French have alfo loft in this battle above a thoufand of the common foldiers ; fo that their victory coft them dear.

The Duke of Enguien, notwithftanding his wounds, marches on the next day with his army to Norlinghen, offering that town a neutrality, and liberty for the garrifon to march out, which confifted of three hundred Bavarians. But receiving a fierce anfwer from the Governor, he caufed the approaches to be made in order to an affault, which was begun that very night, and a breach made in the walls ; upon which the inhabitants were forced to intercede with the Duke, that there might be a ceffation of violence till the next morning, promifing, that then the foldiers fhould furrender at difcretion : which was done accordingly.

There he tarried eight days to refrefh his army. Then he marched to Dunkenfpule, which was defended by a garrifon of five hundred Bavarians. He took this place by ftorm, yet gave quarters to the foldiers, who laid down their arms, and yielded themfelves prifoners. Leaving a garrifon of three hundred French in the town, he remov'd his forces toward Heilbrun. But in regard this place was defended by fifteen hundred men, he forbore to affault it, and only quartered his army in the neighbouring villages.

Since

Since that time, which was about the middle of the laſt Moon, there has been no conſiderable action between the French and the Germans. Yet thoſe who pretend to be vers'd in military affairs, laugh at the ill conduct of the Arch-Duke Leopold, who, when he had the French ſhut up in a narrow Streight, through which it was impoſſible for them to paſs but by ſingle files, neglected that opportunity to cut them off, deferring the victory (whereof he was too ſecure) till the next day, by reaſon of the preſent wearineſs of his ſoldiers. In the mean time Turenne, with his whole army, paſs'd the Streight in the middle of the night, and came to Philipſburgh.

This over-ſight of the General is much talk'd of, becauſe, had he purſu'd his advantage he had not only entirely defeated the French, but in all probability, falling with the whole force of the Empire on the Swedes, he had likewiſe vanquiſh'd them, and ſo put an end to the war. But it ſeems as if the inſcrutable Providence had determined to infatuate the minds of the Germans, and reſerve thoſe two potent nations, their enemies, to be a farther Scourge to the Empire.

Adieu, great Guardian of the eternal Monarchy, and believe Mahmut, when he ſolemnly ſwears by Mount Sinai, and by the Tenth Night of the Moon, that he adores thy conſummate virtue and wiſdom, which never fail thee in extremities.

Paris, 8th of the 9th Moon,
    of the Year 1645.

LETTER VIII.

To Cara Hali, a Phyſician, at Conſtantinople.

I AM weary of writing news of battles and ſieges to the Grandees, and I know, thou ſeldom troubleſt thyſelf with the care of foreign tranſ-

tranfactions. Befides, I have no certain intelligence of moment to communicate. But I can acquaint thee with fomething more agreeable to thy
Studies and Genius.

Here is a man in this city who was not born
blind, but by fome ill hap loft the ufe of his
eyes. Yet Nature feems to have recompenfed
that misfortune in the exquifitenefs of his Feel-
ing. Thou would'ft fay he carried his eyes in his
fingers ends, fince he diftinguifhes thofe things
by his Touch, which are the only proper objects
of Sight. Believe me, I think, there can be no
deceit of confederacy, whereby he might blind
others, inftead of being fo himfelf. I faw him
muffled up with a napkin which covered all his
face, then divers pieces of Eaftern filks, of various colours, were laid on the table before
him. He felt them attentively, and told us the
colour of each piece exactly. I who was never
over credulous of extraordinary pretences, fufpecting that either the finenefs of the linen
which veiled his face, might give him fome
glimpfe of the different colours, or that fome
by-ftander, with appointed figns, might inform
him, caufed all the company to withdraw, except
a learned Dervife, who was intimate with me. We
threw a thick velvet mantle over his face which
reached down to his navel, girding it about his
waift, fo as to leave his arms at liberty. Then
I procured fmall fhreds of filks, fuch as I could
conceal in the palm of my hand: Thefe I
caufed him to touch with his fingers, brought up
as high as his chin, fo that 'twas impoffible for
him to fee them, had he had the ufe of his
eyes; yet he made not the leaft miftake in five
feveral colours. We changed the order of the
filks, and fometimes gave him the fame piece
four or five times together; yet, as foon as
he had felt it, he readily told us, 'twas the fame
colour.

I tell thee, O learned Hali, such an uncommon experiment afforded me matter both of delight and wonder. I concluded from hence, that Nature is no niggard in her gifts, but supplies the defects of one fenfe, by the fuper-abundant accuracy of another. We afked this blind perfon, By what diftinction he thus knew one colour from another without the help of his eyes. He was not able to exprefs the particular manner of this difcriminating fenfation ; but only told us in general, that he felt as much difference between the red filk and black, as he had formerly done during the enjoyment of his eye-fight between the filks of Perfia and the fine linen of Europe : Which, thou knoweft, are as different to the touch as fine paper and vellum.

Thou that daily pryeft into the faculties of human bodies, art better able to judge whether this man's excellency lay in the tenuity and finenefs of his fkin, the fubtilty of his fpirits, or fome unufual, powerful, yet delicate energy of his foul ; or, whether it confifted in all thefe together.

The Dervife who was with me, feemed not much to admire at this rare quality of the blind man : Telling me moreover, that about ten years ago in his travels, he had feen a blind Statuary at Florence, who undertook to make the refemblance of an Image in the chief Temple of that city, which he finifh'd fo much to the life, that his work could no otherwife be diftinguifh'd from the original, than by the difference of the materials, that being alabafter, his white clay, which he fo temper'd and moulded with his fingers, as he continually felt of the other, that no lineament was left unexprefs'd.

Indeed, when I reflected on our Mutes in the Seraglio, and the unaccountable fagacity with which they apprehended thofe words which they never heard, I ceas'd to be furpris'd at what I had feen the blind man perform, or what the Dervife had

had said of the Statuary. I remember in Sultan Amurath's time there was a Mute, in whom the Grand Signior took infinite delight. For, besides a thousand pretty gestures and tricks with which she used to divert that Prince, he often made her his Secretary, employing her in writing letters to his Bassa's and others, whilst he dictated to her by signs. Although she could never receive the sound of words, nor utter any that were articulate; yet I have seen her transcribe a whole Chapter in the Alcoran, containing a hundred and seventy Versicles, in as fine a character, as the most celebrated Scribes of the Empire; and when she had done, would explain what she had thus written by signs, which made it evident that she perfectly understood the Alcoran.

These are rare gifts, my friend; yet were all the Mutes educated with as much diligence and care, as was Saqueda, ('so she was call'd) 'tis possible they would attain to greater perfection. I have been told, that her Tutor, one of the learned'st men in Arabia, bestow'd many years in teaching her this method of reading, understanding, and writing.

This puts me in mind of a man who was bred a Mahometan, but being taken captive by the French, embraced their religion, not in his heart, but only in outward profession. When I first came to Paris, I fell into his company by accident, and understanding that he was an African, I desired to ask him some questions, but he was dumb, so that I had almost laid aside my hopes of conversing with him; till perceiving that he moved his lips, and opened his mouth, as one that was talking, I offered him pen, ink, and paper, making signs to him, that I would gladly know his mind in writing. He accordingly writ in Moresco, That he was struck deaf and dumb about eighteen years since, telling me also the place of his nativity, and how he came hither; I took the pen, and in the same language express'd my compassion of his

mis-

misfortunes. When he faw that I underftood Morefco, he writ again, fignifying to me, that if I opened my mouth wide at the pronouncing of every fyllable, he could underftand my meaning by the pofture of my lips and tongue. I found his words true, to my no fmall admiration ; for he could write down what I had faid. We converfed together often ; and at length I procured his efcape in the retinue of a Chiaus that was returning from hence to Conftantinople.

I befeech the wife Architect of Nature, and Repairer of human Defects, either to continue to us the ufe of our fenfes, or to fupply that want by fome fuperlative endowments of the mind.

Paris, 20th of the 9th Moon,
    of the Year 1645.

LETTER IX.
To Ufeph, Baffa.

THOU wilt fay, I am unmindful of my duty in not congratulating thy new Honour before this ; and that I forget the good offices which formerly pafs'd between us in the Seraglio. I tell thee my obligations are infinite, not only to thee, but to many others of my friends at the Port : It is impoffible for me to acquit myfelf of fo many engagements. As for the Dignity to which the Sultan has raifed thee, I received the firft news of it within thefe fourteen days. And I dare affirm, That none of thy friends, or of thofe whofe dependence is on thee, could with greater complacency behold thee vefted by our moft auguft Emperor, than I read the letter which conveyed to me this welcome intelligence.

Long mayeft thou live to enjoy the bleffings which thy good fortune has heaped on thee. Yet I counfel thee to enjoy them fo, as not to forget thou muft die. Let not the Grandeur of thy Station

tion render thee proud and wilful : But remember, when thou art ſurrounded with a crowd of adoring ſuppliants, That Death ſhall level thee with the meaneſt of thy Slaves. Thus the ancient Philoſophers ſpared not to perform the office of monitors to their Kings and Princes : And I hope, thou wilt not take in ill part the wholeſome advice of Mahmut, who diſcovers a temper void of hypocriſy, in the freedom he aſſumes. If thou giveſt ear to flatterers, they will compliment thee to thy ruin ; and when thou art on the brink of a precipice, they will perſuade thee there is no danger, though, if thou goeſt on, they know thy fall is inevitable. They will pride themſelves in the dexterity of their malice, and inſult over thee with ſcornful Sarcaſms, whom not long ago they idolized.

The eminent command thou haſt, requires thy frequent preſence in the Sovereign Divan : And that thou may'ſt not ſit there, only as an auditor of other men's counſels, and incapable of making one in the number of thoſe, who become remarkable by their orations, or reports of foreign events ; I will now entertain thee with ſome paſſages, which have happened in Europe ſince the beginning of this year, whereof the other Baſſa's may poſſibly be ignorant.

The Diet of Francfort, which had continued for three years, was diſſolved on the 12th of the 4th Moon. This may be known at the Port, while they remain ſtrangers to the reaſons of it. There are a Sort of Chriſtians in Germany, whom they call Evangelics. Theſe are oppoſite to the Roman Church, both in Religion and Intereſt : And their cauſe is chiefly eſpous'd by the Dukes of Saxony and Brandenburgh. It was to comply with theſe, that an Aſſembly was appointed at Oſnaburgh ; but the Emperor and the Catholics were either for continuing that at Francfort, or tranſlating it to Munſter. While the contending parties were bickering and ſtriving to gain their ſeveral ends, the

C 3 Deputy

Deputy of the Duke of Bavaria, tired out with such intolerable delays, departed from Francfort, whom the reſt of the Deputies followed. And this thou may'ſt report for the true occaſion of the Diſſolution of that Diet.

Thus, at the beginning of the year, the diſputes which thoſe Infidels raiſed about ſafe conduct, exactneſs of titles, priority of addreſs, and many other vain Punctilio's, hindered them from coming to any concluſion about a Peace, which was the principal cauſe of their aſſembling. And this is a folly peculiar to the Nazarenes, that in all public Aſſemblies the very ſtrength and vitals of their counſels are ſpent in a vain adjuſting of empty Ceremonies.

It is credibly reported here, That the King of Poland earneſtly ſolicits a match with Queen Chriſtina of Swedeland, but has not hitherto had any poſitive anſwer, or effected any thing in it. In the ſecond Moon of this year, that Queen ſent an Ambaſſador, to give the King of Poland an account, That ſhe had taken the Government upon her. While he tarried in the Poliſh Court, there were not wanting ſuch, as by the King's order, ſifted his inclination, in reference to this affair. It was propoſed to him that this Match would be a happy occaſion to unite the two Kingdoms in a firm and durable League: That the Evangelics in Poland would be much eaſed thereby: That Uladiſlaus was not much decay'd in his natural vigour: That Swedeland might in the mean while be govern'd by the Council, with many other propoſals and encouragements, to this purpoſe. Among which I muſt not omit, that it was ſuggeſted, how eaſy 'twould be for two ſuch potent crowns, in Conjunction, not only to humble the Germans, but alſo to put a ſtop to the victorious arms of the Ottoman Empire. But all this came to nothing, that wary Queen ſuſpecting that there was a deeper deſign in the courtſhip of this old
fox;

fox ; and that by fuch a Match, the Kingdom of Swedeland, in default of the Iffue Royal, might be fubjected to a Foreign Crown.

However, it is eafy to apprehend from this, that if the Poles maintain at prefent their accord with the Sublime Port, 'tis for want of ftrength to break it ; and that they only wait an opportunity to make fome potent and firm alliance, which may fecond the defigns formed by that Court againft the Firft Throne on Earth, whereof thou art one of the principal Pillars.

Remain firm in thy Station, and let neither the tempefts of war, nor the convulfions of ftate, fhake thy conftancy. But above all, fuffer not thy Integrity, which is the Bafis of all Virtues, to be undermin'd by Bribes.

If thou followeft this counfel, God and his Prophet fhall eftablifh thee, all men will honour thee, thy Sovereign fhall exalt thee ; and Mahomet will rejoice to fee thee in time become the Atlas of the Eternal Empire.

Paris, 5th of the 10th Moon,
of the Year 1645.

LETTER X.

To Ichingi Cap' Oglani, Præceptor to the Royal Pages of the Seraglio.

THERE is a vaft difference between thy letter, and that of Shafhim Iftham. He is eloquent in the acknowledgment of his crime, thou rhetorical in thy own juftification. Thou haft plunder'd Demofthenes and Cicero, and robb'd 'em of all the Flowers and Tropes of Oratory, to drefs up a faint, lifelefs excufe. Such an artificial apology, inftead of cancelling, heightens thy offence. It might have procured thee the applaufe of the Academy ; but it comes fhort of giving me fatis-faction for the injuries I have received at thy

hands : I have reafon to efteem them fuch ; becaufe fo defign'd, altho' they took no effect. For
wrongs of this kind ought to be meafured by the
intention of the author, not by their fuccefs.
The Minifters of the Divan will hardly be prevailed to fufpect Mahmut, who has given fubftan-
tial proofs of his fidelity.

Tell me, in the name of God and Mahomet,
What was the motive that induced thee to flander me ? Wherein have I merited this perfecution
at thy hands ? It could not be revenge, becaufe
I never gave thee occafion ; unlefs thou ftill re-
taineft a grudge on the fcore of my ftudying in
the Academies ; and that at my return from Palermo, thou wert not able to expofe me in the prefence of the Mufti, in any point of language or
learning. But I had rather charitably believe 'twas
thy ambition, not thy malice, which gave birth
to thofe calumnies thou haft vented againft me.
Thou envieft me the honour of ferving the Grand
Signior in this ftation, thinking thyfelf capable of
difcharging this office more fuccefsfully than Mahmut. I cenfure not thy abilities ; but think 'tis beft
for every man to be content with his own condition,
fince Deftiny diftributes the employments of the
world among men, by rules into which we cannot
penetrate.

Thou art mafter of the French tongue; but doft
thou think that a complete qualification for a
man in my poft ? Art thou fit to converfe in the
Court of a Foreign Prince, who canft not govern
thy tongue in that of thy native Sovereign ?
Thou art yet to learn a Courtier's mafter-piece,
which is, To diffemble even the neceffary art
of diffimulation. That is, as the Arabians fay,
" To have a veil upon a veil ;" or as the Italians,
" To have a mafk with a natural face on the out-
" fide." Thou art fo far from this, that thou canft
not yet draw perfectly the firft rough ftrokes of a
counterfeit.

To

To fpeak plain, Hadft thou by any artificial feigning of friendfhip to me, made way to infinuate thy ftory into the belief of the Grandees, thou mighteft have praifed me to my ruin. But to go bluntly to work, without preventive Encomiums, difcovered at once the weaknefs of thy judgment, and the ftrength of thy paffion; giving the Minifters occafion to think there was lefs of truth, than of defign in thy accufations.

For the future, I advife thee to mind thy books and fcholars, and meddle not with Mahmut, whofe bufinefs is to ftudy men. Adieu.

Paris, 5th of the 10th Moon,
of the Year 1545.

LETTER XI.

To the Reis Effendi, Principal Secretary of State.

WITH extreme joy I have received the certain news of the taking of Canea by the invincible Ottoman arms.

I muft confefs, when I firft apprehended the intentions of Sultan Ibrahim, to make war with the Republic of Venice, I was apt to hearken to fome thinking men in this Court, who, making their obfervations of the Sultan's indulging himfelf in female pleafures, conjectured from thence (as by a common rule) that he would not have difcovered fuch a martial and active fpirit, in afferting the honour of the Ottoman Empire. His dextrous concealing his defigns, even to the very execution of them, has ftruck a damp into all the Courts in Europe, infomuch as Cardinal Mazarini this day told the Queen Regent, That he doubted left Sultan Ibrahim would prove another Junius Brutus, who being the Nephew of Tarquin, one of the Primitive Kings of Rome for fome years, counterfeited

C 5 an

an extraordinary fimplicity and weaknefs of fpirit: But having privately fecured a faction to his own interefts, by popular arts, he, to gain the Sovereignty, changed the Form of Government, procured himfelf to be made Conful, and difcovered a Genius, furpaffing in policy and mature judgment, all his predeceffors.

Though the Cardinal's comparifon be difproportionate to the Grandeur of the Sovereign Emperor of the World, who cannot without a vaft injury be poftpon'd in virtue, wifdom or power, as a Second or Imitator of any Prince upon Earth: Yet the character holds good in the main, That he has timely and maturely diffembled the moft fublime abilities and endowments a Sovereign Prince is capable of, rendering thereby his enemies fecure and carelefs: Till at length all thofe illuftrious attributes exert themfelves on a fudden, breaking forth like the Sun from an Eclipfe; at once dazzling the aftonifh'd world, and furprifing the enemies of the Ottoman Empire, in the flumbers which proceeded from the contempt of his facred Majefty.

I thought indeed once that the Venetians would have been in a condition to have faced the Ottoman Navy, and difputed their farther progrefs on the feas. I expected no lefs than that they would have made fome huffing attempts on the Ifles of Archipelago; that they would have enter'd the Hellefpont, brav'd the Dardanels, and failing forward would have block'd up the Ottoman Navy in the Propontis, or driven them into the Euxine Sea for fhelter. And who could have thought otherwife, had they been provided for a war? But our fage Emperor, by fecrecy, which is the very foul of all great undertakings, hath anticipated their very fears, and leap'd upon the prey, while the keepers were afleep.

Had the Chriftian Princes and States laid afide their private punctilio's and animofities, when the Venetians firft made their application to them for affiftance, it might have proved a doubtful war. But

But inftead of generoufly uniting their forces in the common defence of Chriftendom, they begin to divide their interefts and hearts one from another, and that upon the vaineft motives in the world, one State difputing with another about precedency of pofts in the army, which proceeded to that height, as to fruftrate the main defign: For the Pope himfelf at laft is forced to raife the greateft aids the States of Venice are like to have; joining his gallies with theirs, and fending a thoufand foot on board at his own coft.

Thus does Divine Providence, out of the difcords of Chriftian Princes, draw occafions to enlarge the facred Empire of the Muffulmans, and to fpread the Ottoman conquefts o'er the Weftern World.

Paris, 20th of the 11th Moon,
   of the Year 1645.

LETTER XII.

To the Magnificent and Redoubtable Vizir Azem.

IT appears that the Queen of France is very indulgent to her Generals, having called home the Duke of Enguien from the toils of war. This Prince neglecting the wounds he received in the battle of Allerfheim, not many days after, fell into a violent fever; fo that he was carried in a horfe litter to Philipfburgh, with no fmall danger of his life. As foon as he recovered his health, he was commanded to return to France, and the charge of the whole army committed to Marefchal Turenne.

Such tendernefs is never fhew'd to the invincible Ottoman Generals, neither would they efteem it a favour, but a difgrace. When they go to the wars, they make no under-hand leagues with the elements to fpare their bodies, but are refolved to combat with cold, heat, hunger, thirft, and all the hardfhips to which foldiers are liable, as well as with the fwords of their enemies. They take no other armour againft the rigorous frofts of a Ruffian winter, or the fcorching fands of a Perfian fummer, but an unfhaken refolution, and invincible patience, and a mind incapable of bowing under the worft misfortunes. They are not angry with the weapons of their adverfaries, when they carve in their limbs, the marks of an honour, which will far out-laft the pain of their wounds ; and in their flefh hew deep characters of an immortal fame, and a renown which fhall know no period. They are not parfimonious of their blood, but court their enemies to fpill it on the ground, from whence it will fpring up in laurels and wreaths, to crown them with triumphs and glory whilft they live, and for to fweeten their memory with the praife of future generations.

Thus, magnanimous Vizir, do the Muffulman Heroes, the Props of the firft Empire, manifeft their courage, in defying of dangers and wounds, and fcorning to capitulate with fortune, for eafe and exemption from death. They know, that when they march againft the Infidels, 'tis in vindication of the eternal Unity ; and therefore, inftead of endeavouring to fhun, they court a death fo glorious, as that which will immediately tranfport them to the Bofom of our Holy Prophet, and to the inexpreffible Delights of the Gardens of Eden. Where this truth is firmly rooted, there is no room for fear to plant itfelf. But the cafe is otherwife with Infidels, who blafpheme that pureft undivided Effence. They affert and believe a Plurality of Gods, and therefore, in time of danger, amongft fo many Deities, they know not whom to addrefs, or whom to confide in. The apprehenfion of death is terrible to them, whofe hope is only in this life ; whofe confciences are ftained with a thoufand pollutions, and

and yet renounce the very method of being clean.
Who not only err themfelves, but by their evil
example and influence, (for I fpeak of the Princes
and Great Ones) draw innumerable after them, to
tafte of the Tree Zacon, which grows in the Middle of Hell.

People fpeak varioufly of the Duke of Enguien's
conduct in the battle of Allerfheim. His creatures
extol his valour and experience with Hyperboles;
whilft his enemies endeavour to leffen his reputation. Some fay, he owes his revocation to the
Queen's diflike; others attribute it to the extraordinary concern fhe has for his health. But fuch as
would be efteem'd the wifer fort, fay, his return is
voluntary, and fought by himfelf, fcorning to hold
his Commiffion any longer at the pleafure of Cardinal Mazarini, who, 'tis thought, firft procured
him this employment, only to have him out of the
way, and take off his application from the domeftic affairs of France. Thefe are the difcourfes
of the people at prefent, who yet perhaps may
change their opinions before the fun goes down.
They will always be cenfuring and defcanting
on the actions of their Superiors; few being willing to think their tongues were given them to lie
idle. It is but a little member, but often does great
mifchief by its activity. One of the Ancients gave
no good character of it, when he called it a Dæmon.
Yet we are not bound to believe all that the Philofophers faid. Æfop gave the moft impartial account of this member, when he faid, " 'Twas the
" beft, and the worft." Sometimes I fit filent many
hours together; not for want of company, (for
here's a glutt of that in this populous city;) nor
becaufe I know not what to fay, (for I could fpeak
a great deal more than 'tis fit for others to hear)
but that I may ftudy with lefs interruption, how to
ferve my great Mafter. For much talking enervates
the judgment, and evaporates the mind into air.
Befides, by thus practifing filence in private, I
learn the art of reftraining my words in public,
when

when it is requifite to promote the ends at which I
aim.   'Tis not for a man in my ftation to be open
and talkative ; but to diftinguifh perfons and fea-
fons ; to underftand the due ftops and advances of
my tongue ; fometimes to fay much in a little, at
other times to fay little or nothing at all ; but ever
fo to fpeak, as not to lay myfelf naked to the hear-
ers ; yet to feem a very frank, open-hearted man,
in what I difcourfe of.

I would not have thee conclude from what I
have faid, that Mahmut ufes any referve to the
Minifters of the Divan, who are Mines of Science
and Wifdom, and can eafily difcern tne heart thro'
the moft artificial veil of words.   But it is abfolutely neceffary for me to ufe diffimulation in this
Court, feeming many times ignorant of what I
really know, that I may not be thought to know
more than they would have me.   I was never yet
fo indifcreet, as to publifh any fecret that was committed to my charge, whereby I have gain'd great
confidence with men who delight to unbofom their
intelligence.   They efteem me a man of integrity,
and fit to be trufted.   Thus am I made privy to
many intrigues of the Grandees, and a repofitory
of the Court news : Whilft they whifper in
Mahmut's ear what is tranfacted in the royal bed-
chambers, and private apartments.

By this means I am acquainted with an amour
of Cardinal Mazarini, which is known but to a
few.   This Minifter has none of the worft faces,
and a proportionate elegance in his fhape : Much
addicted alfo to the love of women ; yet he ma-
nages his intrigues with that caution and privacy,
as not to expofe the honour of his Function.
Among the reft, he had frequent accefs to the
chamber of a certain Countefs Dowager, her
hufband being lately deceas'd.   This was not carried on fo privately, but 'twas whifper'd about, That
a man was feen often to come out of this lady's
chamber a little before day ; but nobody knew
who it was (for the Cardinal went difguifed.)   At
laft

laft it came to the Queen's ear, who was refolved to unravel this intrigue. She caufed Spies to be placed at a convenient diftance from the lady's chamber-door, which opened in a gallery of the Royal Palace, with orders to trace him home. That night the defigned Watch was firft fet, it fortuned that the Cardinal being in the Countefs's chamber, her maid, who was privy to this amour, overheard thefe Spies talking to each other concerning her lady, which made her more attentive (being in a place where fhe could not be feen) till at length fhe plainly difcovered, That they lay in wait to find out who it was that had been feen coming out of the chamber. She quickly acquaints the Countefs with this news. She confults the Cardinal what was beft to be done to avoid difcovery. In fine, it was agreed between them, that the Countefs fhould put on the Cardinal's difguife, and he a fuit of her cloaths; that fhe fhould go out at the ufual hour of his retreat, and walk in the gardens; that if examined, fhe fhould pretend this difguife was to guard her from the rude attempts of men, who if they found a lady alone in the night time, would not fail to offer fome incivilities; that foon after her departure, the Cardinal fhould go forth in her drefs, and fhift for himfelf. This was perform'd accordingly. The Countefs walk'd into the gardens in the Cardinal's difguife, follow'd by the Spies, whilft he goes to an intimate friend's houfe, (an Italian, whofe fortune depended on this Minifter) and changes his female accoutrements for the proper apparel of his fex. The Countefs having walked about half an hour in the garden, was feiz'd on by fome of the Guards, under fufpicion of fome ill defign. She was carried before the Queen, and examined. She then difcovered herfelf, begging the Queen's pardon, and telling her, that a particular devotion had obliged her to take that courfe for feveral mornings; but if it offended her Majefty, fhe would hold herfelf difpenfed with, and would forbear. The Queen

3   feeming

feeming fatisfied with this anfwer, difmiffed her. Thus the amours of the Cardinal and the Countefs remain'd a fecret; and there are but three perfons (befides themfelves) that know any thing of it, among which Mahmut is one.

Thou fceft, illuftrious Minifter, that the reputation of my fecrecy has gain'd me the confidence of one of the Cardinal's Privado's ; for I had this relation from the Italian whom I mention'd, at whofe houfe the Cardinal changed his difguife. I am not without hopes, by the prudent management of this difcovery, to penetrate farther into the Court intrigues. For he that told me this ftory, confidered not that he made me thereby mafter of his fortune, and that it is no longer fafe for him to deny me any intelligence I require of him. He has put a key into my hand, which will open his breaft at my pleafure.

Yet I need not magifterially claim difcoveries from him, as the only conditions on which he is to expect my concealing what he has already difclofed. There is a more dexterous and ferviceable way to become his Confeffor, without fuch an ungrateful infult ; whilft with a well acted candour I feign a relation of fuch things as I fufpect, yet cannot be certain are true, till attefted by himfelf, profeffing at the fame time not to believe thofe pretended reports I heard. If I fhall be fo happy as to do any effectual fervice to the Grand Signior by this engagement, it will anfwer my ends, and I fhall not repent of my craft.

Mahmut falutes thee, Sovereign Baffa, in the humbleft pofture of adoration, lying proftrate on the ground, in contemplation of thy grandeur. Befeeching God that he would grant this favour to thee, to live happily, and to die in thy bed.

Paris, 20th of the 11th Moon,
    of the Year 1645.

LETTER XIII.

To Egri Boinou, *a* White Eunuch.

THOU giveſt me abundant proofs of thy affection and friendſhip, in frankly telling me
what they ſay of Mahmut in the Seraglio. I do
not expect to be free from cenſure; and am ſo far
from being diſcouraged at the obloquies ſome men
faſten on me, that it adds to my comfort; it being
an aſſured mark of innocence to be traduced. I am
not deſirous that the Arabian proverb ſhould be
verified in me, which ſays, " That he deſerves
" no man's good word, of whom all men ſpeak
" well." I dread to be popular at ſuch a price,
and will rather court the ſlanders of the envious,
by a ſtedfaſt perſeverance in my duty, than lay a
train for the compliments of flatterers, by favour-
ing ſedition. Thou knoweſt what reaſon I have
to ſay this. There needs no interpreter between
us. Though the Black Eunuch has recanted his
aſperſions, yet there are others who perſiſt in their
malice; and it will be difficult for the Maſter of
the Pages, with his beſt Rhetoric, to exempt himſelf from the number.

I have received both their apologies, and have
anſwer'd them. I wiſh they would reform this
vice; not ſo much for my ſake, who am proof
againſt their accuſations, as for their own: For the
injury they intended to do me, will redound moſt
to themſelves. Miſery is on him that perſecuteth
his neighbour.

He that is merciful and gracious, who hath ſe-
parated the brightneſs of the day from the obſcu-
rity of the night, defend both thee and me from the
malice of whiſperers, from the enchantments of
wizards, and ſuch as breathe thrice upon the Knot
of the Triple Cord.

Paris, 20th of the 11th Moon,
of the Year 1645.

LET-

LETTER XIV.

To Muſtapha, Berber Aga.

THOU wilt laugh at the hypocriſy and folly of the Nazarenes, when thou ſhalt know the Articles agreed upon between the Elector of Saxony, and Koningſmark, one of the Swediſh Generals, on the 27th of the 8th Moon.

The Swedes had prevail'd on the ſon of the Elector, to intercede with his father for a Truce; but the old Duke would not hearken to any thing of that nature, till Torſtenſon gave orders to the Swediſh army in thoſe parts, that they ſhould oppreſs the Elector's ſubjects, by exacting from them unreaſonable taxes and contributions; and that they ſhould lay deſolate all the countries about Dreſden, if they refuſed to pay what was demanded of them. Accordingly they took a caſtle, which commanded a large valley of meadows and corn-fields. The Swedes burnt the corn on the ground, led away the peaſants captives, and demoliſhed many towns and villages; yet not without ſome loſs on their ſide: For the Saxons one night ſtole upon them while they were ſecurely ſleeping, and ſlew an hundred and twenty, taking above three hundred priſoners. Thoſe who were left in poſſeſſion of the caſtle, met with no better fortune; being compell'd in a few days to ſurrender this their new conqueſt, with five enſigns, and a hundred and fifty priſoners, which were all carried in triumph to Dreſden.

One would have thought that theſe ſucceſſes ſhould have confirm'd the Elector in the averſion he had already conceived for a Treaty; that he would rather have purſued his good fortune with arms; eſpecially when by entering into a private ſeparate Treaty with the Swedes, he muſt needs give a great ſuſpicion to the Aſſembly of the Deputies.
But

But the old Duke doted; and what neither the repeated folicitations of his fon, nor the continual ravages which General Koningfmark made in his territories, could procure from him, that he granted to the charming addreffes of a beautiful lady.

The Elector's fon adhering much to the Swedifh intereft, and finding all other means ineffectual to oblige his new friends; it was agreed upon between him and Koningfmark, that he fhould at leaft perfuade his father to a Truce of a few days: That, during the ceffation of arms, the fon fhould invite his father to a banquet, where Koningfmark fhould be prefent, with fome of the principal Swedes in his army. All this fucceeded according to their wifhes. The good old man confented to a ceffation of arms, and to give Koningfmark a meeting at his fon's banquet. The German gallantry, and indeed that of all North Europe, confifts much in their exceffive drinking: He is efteemed the moft polite man who can bear moft wine, with leaft alteration of his temper. This they call Caroufing. The fon had provided plenty of thofe wines which grow on the banks of the Rhine, efteem'd the wholefomeft and moft delicious of all thefe parts. It is not neceffary to repeat particularly the firft falutes and addreffes: Both parties feemed emulous to exceed in civilities. They fell to the wine with freedom and mirth, after the manner of the country. When in the midft of their glaffes, whilft the heart of the old Duke was elevated with the juice of the grape, came into the room a tall perfonage all in armour, and making his obeyfance to the company, delivered a letter to General Koningfmark; the General having received it, the ftranger was invited by the Elector's fon to fit down with them. He was mafter of the feaft, and only Koningfmark and the ftranger, befides himfelf, were privy to the intrigue.

The ftranger unbuckled his helmet, and pulling

ing it off (for all the reft of the company were
uncovered, it being the hotteft day in all the fummer) difcover'd a face and hair, much like one
of thofe Nymphs defcribed by Poets and Painters.

The Duke could not withdraw his eyes from this
furprifing beauty, nor fix his roving thoughts:
Sometimes it put him in mind of Ganymede,
the difcarded minion of Jupiter; but Ganymede
was never feen in armour. Then he thought of
Adonis, then of the Babylonian Pyramus, the Indian Atys. In fine, he run over all the celebrated
youths of the Eaft, to match the beauty of this illuftrious ftranger. He drank and gaz'd whilft his
fon and Koningfmark were pleas'd to fee the baits
take. From ruminating on our fex, he pafs'd to that
of women: And remembring that in fome former
battles between the Swedes and Germans, feveral
ladies had difguifed themfelves in armour, and followed General Torftenfon to the field, he concluded prefently, that this was fome beautiful female of Swedeland.

This thought put the old Duke into a pleafant
fit of raillery, yet not without fome mixture of paffion for this lovely Heroine. There was fomething fo peculiarly graceful in all her carriage and
addrefs, as charm'd the Elector's heart. The women in thofe parts of Europe are not fo precife in
their converfation with men, as in the Eaft. And
'tis a great point of education, fo to adjuft the
Punctilio's of their deportment, as neither to appear
too open, nor too referv'd. This was her mafter-
piece, for fhe fo equally divided the parts fhe was
to act, both of a maid and foldier, that neither en-
trenched on the other, but fhe acquitted herfelf with
excellent honour and gallantry.

The next day after the banquet, the fon renew-
ed his mediation for a Treaty, but the Elector feem'd
cold. All his thoughts were bufied in ruminating
on his fair enemy.

Not to detain thee longer in expectation of the
iffue, the love of this young Amazon had taken
fo

fo deep root in his heart, that he would grant nothing but for her fake, neither could he deny any
thing which fhe defired. Thus, by this ftratagem,
they accomplifh'd their aims, and he condefcended
to a Treaty, after fourteen days debate on the Articles:
Of which I here fend thee a true and particular
copy, that thou may'ft find fome divertifement in
the folly of the Infidels. The Articles are as follow :

" THAT it fhould be lawful for the Duke to
" keep due Faith to the Emperor ; nor fhould
" he be obliged to admit any thing contrary to the
"intereft of the Empire.
" That the Elector fhould not lend the Emperor
" above three regiments of horfe, nor fhould per-
" mit him to raife foldiers in his Principality.
" That the Swedes fhould have free and fafe paf-
" fage through Saxony, provided they came not
" within three miles of Drefden.
" That there fhall be free traffic between the
" Elector's fubjects and the Swedes, by land and
" water.
" That at the end of three months, each party
" fhould be obliged to declare, whether they would
" prolong the Truce, or break it off.
" That the Elector fhould again enjoy his reve-
" nues, except thofe which were drawn from Leip-
" fick. That he fhould pay the Swedes eleven
" thoufand rix-dollars a month, and a certain quan-
" tity of corn.
" That the Elector fhould do nothing which
" might hinder the fiege of Magdeburgh."

Thefe Articles at firft fight appeared to be
equally favourable to the Saxons and to the Swedes.
But in reality, they ferved only as an umbrage to
deeper defigns, which the Swedes had in agitation.
For this was the firft ftep to draw the Saxons off
from the Emperor's party; and Torftenfon was now
fecure, that whilft the Swedes rufhed farther into

4 Ger-

Germany, the Saxons would not moleſt them behind.

For my part, I neither underſtand the Policy nor the Integrity of the Elector, in ſigning theſe articles; nor how he can reconcile the firſt of them with any of the reſt: To give ſafe conduct, and kind entertainment to the enemies of his Sovereign: To be obliged not to lend him any more aſſiſtance than his enemies ſhall allow, nor ſuffer him to raiſe forces at his own charges: To be cheated of his own revenues, and tamely yield to pay a monthly tribute beſides: To be tied up from ſuccouring one of the principal towns in his Principality, at that time beſieged by the Swedes: This is a new method of keeping due Faith to Sovereigns, or of obſerving common prudence for one's ſelf. But "Women and "Wine cauſe a wiſe man to ſtumble," as the Arabians ſay. And this old Prince is bleſs'd in a hopeful ſon, who is not aſhamed to turn Pimp, that he may betray his father to his mortal enemies. But let the Chriſtians proceed in their falſehood and treachery one againſt another, whilſt every good Muſſulman proſtrates himſelf five times a day; and prays in his integrity for the conſummation of that time, wherein God has determined to put a period to the Monarchies of theſe Infidels, and to reduce them to the faith and obedience of his holy Law.

I wiſh ſome of my friends would ſend me ſome relation of what paſſes in the Eaſt: I have heard nothing of moment out of Aſia theſe many Moons. I could almoſt think myſelf baniſhed from the Eternal Providence, whilſt I reſide among theſe Uncircumciſed.

Think ſometimes on Mahmut; and if thou canſt not relieve his melancholy, at leaſt pity him, whom all the honours and pleaſures of the Weſtern parts would not be able to exhilerate, ſo long as he apprehends himſelf forgotten by his friends at Conſtantinople.

Paris, 20th of the 11th Moon,
   of the Year 1645.

LET.

LETTER XV.

To Mahummed Hogia, Dervife, Eremit, Inhabitant of the Sacred Cave at the Foot of Mount Uriel in Arabia the Happy.

THY remembrance is as the dew of the evening, or the midnight breezes in Africk, after the fcorching fervors of a fummer's day, when neither trees, nor houfes, nor higheft mountains, afford any fhadow. Such are the employments of ftate, keeping the mind in as reftlefs an activity, as that which the Philofophers fay is the occafion of heat. Such alfo is the refrefhment I find in thinking on thee, whofe foul is a manfion of tranquillity, an Umbrella of temperance, and all virtue. Thither I retreat for refpiration from the fatigues of worldly bufinefs. Pardon the bold accefs of an humble flave, who cannot be fo happy as to vifit thee any otherwife, than by letters, yet would be miferable in the want of this privilege.

Ever fince I had the honour to kifs the duft of thy feet in that facred Retirement, I was filled with love and admiration of thy fanctity. Thrice happy are the neighbouring fhepherds, whofe flocks feed under thy aufpicious protection. No fierce lions, no ravenous tigers, dare violate that fanctuary, or hunt for prey within thofe meadows, confecrated by thy prefence. That rich and flowery vale was firft fecured with an eternal immunity from fpoil and rapine, by the blefling of our Holy Prophet. Now that blefling feems to be redoubled by thy prayers and abftinencies, who inheriteft his fpirit as well as his abode. 'Twas in that Holy Cave, the Meffenger of God fafted for the fpace of three Moons. Thy whole life there is one continued abftinence. When thou lifteft up thy venerable hands to Heaven in prayer, the enemies of our Holy Law are feized with fear and trembling: Thou art the Guardian Angel
of

of the Ottoman Empire. Thy body attenuated with twenty years fasting, is purified almost to Immortality: Thou art become a Denizen among the Spirits. Neither the beasts of the earth, nor the fowls of the air, nor the fish of the sea, will charge thee with their blood. Thy table never smoak'd with slaughter'd dainties. Every tree affords thee a feast, and the meadows regale thee with a thousand harmless delicacies. Thy thirst is allay'd with the crystal streams; and when thou art disposed to banquet, the Arabian sheep supply thee with Nectar. Thus, like a prudent traveller, thou accustomest thyself beforehand to the diet of the country whither thou art going: Thou livest the life of Paradise here on earth.

Thou art not privy to the wickedness of the age: That cell guards thee from other mens vices, while thy incomparable humility defends thee from thy own virtues. Thou art not puffed up with thy sublime perfections. Pride is a serpent which commonly poisons the root of the fairest endowment. But thou hast crush'd this serpent in the egg.

In that solitude the Angel opened the heart of the Sent of God, and took out from thence the Devil's Seed Plot. When Mahomet awaked (for this was done while he lay in a Trance) he said, " I am a Worm." When Gabriel saw his humility, he pronounced a blessing on the place, That whosoever would dwell in that cave, " should be meek as Abra-" ham, chaste as Joseph, and temperate as Ismael." Thou hast experienced the effect of his benediction.

There is another happiness also attends thy retirement; thou livest free from cares and anxieties; thou committest the public good to the conduct of thy Sovereign, and thy private welfare to the protection of Providence; neither disquieted for the one, nor solicitous for the other. Who rises, and who falls, in the favour of the Sultan; who purchase the government of the Empire by their merits, or who by their money; whether it be better to remain in the Seraglio, or to be made Bassa of
Egypt,

Egypt, are cares that never moleſt thee. Thou
canſt ſit in that Sanctuary of Peace, and pity thoſe
whom ambition, and the love of glory, has driven
into the Toils of War. Thou canſt behold with
compaſſion the burthenſome attendants of the great;
their labours by day, and their watchings by night;
their reſtleſs thoughts and buſy actions; macerated
bodies, and uneaſy ſouls; while with indefatigable
pains they purſue mere ſhadows; and endeavour to
graſp the wind, or ſecure to themſelves a bubble,
which is no ſooner touch'd, than it vaniſhes. Thou
in the mean time art filling thy mind with ſolid
knowledge, and laying up poſſeſſions which ſhall
never be taken from thee: For the ſoul carries her
goods along with her to that other world.

I often wiſh myſelf with thee; and the remembrance of what I once enjoyed in thy converſation,
cannot be effaced by diſtance of time and place.
The farther I am from thee, the more ardently do
I long to ſee thee. But even in theſe innocent de-
ſires, there is a neceſſary mortification; ſince we
are not born for ourſelves, but to comply with the
myſterious ends of Fate. I am appointed to ſerve
the Grand Signior in this place; where I endeavour
to acquit myſelf a faithful Slave, and a good Muſſulman. If I fail in the firſt, my great Maſter will
puniſh me; if in the laſt, God and his Prophet will
revenge it. Yet I hope every frailty will not be
deem'd a tranſgreſſion, ſince the heart and the hands
go not always together. I often ſtrive to imitate thy
abſtinence, but my appetites are too ſtrong for me:
I return to my old courſe again, like a bow that is
forcibly bent. Yet I ſin not in this, ſince it is not
required at my hands.

Pray for me, holy Man of God, that while I aim
at the beſt things, I may not fall into the worſt;
and by ſtriving to aim at Perfection, I may not
crack thoſe powers which are requiſite to keep me
ſtedfaſt in the high-way of moral Virtue. I leave
thee

thee to thy contemplations, and the fociety of thy courteous Angels, who ever wait at the door of thy Cell.

Paris, 20th of the 11th Moon,
of the Year 1645.

LETTER XVI.

To Ufeph Baffa.

I Formerly acquainted thee, That Uladiflaus, King of Poland, fought Chriftina, Queen of Sweden, in marriage; but that his propofal was rejected. Now thou mayeft know that this Monarch has made a more fuccefsful amour, being married to Louife Marie de Gonzague, Princefs of Mantua. The nuptial folemnities were performed in this city by the Ambaffador of Poland, who was his Mafter's Proxy. The greateft part of the laft Moon was fpent in mafks, banquets, and court-revels, to honour the Efpoufals of this new Queen, who is fince gone towards Poland, being attended to the frontiers by a numerous train of the nobility, with all the ceremonies and regard due to a perfon of her rank.

The French, who are never fparing in words, are too liberal in the praifes they beftow on this Princefs. For if all were true they fay of her, fhe might be lifted in the number of Angels; whereas, fome more impartial eyes have difcovered fuch imperfections, as fpeak her yet on this fide a Saint. But ordinary virtues in Princes dazzle the multitude, borrowing a greater luftre from the nobility of their blood, and the eminence of their quality; whilft their vices are either fhrouded from the vul-

gar,

gar, or made to pafs for virtues, in the artificial drefs which flatterers put on them. 'Tis under this advantage the new Queen of Poland is cry'd up for a Diana; tho' a late Satyrift vindicates her from being half fo cruel as that Goddefs. It being no fecret that a young Italian Marquis had fomething kinder ufage than had Actæon, when he accidentally encountered this Princefs, as fhe was walking alone one evening in a grove belonging to her palace.

I am no patron of libels; nor would I fpeak irreverently of thofe whofe royal birth claims refpect from all mortals. But the ftupidity of the Nazarenes provokes my pen, who allow their women all the uncontroulable freedom and opportunities, that commonly give birth to the moft irregular amours, and yet believe them innocent. They are perfect idolaters of that fex, not having learned, with the illuminated Muffulmans, That women are of a creation inferior to that of men, have fouls of a lower ftamp, and confequently more prone to vice; and that they fhall never have the honour to be admitted into our Paradife.

But thou who believeft the doctrines clear and intelligibly, and haft kifs'd the garments of the Sent of God, wilt not fuffer thy reafon to be blinded by the enchantments of thefe deluding fair ones; but fo love women, as ftill to remember thou art a man, which is fomething more fublime.

Paris, 1ft of the 12th Moon,
   of the Year 1645.

       L E T-

LET|TER XVII.

To the Kaimacham.

IT is hard to guefs where the French victories will terminate. Either fear, or the defire of novelties, opens the gates of moft cities to them ; and when that will not do, the force of their cannon makes a paffage into the ftrongeft holds of their enemies, and puts whole Provinces under their protection.

Their enemies fay, that the French never befiege a town, but their firft affaults are made with bullets of gold ; and when that will neither prevail on the Governor, nor win a party, then they only try the force of the coarfer metal. Yet this will appear but a flander, if thou confidereft a late action of the Duke of Orleans, when he lay down before Bourbourgh.

He had fcarce finifhed his trenches, when the next morning an arrow was found with a letter faftened to it, not far from his tent. The letter was directed to the Duke, and fubfcribed by the Governor of the town. The contents of it were, to fignify to him, That if he would give him fifty thoufand pieces of gold, and continue him in his office, he would the next night open the gates, and let in his army; and, that before mid-day he would fend a meffenger to know his pleafure. The Duke waited the arrival of the meffenger, who feconded what his Mafter had faid. But the magnanimous Prince, inftead of accepting this offer, fent him back to his Mafter, with this meffage, That he came not before the town as a Merchant, to purchafe it at the price of a needlefs treafon ; but as a Soldier, at the head of an army, flufh'd with continual victories ; fummoning him forthwith to furrender at difcretion, That being the only way to experience his generofity.

This

This year has been fignalized with much action in Flanders, Catalonia, and Italy. The field was fhared among many brave Generals.

The Duke of Orleans had the command of the army in Flanders, where he took the Forts of Vandreval, Bourbourgh, Link, Dringhen, Bethune, S. Venant, Guifca, Lens, Mardyke, Lillers, Mening, and Armentiers.

Thefe places were won by feveral parties, under the command of the Marefchals de Geftion, de Rantzau, and the Duke of Guife, who all acted in feparate bodies under the Duke of Orleans.

Nor was the Count d'Harcourt idle in Catalonia, where he fucceeded in the charge of the Marefchal de la Mothe. The firft effort of his arms was the retaking of Agramont, which the Spaniards had feized; a ftrong city, and which kept a large part of Catalonia in fubjection.

From hence he marched towards Rofes, one of the moft important places for ftrength under the Spanifh King's dominions, and governed by an experienced foldier, who failed not to defend the place to the laft extremes; but after a fiege of two Moons, was compelled to yield for want of provifions.

After this, the French General cut off feven hundred Spaniards, who were pofted to hinder his paffage over the river. The next day the whole armies meeting in the plains of Liorens, there was a furious encounter, in which the Spaniards loft ten regiments of horfe on the fpot; the reft threw down their arms and yielded. The Marquis of Mortare, one of the Spanifh Generals, was taken captive, with other perfons of note; among which was the Standard-bearer of Spain.

But this was but the engagement of one Wing. For when the other entered the combat, the flaughter was dreadful. Of the Spaniards were flain fix thoufand horfe, and fixteen hundred foot; and three and twenty hundred of them were made prifoners.

The

The French loft not above three hundred in all, and they had but a few wounded.

This battle has brought infinite glory to the Count d' Harcourt. After which there happened nothing remarkable in Catalonia, fave the taking of Balaguier, which is like to end this year's campaign on that fide.

Prince Thomas of Savoy commanded in Italy, but had no great number of French in his army, the main Body being drawn off to ferve in Catalonia. Yet vexed to fee the fuccefs of the Spaniards, who had poffeffed themfelves of a ftrong caftle, and kept the field in bravado, as if he were not able to face them; he raifed fome recruits, and entered the Milaneze, where he took the city and caftle of Vigevano. After this, defigning to return into Piedmont, he found all the paffages blocked up by the Spaniards, who had a far greater army than his. Yet affuming courage, he attempted to pafs the river Moura; and the enemy prefenting themfelves to oppofe his defign, he gave them battle, and killed five hundred and threefcore of them; among which were nine officers of principal command and quality: On his fide were loft two hundred common foldiers, and twelve officers; among which was his brother, Prince Maurice of Savoy. Thefe are the chief actions on that fide. As for Portugal, there has happened nothing in that kingdom worthy of remark.

I have in this letter, fage Governor of the Imperial City, obferved the method thou enjoinedft me; I have acquainted thee, with whatfoever has occurred in the prefent wars of France and Spain during this year.

'Tis difcourfed here, that the Venetians will lay fiege to Canea, next Spring, in hopes to recover that important place from the arms of the victorious Ottomans.

The Duke of Orleans will be on his march to Flanders, toward the latter end of the next Moon, resolving

refolving to make an early campaign, being alarm-
ed with the late lofs of Mardyke, which the Spaniards took by furprize, without much bloodfhed,
having not the fourth part of an hundred men
killed on their fide. Whereas, when the French
took it from them, it coft five thoufand lives of
the beft foldiers the King of France had in his
army.

The hour of the poft will not permit me to fay
more, than that I am the humbleft of thy Slaves.

Paris, 14th of the 12th Moon,
of the Year 1645.

LETTER XVIII.
To Dgnet Oglou.

I Will not make trial of the virtue of friendfhip at
this time, in the way that Philofophers propofe
to be ufed between fuch as own that title. I will
not complain of the dolors I undergo, that fo by
making thy compaffion fhare them with me, I may
eafe myfelf of a part. It appears to be a pufillani-
mous, if not an unjuft action, for a man to transfer
his fufferings by difcovering them to his friend, and
defignedly throw that upon another, which is fcarce
tolerable to himfelf.

I am fick, and cuftom has rendered this almoft as
natural to me as health. My conftitution is not
proof againft the envenom'd arrows that are fhot
from the Stars. Nor am I conftellated to refift the
fecret contagion that lurks in the Elements. The
herbage of the field languifhes, when poifoned with
invifible atoms from above; and all the leaves of the
foreft wither, when touched with the baneful emif-
fion of certain Meteors, or fcorched with the winged exhalations of the night. So our bodies receive
a thoufand impreffions from things without us, and
not a few maladies from ourfelves. The very chan-

nel

nel of life proves many times the vehicle of death, while our lungs fuck in unwholefome airs, and our very breath becomes our bane. We have radical poifons in our complexions, which though they do us no hurt, while we let them lie dormant, yet once excited by our paffions and vices, they become noxious and fatal, hurrying us into the chambers of death, by unaccountable difeafes, and pains, which are under no Predicament.

This makes me bear my prefent diftemper with an equal mind, becaufe I know its original, and 'tis not in the lift of thofe maladies which have no name; whereby I can eafily calculate its duration, and almoft appoint a day when I fhall be well again. For, 'tis in the number of thofe, Phyfi-cians call Acute; and the anguifh it inflicts con-firms that Title.

Take not this for a complaint, nor what I am about to fay for a Paradox, when I tell thee, That I know not which is greater, my pleafure or pain, during this excruciating Fever. Thefe afflictions border fo near upon one another, that I find it dif-ficult to diftinguifh them. They feem to be inmates to each other, and blended together in their roots. Sure I am, they are fo twifted and interwoven in my conftitution, that I never felt one without the other. Every man may experience, that his ftrongeft defires are compounded of thefe two paffions, and the very moment of fruition itfelf cannot feparate them. The minute of enjoyment is but confe-crated to his lofs, while the heighth of his joy is the rife of his grief, fince the fmalleft particle of time cannot diftinguifh the life and death of his pleafure.

Do but reverfe this contemplation, and apply it to my ficknefs, and thou wilt find no riddle in my words, when I affure thee, that as the torment of my Fever advances, fo does my eafe; Pleafure and Pain fit and fhake hands in my heart, embrace, and equally divide its Syftole and Diaftole between them.

Yet

Yet I muft needs own, I am indebted for this al-lay of my dolors, to the prefence of my mind, which I fuffer not to be torn from itfelf, or carried away by the violent motion of my agitated fpirits. Were it not for this, a Fever would prove a Hell upon Earth, and every Pulfe a tormenting Fury. My very drink (which is all my fubfiftence now) would appear but the loathfome diftillation of that Tree, whofe unpalatable and fcalding Gum is appointed for a Beverage to the Damned. The fofteft enter-tainment of my bed, while awake, would be but a tranflation of the torments of Ixion and Sifyphus; and the flattering intervals of fleep would but re-new the fufferings of Tantalus. Whereas now, whether afleep or awake, my mind keeping aloft in her proper fphere, bufied in the contemplation and enjoyment of herfelf, and fuperior objects, partakes not in the Fever of my body, but as if on the cool top of fome high mountain, furveys all the val-leys beneath, without being fenfible of their raging heats.

I owe this tranquility, in the midft of bodily per-turbations, to the Examples of ancient Philofophers, which thou knoweft have far more influence than Precepts. But ever fince I read that Plotinus could chafe away the racking tortures of the gout and ftone, by the fole force of his thought, I daily try'd the experiment, fpurr'd on by emulation of his virtue; as judging it ignoble in a Muffulman to give the palm to a Pagan, in any point of mafculine bravery.

'Tis recorded of the fame Philofopher, that by the mere ftrength and majefty of his mind, he diffi-pated the Enchantments of Apollonius Tyanæus; and the Infernal Spirits confefs'd they were baffled by that thinking Man: As if his foul were of the nature of Medufa's head, which turn'd all into un-active Statues, who did but look on it.

Surely, great is the efficacy of contemplation, hinted at in the Arabian Proverb, which fays "He "that can fee his own eyes without a glafs, fhall

"be

" be able to move the Bull's Horns." Which myfterious expreffion is thus interpreted by the learned
Avicen. A Prophet, or Spiritual Man, who always
converfes within, fhall have power to fhake the
Foundations of the Earth; which, thou knoweft,
reft on the Horns of a Bull, according to the Doctrine of the Holy Law-giver.

I need fay no more to convince thee, that I am in
a Fever. My thus expatiating and running from one
thing to another (when I thought to have faid all
in a few words) will fatisfy thee what temper I am
in. Yet recollecting myfelf, with comfort that I
know my diftemper, I will crave leave to tell thee
a fhort ftory of a man who was fick for many years,
and yet the ableft Phyficians in Paris could not
difcern his Malady.

This perfon was an Officer of the city, whofe
bufinefs 'twas to arreft men that were in debt. He
was obferved to be the fubtleft of all his brethren,
and the moft dextrous at plotting another man's
ruin. This augmented his eftate, and he grew extremely rich. But in the one and fortieth year of
his age, he was feized with an unknown malady, a
diftemper to which the moft fkilful were ftrangers.
He languifhed five years, in a condition which
moved all men to pity. It will be tedious for to
recount the fymptoms of his illnefs. At length he
died, and according to his own will was diffected.
The Phyficians found all parts of his body decayed
and wafted; but when they came to his head, they
were above meafure aftonifhed to fee a neft of Serpents inftead of brains. This was concluded by
all to be the fource of his diftemper; and people
defcant varioufly on it. Some fay, 'twas a Judgment of God inflicted on him for his cruel fubtlety,
in trepanning men out of their liberties by a thoufand wiles. Others are of opinion, that it is a
natural product, it being ufual in fome conftitutions, for this fort of creature to be bred out of their
vitals. A Merchant that had been at Paris, told
me, that in a Province of that Empire, there were
people,

people, who by drinking the water of a certain river, had Serpents often engendered in their bowels; that he had seen one presented to the King of Spain, which was taken out of a dead man's heart, a cubit in length. He said 'twas of a crimson colour, without scales or eyes; neither was it venomous. This he asserted very solemnly, and with imprecations.

I tell thee, dear friend, if these things be true, who can be sure he harbours not some such loathsome inmate in his body; yet I would not have thee grow melancholy upon it, and disturb thy repose. The day will come, when we shall all be metamorphosed into Worms and Serpents in the Grave.

In the mean while live thou happily, in the Favour of thy Sovereign, in the Enjoyment of thy Health, the Vigour of thy Senses, and have sometimes in thy thoughts a man full of infirmities, without murmuring, Mahmut, that loves his friend in all conditions.

Paris, 26th of the 12th Moon, of the Year 1645.

LETTER XIX.

To the Selictar Aga, or Sword-Bearer to his Highness.

I Wish I could time my letters so, as to gratify all the Ministers of the Blessed Porte, by making each alternately, the first relater of some acceptable news in the mysterious Divan, where all human events are scanned with impartial judgment. But every Moon does not present us with sieges or battles; neither can I receive intelligence of all remarkable events, so soon as they come to pass. What I shall now transmit to thee, is an account of what has

has been omitted in my Difpatches to the other Minifters.

Europe is a field, fertile in Rebellion, Tumults, Diforders, and unnatural Wars. No part of Chriftendom, which is not polluted with treafons, perfidies, and maffacres ; no corner undefiled with human blood. The fon confpires the death of him who firft gave him his life. The brother lays trains to enfnare the partner of his blood, the offspring of her that bare himfelf. No bond of affection, or tie of confanguinity, is of force to reftrain thefe Infidels from purfuing each other with malice. Neither has their religion any more influence on their paffions, than the Fables of the ancient Poets. In public and private, all things are governed by intereft. Thus while every man, and every State, are only biafs'd by the narrow principles of felf-prefervation ; they abandon the general good of Chriftendom, and expofe it as a prey to the next daring invader.

There is no reafon that we fhould grieve at this folly of the Nazarenes. 'Tis from their impiety and vices the virtue and wifdom of the victorious Muffulmans receive the greater luftre, who are created to difplant thefe Uncircumcifed, and inftruct the nations which they poffeffed, in the Faith free from Blemifh.

Yet fince the depredations which the Swedes have made in Germany and Denmark, the neighbouring Crowns and States, notwithftanding their infincerity, have feemingly interpofed their endeavours, to prevent the worft effects of a war, fo deftructive to the common intereft of Chriftendom. Deputies were fent from all parts to Munfter and Ofnaburgh, with inftructions from their refpective Sovereigns. They have fquandered away much time in overtures of Peace ; whilft the Swedes daily get ground on one fide of the Empire, and the French are not unfuccefsful on the other.

The enemies of France, fenfible that they cannot reduce this crown by open force, have recourfe

to

to artifice. They endeavour to corrupt her allies, and infinuate into the minds of the United States of the Low Countries, all thofe apprehenfions which may ferve to improve the jealoufy they had already conceived of the French neighbourhood. Suggefting that the Spanifh Netherlands are the only bar which ftops the armies of France from over-running Holland, and the reft of the United Provinces. In fine, they have prevailed on them to enter into a feparate Alliance, and not to treat in conjunction with the Minifters at Munfter.

On the other fide, the French, by their Agents in Holland, endeavour to unmafk the artifice of the Spaniards; reprefenting that they have no other defign in thefe infinuations but to breed an ill underftanding between this Crown and the United Provinces, that fo by their ill offices, in time, things may come to a rupture, and the States be deprived of the friendfhip and protection of France, which alone is able to fupport that Commonwealth againft the pretenfions of their old enemies, the Spaniards. All Europe is aftonifhed to fee, that notwithftanding the utmoft condefcenfions of the French Court to conferve Peace, yet the States, led by their ill Deftiny, fhould embrace the propofals of Spain. This makes a great impreffion on all the Minifters affembled at Munfter and Ofnaburgh, who now conclude, that the Spaniards only feek occafions to perpetuate the war in Europe; that whilft the Princes of the Empire are engaged in a defence of their territories, and the Swedes and French are bufied in purfuing their conquefts, they may pick a quarrel with their new friends, whom they are deprived of a more powerful protection, and re-eftablifh themfelves in the Revolted Provinces.

The Deputies have had feveral conferences about this important affair; and the refult of their counfels, is to folicit the French Court, to ufe its utmoft power to prevent the ill confequences which this feparate Treaty will bring along with it.

'Tis

'Tis difcourfed here, that Monfieur de la Tuil-lerie will be recalled from the Court of Swedeland, being efteem'd the fitteft man to diffuade the Hollanders from this new Alliance; he having been already employed in feveral negotiations with the States, and as well vers'd in the methods of treating with that nation.

This fome judge to be the reafon of the Sieur Chanut's being fent to Swedeland, that he may refide at Stockholm; and continue to act there in the abfence of la Tuillerie.

So nice and delicate is this affair, that all France cannot afford another man duly qualified, to manage it with any probability of fuccefs. If he fhew not more candour in this negotiation, than he did when he was fent to mediate a peace, between Swedeland and Denmark, he will receive but flender thanks at his return. But if he fucceeds, 'tis faid, That Cardinal Mazarini has declared, he will merit to be inftall'd in the Order of the Holy Spirit. I have formerly fpoke of this in one of my Letters, as the moft eminent Order of Knighthood in France.

I wifh the Chriftians may ever find difficulties to obftruct the meafures they take to eftablifh an univerfal Peace, and may continue to amufe and vex one another, till the Day of the Scourge.

Paris, 20th of the 1ft Moon,
of the Year 1646.

LETTER XX.

To the Reis Effendi, Principal Secretary of the Ottoman Empire.

IT is not yet publicly known what defigns have moved this Court to order a mighty fleet to be fitted out to fea; but it is privately whifper'd, that they will fail to the Levant, to affift the Venetians againft the Turks.

People

People difcourfe varioufly, according to the ftrength or weaknefs of their reafon ; and five days ago an old man went to Cardinal Mazarini, pretending to fpeak by Infpiration : He told him, That 'twas in vain to truft to their winged caftles, (fo he called the fhips) the multitude of their armies, or in the treafures of their money ; for a Decree was fign'd in Heaven againft all the nations in Europe ; that the War was begun Above, between the Potentates who have the Cuftody of Kingdoms and Empires ; that they fhould foon fee the Banner of the Eternal difplay'd in the Firmament ; that the Stars fhould fight in their courfes, againft the wicked Profeffors of Chriftianity ; that the Ifmaelites fhould come out of their holes, and fhould flow down like a torrent from the mountains of the Eaft, over-running all Chriftendom. In fine, that Germany, France, Italy, and Spain, fhould be laid defolate, their beautiful cities fack'd, and the inhabitants led into captivity ; that the Pope, with all his Priefts, fhould be exterminated ; and that all nations fhould embrace One Law.

They put him in prifon, but he was found walking next day in the ftreets. The Keeper chained him in irons, but in the morning he was ftanding at the gate of the prifon, preaching to the people. Some fay he is a Chymift, and has found out the Mafter Secret ; others fay he is a Prophet ; but moft judge him to be a Magician. He feems now to have loft his vigour, not being able to releafe himfelf from the chains, which faften him to the ground where he lies, yet he continues to foretel the ruin of Chriftendom. 'Tis faid he will be fent to Rome, there to receive Sentence of the Holy Father, according to his demerits. I am no admirer of Vifionaries ; yet there appears fomething extraordinary in the conftancy of this man. Time will demonftrate, whether he be a true or a falfe Prophet.

A Courier came to this city laft night from Swedeland, who brings letters from Monfieur, Chanut,

Chanut, which fay, that he has receiv'd great encouragement to hope for the fhips which he was to buy in Swedeland. Thou haft already heard, that Monfieur la Tuillerie, Ambaffador for this Crown to Queen Chriftina, was thought the only proper inftrument to diffuade the United States of the Low Countries, from entering into a feparate Treaty with Spain; and that therefore Monfieur Chanut was fent to refide in his abfence at Stockholm, to obferve what paffes, and to continue the Alliance between the two Crowns.

This Minifter arrived in Swedeland the 15th day of the Moon of December, in the laft year; where Monfieur la Tuillerie had prepar'd all things ready for a fpeedy difpatch of his negotiation; having the day before his arrival made known to that Court the pleafure of the King of France, and the Queen-Regent, whofe letters were receiv'd by Queen Chriftina, with all the marks of royal affection; fhe telling the Ambaffador, that fhe infinitely honoured the perfons of the King and the Queen-Regent; and, that fhe would give them fuch proofs of the integrity of her friendfhip, as would demonftrate, That fhe was fenfible of her obligations to them, for what they had contributed to the good fuccefs of her affairs: And that there was nothing more dear to her, or more fixed in her refolution, than to conferve inviolably the League that was between them. She farther told the Ambaffadors, that it was with no ordinary complacency fhe now beheld two Minifters of France in her Court, after fhe had been without any for a long time. In fine, fhe affured them, That whatfoever could be fpared from the neceffary defence and fervice of the kingdom, whether fhips, arms, or men, fhould not be wanting to the aid of the King of France.

By this thou mayeft perceive, That though the King of France has powerful armies by Land, yet he is defective in Naval Forces: or, if he has fhips enough to defend his own realms by fea, and to

serve

ferve as convoys to his merchants, it muft be concluded, That fome foreign expedition is defign'd,
which has put him upon this extraordinary method
to increafe his fleet.

I thought it highly neceffary to acquaint thee
with this paffage, that the Minifters of the Porte,
auguft and ever happy, may confult what meafures
to take with this Prince, if it be true, That he defigns to break the League which he made with
Sultan Ibrahim four years ago. There is but little
confidence to be repofed in the moft folemn oaths
of Chriftian Monarchs, who hold not themfelves
obliged to keep Faith with thofe whom they efteem
Infidels ; and, thou knoweft, that is the beft Title
they can afford the Obfervers of the moft perfect
Law in the World. Yet the French, among all
the nations of the Meffias, feem to bear the greateft
refpect to the Ottoman Empire. But they are inconftant and changeable, which is an argument of
infincerity. They are very prompt and warm in
contracting friendfhips, and as ready to infringe
thofe facred bonds, on the leaft occafion, efpecially
where intereft and ambition have the afcendant.

The Venetian Refident at this Court makes daily
vifits to the Queen Regent, and has frequent conferences with Cardinal Mazarini. Many Couriers
pafs between Munfter, Stockholm, and this city.
Yefterday one arrived from the Venetian Ambaffador at Munfter, giving an account that the Secretary of that Embaffy, whom he had fent to Queen
Chriftina, was return'd, with the promife of eight
fhips of war, lent by the Queen to the Republic,
to affift them againft the all-conquering Muffulman.

It feems as if Sweden were become the common
Arfenal of Europe, from which the other kingdoms
are fupply'd with all the inftruments of war. But
what is moft obfervable, is, that the Venetians obtain'd not this favour, without the mediation of the
French Minifters at Stockholm. By which it feems
evident, that this Court has newly enter'd into a
private

private League with the Republic; and that they
defign to furprize the Ottomans with fome fudden
enterprize by fea.

I fhall not let a moment efcape which may prefent me with the leaft opportunity, to difcover what
is in the hearts of the Infidels.

If thou wilt favour me with thy inftructions,
I fhall make the fafer fteps. God, whofe eye pene-
trates into all obfcurities, enlighten us with a ray
to that wifdom, which once reveal'd to his Meffenger the fecret confpiracy of the Corei's, when
they plotted to deftroy the Temple built without
hands.

Paris, 17th of the 2d Moon,
   of the Year 1646.

LETTER XXI.

To William Vofpel, a Reclufe at Halmer-
ftadt in Auftria.

I Receiv'd thy letter with abundance of complacency, in that it argues the continuance of thy
friendfhip ; and that I trace therein no footfteps of
an angry pen, notwithftanding the liberty I took to
defcant on thy manner of life. On the contrary,
thou fendeft me an apology full of meeknefs. Thy
reafons have a marvellous force in them ; they feem
to fpring from a foul vegete and living, and yet dead
to paffion. Thou almoft perfuadeft me to affect
a monaftic life, which may not unfitly be term'd
a fociable Solitude.

I much admire what thou fay'ft concerning Silence, and wifh I could practife that paffive Virtue.
It is the firft ftep of wifdom, the nurfe of peace,
and the guardian of virtue. Words do but ruffle
and difcompofe the mind, betraying the foul to a
thoufand vanities. Therefore Pythagoras enjoin'd
his difciples five years filence, before he admitted
them to his myfterious Philofophy.

But

But tell me why thou didſt not rather chuſe to live in a Deſart remote from men, where thou would'ſt have no temptations to ſpeak, unleſs thou wert diſpos'd to hold a conference with the trees or beaſts, or hadſt a mind to ſport thyſelf, and have thy words retorted by mocking Echo's? If a recluſe life be thy choice, for the ſake of contemplation, I would adviſe thee to turn Hermit. But perhaps thou dareſt not venture thyſelf among the Satyrs of the Wilderneſs, or thou art afraid of the wild beaſts. As for the firſt, they are either the dreams of the Poets; or if there be any ſuch beings in reality, they will not hurt thee, ſince thou voluntarily forſakeſt the company of men, to become a Sylvan, as they are. As for the latter, I muſt confeſs, I cannot diſcommend thy fear, there being no friendſhip or intelligence common between us and the lions, tigers, bears, &c. of the foreſts. Yet I can tell thee for thy comfort, That by long and aſſiduous practice, the fierceſt of theſe creatures have been taught to converſe with men, to obey their commands, and to perform the parts of diligent ſervants, and faithful friends.

This Wilderneſs will afford thee a fair opportunity of ſtudying the natures of plants and animals, the various alterations of the elements, the influence of the winds and rains, meteors and exhalations, with many other ſecrets which are hid from the greateſt part of men, who are buried alive in populous towns and cities, baniſh'd from the familiarity of their mother earth, and moſt of her genuine products.

In the Deſart, the unforced harmony of birds ſhall lull thy ſoul in innocent and grateful ſlumbers; the gentle winds ſhall waft immortal whiſpers to thy raviſh'd ears, breathing unutterable ſounds from Paradiſe. The murmuring ſtreams ſhall warble forth their ſoft and ſweet eternal Stories. All ſhall conſpire to ſerve thy contemplation, and tranſport thy mind with ſacred Ecſtaſies.

If

If after all this thou fhall prefer the monaftic enclofure, follow thy refolution, and be happy. Only remember, That though thy body be fhut up within thofe walls, yet if thy mind ftraggle in vain and worldly thoughts, thou art no longer a Reclufe. Adieu.

Paris, 25th of the 2d Moon, of the Year 1646.

LETTER XXII.
To the Captain Baffa.

IF all be true that I have reafon to fufpect, thou wilt find a warm divertifement at fea this Spring. Though the Europeans have feem'd flow in their preparations to affift the State of Venice, fuffering their feparate interefts to fuperfede the care of that Republic, yet now they turn their eyes thither. Their backwardnefs hitherto is owing to the fecrecy with which our fage Emperor meditated the prefent war. His counfels were never whifper'd out of the Seraglio, 'till the fame winds tranfported the news, which wafted our invincible Fleet to the fhore of Candy. Now they behold the ocean cover'd with the fhips of the Eaftern Empire, fear furprizes them; the Princes of the Nazarenes tremble. They look no longer on the Republic of Venice with the eyes of envy, becaufe of her preeminence in traffic, but with another regard: They confider her as the Bulwark of Chriftendom, the only bank which has hitherto ftemm'd the tide of the Ottoman puiffance, and ftopp'd our victorious armies from overflowing all Europe.

I have inform'd the Reis Effendi, of what I knew concerning the naval forces which are fitting out in the feveral parts of the North and Weft, to aid the Venetians; but I have not told him what the Chriftians fay of thee, neither am I willing to believe it. They fpeak of thee, as of a man not

more

more difficult to be corrupted, than was thy predeceffor, who was ftrangled by the order of the Sultanefs Mother. This cenfure, I hope, is an effect of their impotence; while they flatter themfelves with the imagination of bribing him, from whofe courage and fortune they can expect nothing but defeats.

They truft much in the force of thy birth and education, and difcourfe of a certain Magical character, imprinted on thy foul, when thou was baptized, which, they fay, is indelible: And they promife themfelves, That thy native Chriftianity has more influence on thy heart, than forced Circumcifion; and that thou wilt not fight with any zeal againft men of the fame principle, as thofe who gave thee thy breath. But they confide more in the charms of their gold, with which they defign to bribe thee. In fine, they drank healths to the Honeft Renegado. So they term him, who commands the whole fleet of the Ottoman Empire.

I do not give credit to thefe calumnies, having good grounds to boaft of thy integrity. However, I counfel thee, by fome extraordinary fervice to thy Mafter, to give the lie to the Infidels: And fuffer not that, which at prefent may be but a bare fufpicion, to be improved by thy neglect or cowardice, into a palpable evidence, that thou art falfe and perfidious to the Sublime Lord of the Globe.

Paris, 6th of the 3d Moon,
of the Year 1646.

LETTER XXIII.

To Adonai, a Jew, at Vienna.

NOW thou art fix'd, 'tis time to write to thee. Thou haft been a rambler thefe three or four years, and nobody knows where to find thee. I have receiv'd eleven Difpatches from thee fince thy
firft

firſt departure from Genoua; wherein thou haſt informed me of many paſſages of State. Now I deſire thee to ſend me ſome remarks of the different nature of the people thou haſt ſeen, their various cuſtoms and laws, with whatſoever was worthy obſervation in thy Travels.

Italy is a fair field, yet produces Darnel as well as wholeſome Corn. It is a beautiful garden, yet bears Aconite intermix'd with her Roſes: Great virtues, and no leſs vices. The region is famous for the wiſdom of its inhabitants, and for their Proverbs: It is the Arabia of Europe, in many ſenſes; yet much leſſened in its own renown, ſince the decline of the Roman Empire. The Goths and Vandals turned all into Deſarts where they came, and have left ſuch impreſſions of their Northern Barbariſm behind them, as made the people they conquered half ſavages. Hence came the general decay of learning and knowledge in theſe Weſtern parts: Hence the corruption of ancient manners. The great, the noble, and the wiſe, bowed under the yoke of their new Maſters, learned their faſhions, and gloried in their ſhame. Their examples influenced the vulgar; debauchery became modiſh and authentic. Thus a general depravation of priſtine integrity took place, and men became vicious by a law.

Neither has wickedneſs planted itſelf only in Europe: The ſea could not ſtop this boundleſs evil. Aſia is infected alſo, and the vice of Italy is tranſported to the Empire of the true Believers. Thou haſt ſeen all the chief cities between the Alps and Rhegium, which is the utmoſt angle of Italy, to the South: Tell me, whether Sodom could exceed any of them in licentiouſneſs: We will not except even Rome, the ſeat of the Chriſtian Mufti. Theſe Uncircumciſed have learned of thy nation, to call the ancient Philoſophers, Infidels. But had any of thoſe Sages lived to ſee the abominations of the modern Nazarenes, they would have deſpiſed the Faith which produced no better Works.

2   Adonai,

Adonai, put in practice the import of thy name,
be Lord of thyself; and if thou stumbleſt at the
Light of the Muſſulmans, walk in that of Moſes,
but ſhun the Paths of the Chriſtians : For they are
enveloped in darkneſs, and grope at mid-day.
Live according to Reaſon, and thou ſhalt be happy.
Adieu.

Paris, 18th of the 3d Moon,
  of the Year 1646.

LETTER XXIV.

To Muſtapha, Berber Aga.

THE preſent war of Candy is like to render
that Iſland as much the ſubject of the world's
diſcourſe, as it was formerly famous, for being the
Cradle of Jupiter. In thoſe days it was called Crete,
much celebrated in the writings of the Greek Poets.
Afterwards it became a Province of the Roman
Empire; then of the Grecians; next it ſubmitted
to the Saracens. But in the time of the Chriſtian
expeditions into Paleſtine, when Baldwin Earl of
Flanders was crowned Emperor of Conſtantinople,
this Iſland came into his poſſeſſion, which he gave
to a certain valiant commander in his army, a
man of a noble deſcent, of whom the Venetians
purchaſed it; and in their hands it has continued
ever ſince. But now, in all probability, it will
be the prize of arms, which nothing ſublunary can
reſiſt.

The poſts from Italy and the ſea coaſts of this
kingdom, confirm each others news; all agreeing,
That notwithſtanding the utmoſt efforts of the Venetians and Candiots, to hinder the relief of Canea,
yet our General is got into that haven with vaſt
quantities of proviſions, and a ſufficient reinforce-
ment of men. They add, that forty thouſand of
our ſoldiers have made a deſcent in another part of
that

that Iſland, have gained the forts of Ciſternes Col-mi, and Bicorno, and were on their march-towards Suda, with a deſign to beſiege that place. They accuſe our General of barbarous cruelty, in that he cauſed five of the principal Noblemen of that king-dom to be put to death, becauſe they refuſed to be-tray their country, or enter into the intereſts of the Grand Signior.

I muſt confeſs, magnificent Aga, that whatever may be ſaid in commendation of this General's policy and fidelity to his Maſter ; it is no argument of the goodneſs of his diſpoſition. I rather admire the temper of the Duke of Orleans, who, when Graveling was ſurrender'd to him, juſt as he en-ter'd the town, was heard to ſay theſe words ; " Let " us endeavour, by generous actions, to win the " hearts of all men ; ſo may we hope for a daily " victory. Let the French learn from me this " new way of conqueſt, to ſubdue men by mercy " and clemency."

Theſe are heroic ſentiments, and agree well with the character of this Prince, who is ſaid never to have been the author of any man's death, nor to have revenged himſelf of any injury ; yet a valiant ſoldier, an expert commander, and no bad phy-ſician.

It is not hid from the Court, with what a match-leſs virtue he diſmiſs'd a gentleman that was hir'd to murder him. This Aſſaſſin was ſuffer'd to paſs into the Duke's bed-chamber one morning early, pretending buſineſs of great moment from the Queen. As ſoon as the Duke caſt his eyes on him, he ſpoke thus ; " I know thy buſineſs, friend ; thou " art ſent to take away my life : What hurt have " I done thee ? It is now in my power, with a " word, to have thee cut in pieces before my face. " But I pardon thee ; go thy way, and ſee my face " no more."

The gentleman, ſtung with his own guilt, and aſtoniſh'd at the excellent nature of this Prince, fell on his knees, confeſs'd his deſign, and who

employ'd

'employ'd him : And having promifed eternal gratitude for his royal favour; departed without any
other notice taken of him ; and fearing to tarry in
France, entered himfelf into the fervice of the Spanifh King. It was his fortune afterwards to encounter
the Duke of Orleans in a battle in Flanders. The
Duke, at this inftant, was oppreffed with a crowd
of Germans, who furrounded him, and, in the con-
flict, he loft his fword. Which this gentleman perceiving, nimbly ftepp'd to him, and delivered one
into the Duke's hands, faying withal, " Now reap
" the fruit of thy former clemency. Thou gaveft
" me my life, now I put thee in a capacity to de-
" fend thy own." The Prince, by this means, at
length efcaped the danger he was in; and that day
the fortune of war was on his fide. The French
had a confiderable victory.

Thou feeft by this, that heroic actions have fomething divine in them, and attract the favours of
Heaven. No man was ever a lofer by good works ;
for tho' he be not prefently rewarded, yet in tract
of time fome happy emergency or other arifes to
convince him, "That virtuous men are the darlings
" of Providence."

Thou that art near the perfon of the Grand Signior, may'ft find an opportunity to relate this ftory
to him, which may make no unprofitable impreffion
on his mind. Princes ever ftand in need of faithful
monitors.

Adieu, great Minifter, and favour Mahmut with
the continuance of thy protection and friendfhip.

Paris, 25 h of the 3d Moon,
  of the Year 1646.

LETTER XXV.

To Naſſuff, Baſſa of Natolia.

I Received thy letter as an argument of the continuance of that friendſhip which was between us,
when we lived together in the Scraglio.   Since that
time thou and I have been employed abroad, in different ſervices of our auguſt Emperor, who has
now rewarded thy fidelity with a command; which,
if it be not adequate to thy merit, is nevertheleſs
agreeable to thy wiſhes.

I congratulate thy honour, and wiſh thee a gra-
dual increaſe of it; for ſudden and violent leaps
are dangerous.   But our glorious Sultan diſcovers
his abilities in nothing more eminently, than in
adapting places of truſt to the deſerts and capacities
of his faithful Slaves.   So that if he ſhould in time
think fit to exalt thee to the higheſt dignity in the
State, we might from the choice of ſo wiſe a Prince,
preſage thee a better fortune than befel one of thy
name, in the reign of Sultan Achmet III. who
from a Slave ſold in the market for three ſequins,
was advanced to an honour too weighty for his virtue; being made Vizir Azem, and Lord of the
moſt delicious Province in Aſia.   But being ambitious of abſolute Sovereignty, he plotted treaſon
againſt his Maſter, which being diſcovered, the fatal
Firm was ſign'd, and all his deſigns were ſtifled with
a bow-ſtring.

By this thou may'ſt comprehend, how neceſſary
it is for Princes not to overload any man with Dig-
nities, beyond the proportion of his humility and
faithfulneſs.   Yet rewards well placed, give new
vigour to the endearments of a Slave, whereas when
good ſervices are ſlighted, it does but quench the
ardour with which they were performed.   Few men
are ſo ſpiritual, as to do great and heroic things,
purely for the ſake of internal complacency.   And I
doubt

doubt not, but the Decii themselves, in so freely sacrificing their lives for their country, had regard to
human glory. Even Seneca, whom one would take
for the moft mortify'd Stoic of that age by his
Writings, yet is conceived to have found more encouragement in the treafures of gold, with which
Nero's bounty had filled his coffers, than all his
Morals, of which he had fuch refined fentiments
and elegant expreffions.

What I have faid, thou haft wifdom enough to
apply to thyfelf, without being vain-glorious. Let
thofe whom thou employeft in any meritorious fervices, and who difcharge their truft well, be encouraged with the fame proportions of bounty. Munifi-
cence will notonly add to thy glory, but alfo advance
thy intereft, fince thou wilt ever have occafion for thy
Slaves : And he who has once tafted thy liberality,
as a reward for any eminent performance, had he
no other motive than the pleafure of renewing fo
profitable an experiment, will freely hazard his life
to ferve thee in an extremity.

This method thou wilt find of no fmall ufe to'
thee, in the wars to which thou art going, where it
will be neceffary for thee to recompenfe the leaft
fingular bravery of the meaneft foldiers, not only
with applaufe, but with fome preferment in the
army. This will not only prove a fpur to others,
but even to the perfon fo rewarded; and put him
upon new efforts of courage, to attract the eyes of
his munificent General. This will be the way for
thee, in time, to have an army compofed of all captains, or men qualified for fuch.

Yet let not this diminifh the feverity of that difcipline, which is requifite to retain a profperous
army in their obedience. I counfel thee to be ftrict
in requiring the leaft military duty, and induftrious
in performing thy own part, which will be an example to the reft; yet rather be forward to lead in
labours than in dangers : In regard thou wilt be
more ferviceable in a battle, by thy counfels and or-

ders,

ders, than by personally entering the combat. In all things prefer the welfare of the Ottoman Empire, to whatsoever else is most dear to thee, even to thy own Honour, which yet ought to be dearer to thee than thy Life.

If thou thinkest I have taken too much liberty to advise thee, accuse thyself for having honour'd me with thy friendship, which admits of no Reserves in Conversation.

Paris, 7th of the 4th Moon,
   of the Year 1646.

LETTER XXVI.

To the Kaimacham.

IT is a vast disappointment to the Venetians that our General in Candy has so opportunely revictuall'd Canea and increas'd the garrison there. Morosini is blam'd for this, by those that wish him no good. What will not envy suggest, when it beholds a man on the top of honour? This General, to give an enemy his due, is a man of spirit and true fortitude; neither courting, nor shunning dangers in the service of his country; but when once engaged in perils for that cause, he is fearless as a lion. If he has not hitherto had occasion to give the state so desperate a proof of loyalty, as once did the Roman Curtius (who bravely gallop'd into the bottomless Chasm to pacify their angry God;) yet he has often demonstrated, that his courage and fidelity come not short of the ancient Heroes. In a word, he has done too much for the republic of Venice, to escape the spleen of other grandees. All must be Generals, or the war will not prosper. Each man's ambition dictates this to the State, that a man of conduct would soon expel the Turks out of that Island: Thus in his conceit, laying a train for his own promotion.

Would'st

Wouldſt thou know Moroſini's crime, that excites all this paſſion? To ſpeak the truth, it was an over-ſight advantageous to the Ottomans. He got out with his whole fleet to ſea, and left the Port of Canea open. By which means, three of our ſhips got in with plenty of proviſions. So that the town is now in a condition to ſuſtain a long ſiege, and the Venetians deſpair of ever recovering it. Yet Moroſini has made ſo plauſible an apology, that the Senate have acquitted him, not judging it conſiſtent either with juſtice or their intereſt, to ſuffer one miſcarriage, the effect of a fair intention, to outweigh his numerous merits and ſervices. For the occaſion of his thus ſuddenly abandoning the avenue of that haven, was, to chaſe ſome of our veſſels then under ſail, not many leagues; and the taking of thoſe veſſels, on board of which were abundance of Slaves, juſtified to the Senate the truth of his pretenſions. However, there are not wanting ſuch as ſay, he held a private correſpondence with our General: Others, that the preſent Governor of Canea has formerly taken captive at ſea a ſon of Moroſini's, whom he now offer'd to reſtore, in caſe he would withdraw his ſhips from before the haven for a few days. I know not how far this may be credited. But 'tis a certain truth that Moroſini has his ſon again, and he defended himſelf by pleading, That he redeemed him by exchanging a Mahometan captive of equal Quality, whom he had aboard his ſhip.

And thou knoweſt, that this manner of barter is lawful in war. Adonai the Jew ſends me this intelligence, and I dare believe him. For ſince the inſtructions I ſent him to Genoua, he has taken care to aſcertain his reports. I wiſh it were as true that Moroſini could be prevail'd on to accept the friendſhip of the ſublime Port. But the character of that General gives me no encouragement to hope for ſo fortunate a treachery, from his ſevere virtue.

E 3 However,

However, I will hope and believe, That the eternal Patron of true Believers, will give fuch a happy iffue to the Ottoman arms in Candy, and all other parts, as fhall difpofe the Nazarenes that remain unconquer'd, to honour HIM whom they have hitherto defpifed and blafphemed ; even the Prophet, who could neither write nor read.

Paris, 7th of the 4th Moon,
  of the Year 1646.

LETTER XXVII.

To Cara Hali, a Phyfician, at Conftantinople.

THE time of the year is now come, wherein the earth turns her infide out, and nature calls forth the hidden virtues of that element, to grace the world with an infinite variety of pleafant forms and colours. The eye is loft in fuch a crowd of different beauties, and every fenfe is ravifh'd with delightful objects. The young men and virgins throng the fields, to behold the refurrection of flowers and herbs; and the old feel new vigour fpringing in their bodies, as though they had been in Medea's cauldron. Even Mahmut himfelf, who has droop'd all the winter, now begins to lift up his head, and partake in the common reftauration of all things.

If I am capable of guefling at the occafion of my frequent ficknefs, I believe it may in part be attributed to the want of frefh air, in the place where I lodge. There is a vaft difference between the ftreets of Paris, and thofe of Conftantinople. I feem to myfelf to be buried alive in this clofe city, where my chamber-window affords me no farther profpect than I can fpit ; whereas in Conftantinople the
gardens

gardens are fo intermix'd with houfes, that it looks like a city in the midft of a foreft; and by the advantage of its fituation, is always refrefhed with breezes from the fea.

Befides the impurity of thefe Infidels, who empty all their filth in the ftreets, fo that the dirt of Paris may be fmelt fome miles off; the uncleannefs of their dirt contributes in no fmall meafure to my diftemper; being forced either to feed on flefh with the blood in it, or live on herbs. They laugh at the nicenefs of the Muffulmans, who will eat no meat that was knock'd down or ftrangled. They feem to be greedy of blood, faving it in veffels, and mixing it with flower of wheat, make a certain bread thereof, which they devour without the leaft fqueamifhnefs. A true Believer would tremble at the fight of fuch impiety. I tell thee, it is impoffible to live among them and not be polluted: They have no method of purification. They wallow, and hug themfelves in their uncleannefs: They are worfe than the beafts.

Now the Spring has provided a new banquet, wherein there is no impurity, I am refolved to live like a Muffulman, and conform to the precepts of our holy Law-giver; who, when he beholds my zeal and abftinence, will fend the Angel of Health from his Paradife, to repair my decay'd conftitution.

The French Philofophers are bufied in an inquifition after certain kinds of birds, which from the fecond day of this Moon, they fay, are not to be found in the whole kingdom, though the woods and fields were full of them in the Winter. Some are of opinion, that they fly to the Moon; afferting, that if their wings will but carry them beyond the Magnetic force of the earth, it will be no pain to glide through the upper airy region, 'till they arrive within the attractive energy of that Planet, where they will naturally feek reft. Others, with more probability, fay, that thefe birds take their flight to fome other region on earth, whofe

climate

climate is more agreeable to their nature, at this time of the year.

I wish I could as easily once a year take my flight to Constantinople, where my heart is Winter and Summer. Adieu, dear Hali, and pity Mahmut, who counts himself unhappy in nothing so much, as in being absent from his friends.

Paris, 7th of the 4th Moon,
  of the Year 1646.

LETTER XXVIII.

To the Tefterdar, or Lord-Treasurer.

IT appears that France has some extraordinary design by sea: When and where 'twill be put in execution is not yet known; but the vast preparations that are making seem to threaten some foreign invasions, rather than a naval combat: it looks as if they had an expedition in hand greater than that of Xerxes; to make a bridge over the ocean, and join the separated parts of the world together. New Arsenals are built in several maritime towns, and all the forests are cut down to fill them with timber for Ships of War: The mountains are left naked of trees, and the stately woods are transplanted into the havens. An infinite number of men are employ'd in making cordage, chains, bullets, anchors, ordnance, and all other necessaries belonging to a navy.

This is Cardinal Mazarini's project, under pretence of setting the poor of the kingdom at work, and disburthening the Commonwealth of vagabonds and idle persons. But Mahmut is not placed here, to be amused with state-umbrages. It is evident, that this Minister designs to render his Master formidable on both Elements. Agents are sent to buy ships in all parts; and the very peasants

are

are forced from the vineyards and fields, to man the greateſt fleet that ever this kingdom fitted out to ſea.

Laſt moon the Sieur de Queſne was ſent to aſſiſt Monſieur Chanut, in purchaſing veſſels in Swede-land. It ſeems there has been ſome demur in his negociation; to remove which, this latter was ſent with freſh inſtructions. But Monſieur Chanut rejected him: And ten days ago came an ex-preſs from that miniſter, deſiring that a more intelligent colleague might be ſent him, in regard he found it difficult to treat ſuccefsfully with a peo-ple too much elated with continual victories.

Upon this, the Court have ſent a Courier to Stockholm, with new orders, whereby he is for-bid to make any further overtures, in order to the continuance of the League between theſe two Crowns: That France may not always appear in a ſuppliant poſture, whilſt the Swedes ſeem careleſs to conſerve a friendſhip which they themſelves firſt coveted.

Theſe miſunderſtandings may in a ſhort time proceed to a greater alienation; and, in the end, to an open rupture. Which has the more pro-bability in that General Koningſmark lately ſtop-ped ſome French troops in their march, under pretence of ſeeing their paſsports; but really, as 'tis thought, to corrupt the ſoldiers, and with-draw them from the fidelity they owe to their ſovereign.

This is highly reſented here; and they begin to diſcourſe of making Peace with Germany.

What the iſſue of theſe things will be, is yet in the dark; but God, from whoſe Throne hangs the Chain of Deſtiny, which reaches to the center of the earth, will, I hope, ſo diſpoſe of all hu-man events, that the quarrels of the Nazarenes ſhall miniſter occaſion to the Oſmans to encreaſe the territories of our puiſſant Emperor.

Paris, 1ſt of the 5th Moon,
    of the Year 1645.

E 5   L E T-

LETTER XXIX.

To Nathan Ben Saddi, a Jew, at Vienna.

I Cannot but highly applaud the resolution thou haſt taken, as thy letter intimates, to enquire into the Grounds of the Religion thou art of. This ſhews, that thou ſetteſt a value on thy reaſon, and thinkeſt thyſelf beyond the pupillage of a child; that thou eſteemeſt thyſelf of years to make a choice of thy Religion, and not to take it upon the bare Credit of thy Fore-fathers. 'Tis certain, that Error may be traditional as well as Truth: And the Pagan Idolaters pleaded a greater Antiquity for the Altars of their Gods, than could the Followers of Moſes, for the Temple of Jeruſalem, the Tabernacle in the Deſart, or the promulgation of the Law itſelf on Mount Sinai: Since there was ſcarce a region on the Continent, which had not eſtabliſh'd Rites and Ceremonies of Worſhip, long before Moſes, or even Jacob, the great Father of the Iſraelites, were born.

Amongſt the reſt of the nations, Arabia, my native country, was peculiarly bleſſed with the foot-ſteps of the illuſtrious Ibrahim, Grandfather to Iſrael, from whom the Jews deſcend. In this happy country that renown'd Prophet ſojourned, converſed with Angels: And, with the Majeſty which cannot be utter'd, he preached the Unity of the Divine Eſſence, converted the People from their Idolatry, built an Oratory at Mecha, and was taken up into Paradiſe.

Iſmael his eldeſt ſon, and heir of his father's ſpirit, as of his territories, trod in the footſteps of the Aſſumpt of God. He brake down the Idols, aſſerted one God, the Reſurrection, the Day of Judgment, the Joys of Paradiſe, and the Torments of Hell. His Off-ſpring multiplied, and peopled all the Eaſt: The Princes of this holy Line ſubdued the Infidel nations, and rooted themſelves

in

in the most fertile regions of Asia, professing themselves Mussulmans, or True Believers. Thus passed the Light of God from the Face of Ibrahim, to his Posterity by successive generations; 'till at length it rested on the Face of Mahomet, our holy Lawgiver, and was encreased with admirable splendor, by the frequent visits of the Angel Gabriel. He took the Root of Evil out of the Prophet's heart, brought him down the Alcoran from Heaven, and gave him victory and honour; call'd him by a new name, THE SEAL OF THE PROPHETS; carried him to the Throne of God, through Legions of Devils, that waited below the Moon to destroy him. And finally, made his Sepulchre glorious, and resorted to by the Believers of all nations on earth.

I sent thee this Abstract of the Mussulman History, to the end thou may'st see what pretensions the Children of Ismael have to the free Law, which you, of the Posterity of Isaac, would monopolize to yourselves: As if God had not sent Prophets to all Nations, to lead them into the right way, and not into the way of Infidels. Nevertheless, take not these things on my credit, but examine the Records of thy own Nation, and the History of past Times. Weigh all things in the ballance; consult thy reason, which is an indeficient light to those who follow it. Your Law was once pure and uncorrupted; but in time the Devil inserted many errors: He seduced your Fathers: They returned upon their steps, and fell back into Idolatry. Then God raised up the Messias, to reform all things; but him ye rejected. And when he was taken up into Paradise, ye reported, That he was hang'd on a Tree. In this the Nazarenes are your fools, and fight against themselves; whilst they assert, as you do, that he who is immortal and triumphant, among the hundred and twenty four thousand Prophets, was crucify'd between Two Thieves: Thus bringing a reproach on the Apostle of God, and on their own Faith, in believing

lieving things inconfiftent with the goodnefs
and power of the Divine Majefty. Without doubt,
Jefus, the fon of Mary, is afcended Body and Soul
into Paradife; who, whilft he was on Earth, faid,
Worfhip one God, your Lord and mine.

Let me not feem importunate or troublefome.
I feek not to circumvent thy reafon, but to direct
it. Think feven times before thou change once.
I will procure the Books of our Law; perufe them
with Judgment, and tell me then, whether thou
haft ever feen any Writings comparable to the
Alcoran? The Majefty of the Style fpeaks it above
Human Original: It is exempt from contradictions
from the beginning to the end; it confirms the
Old Teftament, which thou believeft. It is alfo
over cloathed with light. Doubtlefs it is no other
than a tranfcript of the Book written in Heaven.

If after all thy fearch thou fhalt determine
otherwife, follow thou thy Law, and I will follow mine. We both worfhip one God, Lord of the
Univerfe.

Paris, 10th of the 5th Moon,
of the Year 1646.

LETTER XXX.

To the fame.

LET not the fear of difpleafing thofe of thy
Nation hinder thee from embracing the
Truth. God fhall protect thee from the malice
of Unbelievers. Thy intereft is already great
among the Muffulmans; our auguft Emperor will
augment both that and thy honour. Take
hold of the ftrongeft knot, and adhere not to
Tagot. The cleannefs and delicacy of the
Muffulmans may invite thee, which far exceeds
that of the Jews, and yet is void of Superftition:
We only obey the fincere dictates of Nature,

which teach us, That fo long as the foul dwells
in this manficn of flefh, it partakes, of bodily
pollutions. 'Tis to avoid. thefe, we abftain from
certain meats and drinks, which cannot be
touch'd without contamination. To this end,
do we obferve that fuperlative nicenefs in our
wafhings and purifications, which difcriminates
us from all the world befide. Doubtlefs, our Law
is but the Law of Mofes, refined and fublimated
from the dregs cf adventitious error.

Write often to me, and whatever reafons may
prevail on thee not to change thy Religion, let no
arguments tempt thee to fwerve from thy Fidelity to the Sovereign of Sovereigns on earth, the
Grand Signior, in whofe veins runs the moft exalted blood of human race.

Here is a report in this city, that the Elector
Brandenburgh will demand the Queen of Sweden
in marriage. Let me know if it be true, that I
may inform the Minifters of the lofty Port, from
whom nothing ought to be conceal'd that occurs
of moment betwixt the two Poles.

Inform me alfo, what paffes remarkable in the
Affembly of the Deputies at Munfter, and whether
it be true, that the Danube has lately overflow'd
its banks, and carried away four hundred houfes
in its rapid courfe.

Such ftories are told here, by thofe who know
not how to pafs away their time, but in hearkening after foreign news, to furnifh themfelves
with matter to amufe the credulous, and beget
admiration of their intelligence.

I have fent thee a Watch of my making; if
thou accepteft it with good will, 'tis a fufficient
acknowledgment.

May God, whofe prefence fills the Univerfe,
difclofe himfelf to thee, in the way of Salvation,
and continue to breathe good motions into thy
foul.

Paris, 10th of the 5th Moon,
   of the Year 1646.

LET-

LETTER XXXI.

To the Kaimacham.

ADONAI the Jew has much improv'd himself in his late progress through Italy. He is grown a perfect Statesman; having found out the way to penetrate into secrets, and to dispatch business without any noise. He may prove very serviceable at Venice, during the present war of Candy. His acquaintance in that city gives him access to the cabals of the Senators, who spare not, over their wines, to whisper the counsels of the State, and to descant upon the measures that are taken to defend the Republic, against the invincible prowess of the Ottoman armies.

It is publicly known, that they have sent Ambassadors to the Crown of Muscovy, that of Poland and to the Cossacks, inviting them to enter into a League against the Grand Signior. But few are acquainted with the private Treaty they are making with the Bassa of Aleppo. We owe this discovery to the diligence and wit of this Son of Israel. He has drawn the secret from the mouths of several eminent Counsellors of State; and assures me, That the Senate have made such proposals to the Governor, as cannot fail of inducing him to revolt.

This may prove of ill consequence, if not timely prevented: The pernicious example of this Bassa, may incite others to tread in his steps, especially his neighbours of Sidon and Damascus, who have for so long time meditated a sovereignty, independent of the throne, which first establish'd them in those charges. Besides, the single forces of this Bassa will be able to give a powerful diversion to the arms of the Empire, already engag'd in Candy, Dalmatia, and other parts, by sea and land. He says, The

Venetians

Venetians fpeak much in the praife of this Bafla's juftice, whereof they relate many examples; among the reft, a certain Cook among the Franks of that city, was accus'd of dreffing and felling putrify'd flefh, whereby many that did eat thereof, were infected with the Plague. Complaint being made of this to the Bafla, he fends for the Cook, and examines him about it: He reply'd, that he fold none but good and wholefome meat, for if it happened, that at any time he was forced to keep any flefh in his houfe above three days, he fo feafon'd it with fpices and herbs, as made it very favoury, and without any ill fcent.

The Bafla, not having patience to hear any more of this fetid apology, commands his arms and legs to be cut off, and the veins to be feared up; ordering, That during the time he had to live, he fhould have no other food, but what was made of his own limbs.

They relate one more paffage, of a complaint that was made by a peafant, whofe daughter this Bafla's only fon had ravifhed: The Bafla compelled him to marry her, with this charge, Let me hear no more complaints of thee, except thou art refolved to leave me without a Son.

It is reported here, that the King of Perfia has made a Peace with the Great Mogul; and that they will both turn their forces againft our auguft Emperor.

Here is alfo a Courier arrived from Marfeilles, who brings news of the revolt of Cavarra; the inhabitants of that place having fhaken off the obedience they owe to the Sultan, and put themfelves under the protection of the Venetians; and that General Grimani has taken four fhips of Ragufa, laden with ammunition for our army. He adds alfo, That Morofini has thirty fmall veffels, befides gallies, under the very walls of the Dardanells. I long ago fuggefted to the Vizir Azem, that the weaknefs of thefe caftles would, one time or other, encourage

encourage the Chriftians to perform fome notable exploit in the Hellefpont. But Mahmut's counfel was not regarded.: Now the event juftifies my advice, the Porte will confult the fecurity of that avenue. I wifh they do not practife the Trojan wifdom. The Venetians have a powerful fleet : If they block up the Hellefpont, and hinder our fhips from failing into the Archipelago ; and the Coffacks in the mean while cover the Black Sea with their barks, committing a thoufand piracies and ravages, what will become of the Imperial city? Whence will they provide fuftenance for fo many millions of people as inhabit that city, and the parts adjacent?

Thefe things are worthy of confideration : As thou haft the care of that capital Seat of the Ottoman Empire, thou wilt not blame Mahmut, for putting thee in mind of the danger which threatens even the Seraglio itfelf at this juncture. However, I have done my duty, fage Minifter, and refer the reft to thy wifdom. My letters are all regifter'd ; and if affairs fhould fucceed ill, it will be manifefted, that Mahmut, who watches night and day to ferve the Great Mafter of the World, has not been wanting to give timely notice of what might be advantageous to the Monarchy of the True Faithful.

Thou, who art celebrated for thy juftice and probity, pardon the liberty which my zeal for thy Mafter and mine, renders worthy of excufe.

Paris, 19th of the 5th Moon,
  of the Year 1646.

The End of the FIRST BOOK.

L E T.

LETTERS

WRIT BY

A SPY AT PARIS.

BOOK II

LETTER I.

To the most Magnificent and Illustrious Vizir Azem, at the Porte.

OSMIN the Dwarf, whom I formerly mention'd, remains still in the Court; and continues his good offices in communicating to me such passages as come to his knowledge. He has a subtle wit, and bears no hearty love to the Christians, tho' he be one himself in Profeffion. He frequently visits me, and trusts me with his secrets. One day he convinced me by evident circumstances, that Cardinal Mazarini was projecting to give some secret and sudden blow to the Ottoman Empire for which Osmin seems to be concern'd by a natural inclination; being, as I told thee, born of Mahometan parents, he was uneasy, till he had acquainted me with his apprehensions; and I gave him such instructions, as I thought most proper on this occasion. I set my thoughts on the rack, to prevent so dire a mischief. And having premeditated well on this affair, I pitched on a course, which would at once clear me from the Cardinal's suspicion; and by seeming to
favour

favour his defigns, would abfolutely overthrow them. I went to him boldly one day, and being admitted to his Clofet, I thus addrefs'd that Politician.

"THERE are now nine years elaps'd, great "Minifter, fince I firft breath'd the air of "France; during all which time, I have not only "fhared in common with the natives, the benefits "which have accrued to this noble kingdom, "under the aufpicious Miniftry of Cardinal "Richlieu, and his no lefs eminent fucceffor; "but have alfo received many particular honours "from that illuftrious Prince of the Church, to "which your Eminence has been pleafed to make "fome undeferved additions. 'Tis to you both I "owe the character which has introduced me into "the acquaintance and favour of the Nobility, "who on that fcore have thought me worthy to "inftruct their children in the Greek and Arabic "tongues; have vouchfafed to admit me to their "Salt, and to encourage me with the hopes of "finding a confiderable repofe in the bofom of the "Gallican Church, after a tedious peregrination "from my own country.

"When I reflect on all the accumulated blef-"fings I enjoy, under the protection of your Emi-"nence, bleffings equally tranfcending my ambi-"tion, as they do my merits; I apply all my ftu-"dies to find out fome acceptable way of acknow-"ledgment to my gracious Benefactors. And "becaufe nothing can be more welcome to the "Guardian of France, than the means of advanc-"ing the public good of the kingdom committed "to his care; I now prefume, as a teftimony of "my gratitude, to propofe to your Eminence fome "fpeculations, which, if put in execution, will, "in my judgment, not only render France the "moft formidable and abfolute Monarchy on "Earth, but alfo the whole Catholic world in "eternal obligations to her; and give juft reafon
"to

" to change the Style of the moſt Chriſtian Majeſ-
" ty, from the Eldeſt Son of the Church, to that
" of Father of all Chriſtendom.

" Your Eminence will not wonder at the zeal
" of a ſtranger, or the care that Titus of Moldavia
" takes for France : In being ſolicitous for this
" kingdom, I conſult the welfare of my own
" country, and of all the nations which profeſs the
" faith of Jeſus ; ſince it is eaſy to ſee, that in the
" fate of France, that of all Europe is involv'd.

" It is a long time ſince the diſmembring re-
" liques of the Roman Empire, bordering on Aſia,
" found themſelves too weak to reſiſt the puiſſance
" of the Ottoman arms. All Greece was ſoon
" over-run by the warlike Turks. Tranſylvania,
" Wallachia, Moldavia, with the greateſt part of
" the Upper-Hungary, quickly became Tributaries
" to the inveterate enemies of the Chriſtian Name.
" And Germany itſelf is ſo enfeebled by their re-
" peated incurſions, that all the Emperor can do,
" is to make diſhonourable and coſtly compoſi-
" tions, buying a precarious peace with little leſs
" charges than would ſerve ſome more fortunate
" Prince, to carry on a glorious and ſucceſsful
" war. Neither is the State of Venice in any bet-
" ter condition of defence, the Turks having pared
" away whole Provinces from that once flouriſhing
" Commonwealth, and by their continual invaſi-
" ons and hoſtilities, reduced her to a neceſſity of
" merchandizing with the Ottoman Porte for a
" Peace : which is no ſooner concluded, but on
" the leaſt pretence is broke again, by thoſe who
" hold themſelves not obliged to keep Faith with
" Chriſtians. Behold, at this time without provo-
" cation on the part of Venice, or a declaration of
" war by the Grand Signior, the late League bro-
" ken on a ſudden, and in a moſt clandeſtine manner.
" Behold Candy environ'd by their Fleet at Sea,
" and her fertile plains cover'd with Armies of
" Mahometans by Land. Behold her cities in the
" hand of her enemies, and her villages laid deſo-
" late :

" late : her Nobles put to the fword, and her
" Merchants led into captivity. In fine, Behold
" that afflicted Commonwealth yet ftruggling with
" her Fate, and fending her Ambaffadors to all the
" Princes and States of Chriftendom, demanding,
" or rather, in a fuppliant manner, imploring their
" affiftance. Yet fhe finds little or no help from
" any but the Pope, and the Knights of Malta.
" And his Holinefs has enough to do to preferve
" the Patrimony of the Church from violence. The
" State of Genoua is too intent upon her traffic, to
" regard the calamities of her neighbours. And
" all the Princes of Italy have fuch diverfions at
" home, as render their application to things
" abroad very cold and indifferent. In the mean
" while, the Turks gain gound, double their
" ftrength, and encreafe their victories! O deplo-
" rable ftate of Chriftendom! Is there no redrefs for
" thefe miferies? Yes, furely there is! And fuch a
" redrefs, as only lies in your power, Great Mi-
" nifter, to apply; which, in the experiment, I
" dare affure will prove effectual.

" I do not pretend the Vifions and Infpirations
" of Peter the Hermit, who garbled fecular di-
" vine offices; and arming himfelf in habiliments
" of fteel, went dragooning up and down Chrift-
" endom, at the head of a confufed rabble, to
" render himfelf popular, and acquire the triple
" character of Pilgrim, Prieft, and Captain. The
" ill fuccefs of his rafh Expedition fhew'd, that
" he was only ftung with a religious Caprice,
" and that God approved not his Folly. I do not
" go about to propofe another Crufade, or con-
" trive a way to fhed whole Deluges of human
" Blood, with no other confequence, than to
" ftain Hiftory with the fanguine Memoirs of
" Chriftendom's vanity and misfortune. Befides,
" that would be found impracticable, in this age,
" which was fo eafy to put in execution five or
" fix hundred years ago : The world is not fo
" devout now, as it was in thofe days; neither
" are

" are men fo prompt to run the rifk of their
" lives on religious Errands, for the honour of
" being efteem'd Martyrs. 'Twill be difficult to
" find out a new Lift of Godfrey's, Baldwin's,
" Guy's, and other Heroes, to lead the Champions
" of the Crofs through all the hardfhips of the fea
" and land, fo many hundred miles, into remote
" and defolate regions, to combat not only with
" flefh and blood, but with famine, peftilence,
" and all the miferies of human life : And, as if
" this were not enough, to fheath their fwords alfo
" in each others bowels, for Punctilio's, mere
" trifles of miftaken honour, and ill-timed emu-
" lation : And all this only to purchafe the empty
" Title of King of Jerufalem ; or the precarious
" authority of a Grecian Emperor : Both fhort-
" liv'd honours; the one to be loft in a little time,
" with all Paleftine, to the Saracens ; the other
" depending only on the pleafure of the multitude !
" Such were the glorious fruits of the Chriftian
" arms in thofe days ! Such the triumphs attending
" our victories! Thefe the trophies which our Fathers
" erected to their own difgrace ; when after a war
" of fo many years they left the Holy Land, in a
" worfe condition than they found it ; and of fo
" many hundred thoufand men as marched thither,
" threatening the utter fubverfion of the Saracen
" Empire, there fcarce return'd enough to difperfe
" the news of their own overthrow.

" Waving therefore thefe vifionary rafh Expe-
" ditions, I now propofe to your Eminence an un-
" dertaking, which, though it may make lefs noife
" in the world, yet carries more probability of fuc-
" cefs, and will not only promote the intereft of
" France, but redound to the advantage of all
" Europe.

" No man who is acquainted with Hiftory, can
" be ignorant what claims the Kings of France
" have made to the Empire of the Weft, fince the
" days of Charlemaigne, the royal predeceffor of
" his prefent Majefty, who was dignified with the
" Imperial

" Imperial Title, by the Sovereign Bishop. Nei-
" ther is it unknown, by what artifices the House
" of Austria have procured the Translation of the
" sacred Authority to their own Family.

" Your Eminence is sensible by what tyrannous
" and unjust methods they have maintain'd them-
" selves in this highest pitch of human glory; and
" not content with this, how they have aspired after
" the Monarchy of the whole World! All the
" North have groaned under the burden of that in-
" supportable Tyranny. And their encroachments
" on the South, have render'd that Line little less
" infamous. They spare neither civil nor eccle-
" siastical rights in the pursuit of their ambition,
" not even the Patrimony of St. Peter, which has
" ever been esteemed sacred and inviolable by
" Christian Princes. They have sack'd Rome it-
" self, and led the supreme Pastor of the Church
" into Captivity. What should I speak of the Hol-
" landers, Swizers, Grisons, and other nations,
" which, impatient of the Austrian yoke, revolted
" from their cruel Masters, and have ever since
" asserted their liberty by the force of their arms?
" What should I mention the frequent troubles in
" Bohemia, Transylvania, and Hungary, when the
" inhabitants of those countries grown desperate
" with their daily oppressions, have bravely endea-
" voured to redeem themselves and their posterity
" from perpetual servitude; but for want of a pow-
" erful Protector, have been forced to yield to their
" old Masters! That incestuous Race are grown
" odious to the whole world: Even the Princes of
" the Empire are forced to smother their resent-
" ment, when they elect one to possess the Impe-
" rial Diadem, whom they cannot but hate.

" That therefore which I aim at in this address
" is, To represent to your Eminence, how easy it
" will be in this juncture for his most Christian
" Majesty to recover the Imperial Crown, which
" of right belongs to none but the Successors of the
" renown'd Charlemaigne; and which even the
" greatest

" greateſt part of the Germans themſelves wiſh to
" ſee placed on the head of Lewis XIV. Moſt of
" the Electors are already inclining to the intereſts
" of France : It will not be difficult to win the
" reſt. The Hungarians, &c. long for a deliverer:
" And the other Provinces beyond the Danube
" will freely open the gates of their cities, to let
" in his armies, whom they look on as the Hope
" of all Chriſtendom. The Helvetians, who are
" Allies of this Crown, will not fail to perform
" their part. The Swedes have already plucked
" many Feathers from the ravenous Eagle. And
" the forces of this crown have blunted her Ta-
" lons. Another campaign will quite deplume her,
" enervate her laſt vigour, and end the tedious con-
" troverſy.

" Let not therefore an untimely peace with the
" Emperor, ſo much talk'd of, ſtop the current of
" the French triumphs ! Let not the ſiniſter practice
" of German Penſioners in the Swediſh Court, oc-
" caſion a rupture between two the moſt potent
" and victorious crowns in Europe ! Or rather,
" let Queen Chriſtina reap the ſole glory of ſo for-
" tunate and profitable a war ! His Majeſty has a
" formidable army by Land ; and, in a ſhort time,
" will have an invincible Fleet by Sea. Continual
" victories court the perſeverance of the French va-
" lour, whilſt the juſtice of your cauſe invites to
" the battle.

" All things conſpire to put a period to the Au-
" ſtrian grandeur. Only ſnatch the preſent oppor-
" tunity, which, once loſt, may never be reco-
" vered again. 'Twas only the ſudden and unex-
" pected fate of Henry IV. this King's grandfa-
" ther, of eternal memory, that hindered him from
" putting in execution the ſame deſign I now pro-
" poſe. And if Lewis XIII. did not proſecute it,
" 'twas becauſe he wanted a favourable juncture.
" Now, behold it offers itſelf: It is in your power,
" ſupreme Director of the State; under his Ma-
" jeſty, to build the Fortune of France ſo high,

2   " that

" that all the Nations of Chriftendom may repofe
" under its Shadow. Purfue the fuccefs which
" Heaven has already granted. And when all Eu-
" rope is thus fettled in a durable peace, either
" making honourable friendfhip with, or entirely
" fubmitting to the new Gallic Empire; then will
" be the time to call the Ottomans to an account,
" for the ravages and fpoils they have committed
" in Chriftian countries, and to carry out arms to
" the walls of Conftantinople, and drive thefe Bar-
" barians back to the primitive rocks and defarts,
" from whence they have thus long ftraggled, to
" ruin the moft defirable Provinces of Afia and
" Europe; nay, and of the whole World.

    " There is no other way but this, in my judg-
" ment, to ftop the progrefs of the Turkifh victo-
" ries. Since it is impoffible to make a durable
" Peace among Chriftian Princes, but by con-
" queft; I mean fuch a Peace, as will infpire
" them with the refolution, and put them into a
" capacity, to unite all their forces in a war
" againft the Mahometans. As for the prefent con-
" dition of the Republic, if their loffes were great-
" er than they are like to be, yet they will be in-
" confiderable in comparifon to the mighty gain
" which will afterwards accrue, not only to them
" but to all the Chriftian nations, by advancing
" the French Crown to that height of grandeur
" defign'd for it by Fate. Hitherto the Chriftian
" Princes have only endeavoured to apply a re-
" medy to the part particularly affected; from
" whence if by fortune they chafed the diftem-
" per, it foon brake out in fome other member;
" whence it came to pafs that we loft Province
" after Province, and the Turks are almoft gotten
" into the Heart of Europe. If therefore we de-
" fign to drive them thence, it is neceffary to fol-
" low this method, which will be found the only
" way to pluck this evil up by the roots.

    " Go on then, moft prudent and illuftrious
" Guardian of the Crown, deftin'd to command
" the

" the Earth: Go on, and lift up our great
" Mafter to the Wreath with which the Tutelar
" Angel of Europe is ready to environ his facred
" Temples. Let not the German Deputies at Mun-
" fter any longer amufe you with feigned over-
" tures of Peace. But purfue the propitious Fate
" of France, which wants to lead our armies to
" victories, triumphs, and glories, and to efta-
" blifh a new Empire in the World, to which
" all nations fhall pay homage, and fly for pro-
" tection."

Thou feeft, illuftrious and ferene Vizir, that I
have ufed much flattery in this addrefs. It is a
neceffary vice in the Court of France, where no
Diogenes can have audience. It cannot be expected that I fhould difcover by the Cardinal's anfwer what his fentiments were of my project. He
is of a debonair humour, and would rather feign
Virtues to commend in another man, than put
him to the blufh by mentioning his real Vices.
This is an effect of his natural Difpofitions, which
he is wife enough to improve to the Ends of Policy. There being no fubtiler artifice to gain a popular efteem, than by the reputation of a generous
temper.

However, I think I faid nothing that could juft-
ly offend him, unlefs he were endued with the
incommunicable gift of difcerning hearts. For
otherwife at the worft, he could but tax me with a
loyal prefumption and miftake, in propofing things
altogether impracticable.

Thefe were fuch as thou wilt eafily difcern, when
thou confidereft, that though they appear fair and
eafy in the attempt, as the circumftances of Europe
are at prefent; yet the revolution of a few Moons
may quite change the face of affairs; The Emperor
may make a Peace with Swedeland, the Pope might
interpofe his mediation and authority, the Affembly
at Munfter might have a conclufion according to
their wifhes, the Electoral Princes might be more

firmly faftened to the intereft of the Empire. Befides, another campaign may prove as fatal to the
French, as the former have been profperous. After
all, if they fhould find encouragement to begin this
enterprize, and fhould meet with anfwerable fuccefs
in the profecution of it, yét a thoufand occurrences
would emerge, to hinder them from enjoying their
new gotten empire long; or from being able to
maintain a war againft the Emperor, whofe fubjects are infinite, and treafures inexhauftible.

If thou, who art the light of the Ofinan Monarchy, fhall approve of what I have done, my happinefs will be great; neverthelefs thy reproofs will
not make me miferable, fince they are arguments
of thy condefcenfion and favour.

Paris, 10th of the 6th Moon,
   of the Year 1646.

LETTER II.

To Ifmael Mouta Faraca, a White Eunuch.

THY letter is come fafe to my hands, accom-
pany'd with a munificent prefent from Egry
Boinou, who thou telleft me is deprived of his eyes
by the Grand Signior's order. I condole the calamity
of thy friend, yet accufe not the juftice of him who
is mafter of us all. We are Muffulmans, and
muft not difpute the Pleafure of Heaven, or the
Commands of our Sovereigns. It is an argument of
their clemency, when they retrench their anger,
and fpare the lives of their Slaves. The Sultan is
merciful in a higher degree, in not extending his
hands to the wealth of our friend, but has left that
and his liberty untouch'd, whereby he is ftill in a
capacity of enjoying many pleafures, which are denied to thoufands who have their fight.

I do not write this, as if I were void of compaffion toward my friend. I owe him ftill the
                                  same

fame affection, as when he was able to read the fin-
cerity of it in my face. But I would not have the
lofs of his eyes abate the fight of his foul, which is
his reafon. Let him remember, that a famous
Philofopher has done that voluntarily to himfelf,
for the fake of a lefs interrupted contemplation,
which is impofed on our friend as a punifhment.
There is no outward difafter can hurt the optics
of a mind guarded with patience and fhut up within the circles of its own light. Such a foul is impregnable againft all the affaults of Fortune, and
triumphs over Deftiny itfelf.

Befides, our beloved Eunuch can ftill converfe with
his friends, which is a privilege the Deaf would
almoft give their eyes to enjoy. It is hard to determine
which of thefe two Senfes would be miffed with leaft
regret, efpecially to a man, who, by his excellent
voice and fkill in Singing feems to be the very Soul
of Mufic.

What is it in all this infinite variety of vifible
objects, that affects the eye with fo refined a pleafure, but the harmonious difpofition and fymmetry
of the parts, which compofe the whole fcene of the
univerfe? And may not that pleafure be tranflated to
the ear, when it receives the proportionate meafures
and exquifite cadencies of founds? Certainly Mufic
is no other than beauty to the ear, as beauty is
Mufic to the eye.

But our friend Egry needs not thefe encouragements: He underftands the way to make himfelf
happy, and has wifdom enough to put it in practice.

The Grand Signior's fury is pacified. Egry lives.
He has houfes and gardens; gardens replenifh'd
with all manner of fruits and flowers to gratify his
Tafte and Smell. He is mafter of much treafure
in filver and gold, and of many Slaves. If all thefe
cannot contribute to his felicity, he is Mafter of
himfelf, which is effential Happinefs

Thou who fucceedeft him in that honourable
poft, and guardeft the avenues of the majeftic

Chamber, where the addresses and supplications of all the Princes of the earth are made at the feet of our august Emperor, watch thy senses, and obey thy reason. Remember thy Predeceffor's Fate, and forget not Mahmut: But above all things, forget not thyself. Adieu.

Paris, 20th of the 6th Moon,
   of the Year 1646.

LETTER III.
To Dgnet Oglou.

I AM extremely surprized, and equally troubled at the severe punishment which Sultan Ibrahim has inflicted on Egry Boinou. His succeffor, Ismael Mouta Faraca, sent me the first news of it, but said nothing of the Eunuch's crime. Neither would I requeft that satisfaction of a man, who derives a new luftre from the tragical eclipse of my friend, left my love should have betray'd my discretion, and tempted me to utter that, which is not proper for a Slave to the Sultan to exprefs. Our thoughts are our own whilft we keep them chain'd up in our breafts, but if once we suffer them to take air, in words, they become another man's, who may make use of them to our ruin. I never had familiarity enough with Ismael, to truft him with reflections of this nature. Befides his own letter to me difcovered too much freedom to be void of defign, it being the firft ever pafs'd between us; which for that reafon ought to have been dictated in a ftyle more referv'd. I fet him a pattern in my anfwer, not letting a word efcape my pen, which might fpeak lefs refignation to the will of our Mafter, than tendernefs for my friend's fuffering.

'But with thee I dare use greater freedom: My long experience of thy integrity will juftify this boldnefs. Tell me, my Dgnet, was it not the

blindnefs

blindnefs of Sultan Ibrahim's paffion, which has robb'd Egry of his fight? Anfwer me without difguife: Was it not fome caprice of jealoufy? Was it not becaufe the Mafter thought he faw too much, that the Slave fees not now at all? If that fenfe was not judg'd criminal to Egry, why was it in particular punifh'd? But 'tis in vain to meafure the cruel frolic of a Sovereign Monarch by a Rule, who makes his Will a Law.

The Chriftians fay, The Ottoman Princes are Butchers, and the whole Empire a Shambles; where perfons of all degrees are facrificed to the luft or paffions of a Tyrant. I tell thee, though I approve not the licentious tongues of thefe Infidels, yet it appears too true, that fo uncontrollable a power as the Eaftern Monarchs are invefted with, prompts them to commit many violences, for which juftice can make no plea. It were to be wifh'd, that the practices of the Sublime Seraglio, did not too often verify it. Suffer me to be exafperated a little for the cruel fentence executed on my friend, the moft accomplifh'd perfon within the walls of that magnificent Palace. Doubtlefs, he owes the lofs of his eyes to the grudge of fome envious minion, who would not brook fo dangerous a rival in the Sultan's favour. For this unfortunate Eunuch, who charm'd all hearts, made fome impreffion alfo on the cruel Ibrahim's. He often loved to hear him fing the lively Doric ftrains to chafe away his melancholy; for Egry is a fecond Orpheus, whofe voice, thou knoweft, infpired the tree and rocks with paffion. Befides, he has many other gifts, which render'd his perfon and converfation delectable to all; and taught the whole Seraglio new leffons of Platonic love.

When thou haft received this, I defire thee to give him a vifit: Thou knoweft his houfe at Galata. Embrace him in my name, and give him a kifs of faithful friendfhip. Forget not alfo to return him my acknowledgments for the Diamonds he fent me: And cheer him with this thought, that one

F 3   day

day his eyes fhall be renew'd in Paradife, far brighter than thofe glittering Jewels. Adieu.

Paris, 2cth of the 6th Moon,
    of the Year 1646.

LETTER IV.

To Dichieu Huffein Baffa.

'TIS not eafy to guefs at the motive which induced the Duke of Orleans to begin this year's campaign in fo rigorous a feafon. It was the firft Moon, and the ground was cover'd with deep fnows (an ill time to march in an enemy's country): and when thefe fnows were diffolv'd, floods follow'd. It feems, as if he were thirfty of fame, and would acquire the character of a hardy Warrior; refolving to fhun no fatigue, which might advance the reputation of his arms.

The Duke of Enguien, fpurr'd on with a glorious emulation, foon follow'd with another army, but by a different road. There are four Marefchals of France gone with them. Thefe early marches make a great noife. But little of action could be expected while the wary Flemmings knowing the paffes of the country, and the force of the floods, have kept their winter quarters, fpending the time at eafe, in preparing all things neceffary for a more feafonable campaign, which they have now begun.

In this the Spanifh policy deferves commendation; who would not expofe the health and lives of their foldiers to unneceffary rigours, but waited till the fun had well dry'd up the unwholefome damps of the earth, and fhedding his benigner influence through the air, invited them forth into the field. But when I thus approve the wifdom of the Spaniards, think not that I condemn the fprightly Genius of the French, who
                                    feem

feem to approach neareft the bravery of the Muffulman armies.

The action of a French Officer was worthy of remark, who being fent from the camp with letters to the King and Queen, arrived at the Court, the 24th day of the fecond Moon, whilft the ground was yet frozen hard. After he had delivered his meffage, the Chamberlain of the Royal Houfhold appointed him a lodging for that night in the King's Palace, he being to return to Flanders the next day. But he generoufly refufed it, faying, "It became "not him to lie in a bed of down, when his General, "with the whole army, were forced to fleep on the "frozen earth." Therefore caufing fome ftraw to be brought out of the ftables, he took his repofe thereon, in the open air. The young King, extremely pleas'd with his gallantry, ordered him an hundred Pieces of Gold, and recommended him to the Duke of Orleans as one of the braveft men in his army.

I fwear by the whiftling of the winds, and the ruffling of the leaves, that I honour fuch virtue, even in an Infidel.

Paris, 20th of the 6th Moon, of the Year 1646.

LETTER V.

To Kerker Haffan, Baffa.

THY letter is come to my hands, with the prefent of Kopha, which is fo much the more acceptable, becaufe thou broughteft it thyfelf from the valley of Amoim, the place of my nativity. It is an evident fign that thou haft not forgot thy countryman, in that thou condefcendeft to oblige him in fo peculiar a manner. The place where we drew our firft breath is always dear to mortals; and the remembrance of that delicious vale, affects Mahmut with fingular delight. 'Tis true indeed, I was brought

F 4 from

from thence before I could diſtinguiſh one place from another; but I have viſited that region ſince, and have reaſon to pronounce it the moſt delectable part of Arabia. Had the Grecian Poets ſeen that Paradiſe, they would not have ſo extolled the celebrated fields of Tempe in Theſſaly. Theſe happy vallies, the Elyſium of the World, bleſs'd with an eternal Spring.

Thou art highly oblig'd to the Sultan for the liberty he has given thee to viſit the place of thy cradle, and to ſojourn ſo long among thy kindred. Thy father was famous in that country for hunting of Lions, and other Beaſts of Prey. I have heard ſome of our Tribe praiſe his valour and dexterity, in the chace of thoſe fierce animals. They told me, that in the ſpace of two years, he had preſented the Beglerbeg with twenty Lions heads killed by his own hand: That he had three tame ones in his houſe, which he had taken when whelps, from a Lioneſs of prodigious bulk. That the walls of his houſe were hung with the ſkins of Tigers, Panthers and Lions, the trophies of his indefatigable diligence, ſkill and courage, in purſuit of wild beaſts. In a word, they ſaid, he was the moſt ſucceſsful hunter in all Arabia. If thou inheriteſt his inclinations as well as his blood (for they commonly go together) thou haſt had a fair time to range the Foreſts, and purge the Deſart of thoſe ravenous creatures. Were it not for the enmity of the Gnats, the Eaſt would be over-run with theſe ſavages. They ſay, this little deſpicable Inſect deſtroys more Lions, than all the Huntſmen in Aſia. For ſwarming about them in the heat of Summer, they chiefly faſten on their eye-lids, which they ſting ſo vehemently, that the Lions thinking to eaſe themſelves by ſcratching, often tear their own eyes out, and ſo are famiſh'd.

To underſtand well the different natures of beaſts, is a ſtudy fit for Kings. 'Twas the glory of Solomon to be accurate in this knowledge: And Alexander the Great had ſuch an eſteem for it, that he
beſtowed

beſtowed on Ariſtotle the Philoſopher eight hundred Talents, only for writing a Treatiſe of Animals. Our Holy Prophet was eminent above all other mortals, for his familiarity with the brutal generation, underſtanding their qualities and language, and often diſcourſing with them. When he lived in the Deſarts, a Libard continually waited at the door of his Cave: and did all the offices of a kind and faithful ſervant. Such grace is given but to few.

But, I forget my own opportunity of venting my affections to my country and my friends. I forget that I am writing to one who is newly come from Arabia. Would to God I might ſee thee, were it but for an hour. I have a thouſand queſtions to aſk about my Relations, and what changes have happened ſince I was there.

But I muſt ſacrifice theſe natural fondneſſes to the will of Deſtiny. I am a double exile: And ſince it is for the ſervice of the Grand Signior, I am reſign'd.

Adieu, happy Miniſter; and if Mahmut may be admitted ſometimes to mingle with the train of thy better thoughts, he ſhall count himſelf happy where-ever he is.

Paris, 2d of the 7th Moon,
    of the Year 1646.

LETTER VI.

To Huſſein, Baſſa.

THE taking of Retiino in Candy, has fill'd the Nazarenes with apprehenſions of greater calamities.

The firſt fortunate ſtrokes in a war, make deep impreſſions on the enemy; the vulgar looking on

them.

them as the Index of their future Deftiny.   But re-peated fucceffes chill their vitals, bereave them of courage and hope, leaving them nothing but omi-nous portents, and fuperftitious prefages of their approaching ruin.   So hard a thing it is to judge of human events, without being carried into ex-tremes.   They already give over the whole Ifland for loft.   I wifh and believe it may prove true.   Yet at the fame time I know the fortune of war is un-certain, and another campaign may repair or re-venge the damage they have fuftained in this and the former.

The Venetians loft five thoufand men before the walls of that town, among whom was General Cornaro, the Viceroy of the Ifland, flain in the firft onfet, befides what were kill'd by our foldiers, when they enter'd with the retreating Candiots, and facri-ficed all to the heat of martial paffion.

But that which appeared moft ominous to their caufe, tho' the prefent damage were lefs, was the falling out of the Supraveditor and the Proveditor of the Ifle; who not agreeing about the extent of their different Commiffions, form'd two parties, between whom there happen'd a furious encounter, in which four hundred were flain on both fides.

This finifter event occafioned the Republic to make frefh applications to the Court of France; and an Ambaffador is fent from this Crown to Con-ftantinople, in order to mediate a Peace.   They call him Monfieur de Varennes, a man of a prefumptu-ous difpofition, and who delights to attempt diffi-cult things.   When there could not be found a per-fon, willing to undertake a negotiation, which car-ries fo little probability of fucceeding: This Gentle-man, in a Bravado, offered himfelf; telling the Queen, that he made no doubt of fo reprefenting matters to the Grand Signior, as would infallibly produce a Peace.

It had been eafy for Cardinal Mazarini (whofe counfel the Queen follows in all things) to have hindered

hindered this man's voyage. But thofe who are
acquainted with the pique that is between them,
conclude, that the Cardinal confented to his Commiffion, on purpofe to lay a train for his future difgrace; as knowing the boldnefs of his temper was-
far from being feconded with equal wifdom and.
conduct; and that though he was prone to undertake great and hazardous actions, yet he never had
the good fortune to accomplifh any thing of moment.

They, that know this Gentleman's character,
fay, that any example will encourage him to rufh
into labyrinths and perils. And where examples
are wanting, he is ambitious to be made one himfelf. He fears not to tread in the footfteps of fuch,
as have mifcarried in the moft defperate enter-
prizes; but promifes himfelf fuccefs, where a thoufand have failed. In fine, he is efteemed the rafh-
eft man living.

I fend thee this defcription of the French Ambaffador, that thou may'ft communicate it to the
Sovereign Divan. It will be no fmall advantage
to know the temper and qualifications of foreign
Minifters refiding at the auguft Port: Efpecially
at this juncture, whereon the Fate of Chriftendom
depends. Befides, there cannot be too great caution ufed, to obviate the fubtle trains of Cardinal
Mazarini, who, I fear, is contriving no kind offices
to the Ottoman Empire.

I kifs the hem of thy veft, illuftrious Baffa, and
bid thee adieu.

Paris, 2d of the 7th Moon,
    of the Year 1646.

L E T-

LETTER VII.

To the fame.

THE Captain Baſſa has the reputation of a good Seaman among the French. They highly applaud his expeditious relief of Canea, and no leſs commend the ſecrecy with which he landed his army, and took the town of Retimo. The French are generally great Critics in military affairs, and are not ſo partial to the honour of the Chriſtians, as to deny the praiſes that are due to an expert Leader among the Muſſulmans. Yet they are inconſtant, and ſeldom retain the ſame ſentiments long. Every circulation of their blood begets new friendſhips, new opinions, new cenſures. In this they ſeem to inherit the vices of the ancient Gauls, as well as their country.

A Roman Emperor, who made war in this nation, hath left excellent Memoirs behind him: Wherein, amongſt other things, he deſcribes the Nature of the Gauls, their Diſpoſitions, and genial Inclinations. He that ſhall read his Writings, which were penn'd above ſixteen hundred years ago, and ſhall converſe with the preſent French, will eaſily conclude, that the latter are a living tranſcript of the former; and that their humours and actions are exactly copied from his words. Yet in nothing does the character of the primitive Gauls ſuit more truly to the preſent inhabitants, than in their furious onſets in a battle, and their equal readineſs to flight. Their firſt aſſault ſeems to ſpeak 'em more than Men, their ſecond, leſs than Women; and they ſeldom venture on a third.

Wilt thou know then, how they obtain ſo many ſignal victories? It is by ſtratagems and money. Where they cannot circumvent their enemies, they corrupt a party of them with bribes

and

and penfions. Thus they purchafe their con-
quefts with a more powerful metal than fteel.
The force of gold, to which all things yield, lays
Cities and Provinces at the feet of this invincible
Monarch.

But, I pray Heaven, fo to profper the armies
of the Empire founded on Virtue, that this Infidel
Prince, and all the Nazarenes, may experience
their gold to be as ineffectual as their Swords,
againft the valour and juft revenge of the True
Believers.

Paris, 2d of the 7th Moon,
    of the Year 1646.

LETTER VIII.

To the Venerable Mufti, Sovereign Guide
of the True Believers.

THOU, who art all goodnefs, the arch-type
    of clemency and virtue, wilt not number
me among the importunate, for fo often troubling
thee with difputes of our holy Law. I afk thee
no common queftions, neither am I captious,
feeking occafions to darken what is apparent, or
invalidate the teftimony of him who touch'd the
Hand of God. I revere the holy Oracles, and the
Book not dictated on Earth. Every Chapter I read
in the Alcoran, makes me blefs the Angel who
took fo many flights, to bring down the facred
Pages from Heaven. And my reverence is increas'd towards that Volume of Glory, when I
confider it was not haftily compofed; every Ver-
ficle being the product of divine premeditation.
Doubtlefs it excels all the Writings in the world.
No Scripture before or fince, has approach'd to the
myfterious elegance of thofe celeftial lines. Yet
                                            methinks

methinks I find a great profundity of wifdom in the Treatifes of the Ancients.

'Thou wilt fay, my ftation requires me to read men more than books, being not fent hither to contemplate, but to act for the intereft of my Mafter, and the Ottoman Empire. 'Tis true, my bufinefs now is to unravel the defigns of the Infidels; but bear with me, if I tell thee that in order to this I took no wrong courfe, when in my younger years I apply'd myfelf to books, which are but men turn'd infide out, or metamorphofed into letters; againft whom thus furviving themfelves, the ftroke of death cannot prevail.

Thofe who have erected ftatues of gold, filver, brafs, or marble, to the memory of departed Heroes, can but tranfmit the effigies of their bodies to pofterity ; which, thou knoweft, is the ignobler part of man. And herein they come fhort of the Egyptians, who have the art of preferving the bodies themfelves incorruptible for a thoufand generations. But they who left their Writings to pofterity, have obliged the world with an immortal and lively image of their mind : This is properly the man, and lives for ever; when the body is confumed in the grave, and the ftatue perhaps is eat up by time, or demolifh'd by envy.

Pardon this digreffion, oraculous and unerring Mouth of God. I have a great deal to fay, and cannot comprehend it in a few words. It has been enjoin'd by our holy Doctors, That a Muffulman fhould not read the Books of profane Infidels. But tell me, thou who art the Refolver of Doubts, whether this Precept is extended to all, without exception; or whether a Difpenfation may not be allowed to fuch as read thofe Books with one eye, whilft the other is fix'd on the Law, which balances the mind with truth? The Alcoran tells us, that the Devil has inferted fome Falfities in the beft Writings : But, is it not poffible for a man to feparate the good from the bad? I read in the

Book

Book of Glory, many remarkable things of Alexander the Great: But is it unlawful also to peruse what has been writ by others, of the life of that famous Warrior, and holy Prophet? Both Grecian and Roman Historians have related his adventures in Asia, his battles with Darius the Persian Monarch, and Porus the Indian. They praise his continence and modest regard to Syssigambis and her daughters, when they were his captives; his inviolable friendship to Epheftion, whilst living, and the affectionate tears he shed for him after his death. Yet they condemn him of cruel ingratitude, for sacrificing Clitus to his choler, and the fumes of wine, who was a faithful friend, a valiant soldier, and once had saved his life in a battle. They cannot pass over the burning of Persepolis, without some reflections on the unmanly softness of this warrior; who, to please his concubine, gave orders, that the fairest and most magnificent city in Asia should be set on fire. The Persians boast, that that city was built all of Cedar; that Cyrus had wholly displanted, not only Mount Libanus, but the choicest nurseries of that fragrant wood, through all Asia, to build this glorious city, in emulation of Solomon King of the Jews, who was by other Princes thought to value himself too high, for building the Temple of Jerusalem of the same materials. They add, That Alexander found in this city ninety millions of caracks in gold; that after the debauch was over, and the flames had consumed to ashes this Phœnix of Asia, the Conqueror wept, and commanded the money he had found there, should be expended in raising another in its room, more glorious than he former: But that Thais, who had persuaded him to ruin it, was the only obstacle to its re-edification. For such was her empire over this Monarch, that he could deny her nothing.

What I have said of Persepolis, is recorded by Persian Historians; other writers make some mention of it, but not so particularly. There are some

some also who mention his demolishing of Tyrus, a city so ancient, that 'tis said to be first built by one of the Grand-children to Noah, of whom, thou knowest, the Alcoran speaks often. They tax him also with cruelty, in causing two thousand of the chief Tyrians to be crucified, as a Sacrifice to Hercules. Thou art best able to judge, whether this be agreeable to truth; for what Musfulman will believe, that the victorious Prophet was guilty of so barbarous an Idolatry?

The method he took to subdue this impregnable city, is an argument of his invincible courage; and that there is nothing impracticable, to a mind armed with resolution and perseverance.

Tyrus was situated above half a mile in the sea; when the Macedonian demanded a surrender. The citizens trusting to the strength and height of the rock whereon they lived, (for 'twas a perfect Island) and to their distance from the shore of the Continent, bid defiance to him, whom God had ordained to subdue all nations between the extremities of India, and the Pillars of Hercules. The Conqueror, enflamed at their refusal of offered Peace, prepares for an assault. He attempted, without the Miracle of Moses, to make a path for his army through the sea. He followed the steps of the Babylonian Monarch, who, not three ages before, had joined this proud nest of merchants to the firm land. Twice his industrious soldiers raised a causey above the waves, to the very walls of Tyrus; and as often was their labour defeated by the watchful Tyrians. When the third time he proved successful; and in spite of all their resistance by fire and sword, after a siege of six Moons, he scaled the walls of that queen of maritime cities; and convinced the world, That no human force could put a stop to his conquests, whom Destiny had appointed to chastise the Nations of the Earth.

That Chapter in the Alcoran, which speaks of this renowned Worthy, tells us, "That he march-

"ed

" ed fo far Eaſtward, 'till he came to a country
" where the Sun riſes." This paſſage the Chriſtians ridicule, ſaying, That the Sun riſes and ſets
in all countries ; and that there is no ſtated point
of Eaſt and Weſt in the fabric of the world ; ſince
the ſame place which is Eaſt of one country, is
Weſt of another. Thus the deſpiſers of our holy
Law cavil at the Alcoran, and ſay, 'tis compoſed
of Old Wives Tales ; a rude indigeſted collection
of Eaſtern Romances, and ſuperſtitious Fables, cal-
culated for the meridian of ignorance, firſt pro-
mulged in the ſavage and unpoliſh'd Deſarts of
Arabia, and afterwards propagated by the ſword
through thoſe countries, whoſe vices had baniſh'd
their learning, and render'd them flexible to a Religion, whoſe higheſt pretenſions conſiſted in gra·i-
fying the Senſes.

These Critics conſider not at the ſame time,
that they argue againſt the Old and New Teſta-
ment, (which is eſteem'd the Alcoran of the Chriſtians) wherein there is often mention made, of the
riſing and going down of the Sun ; of Eaſt and
Weſt, as proper points or marks, from which to
take the ſituation of countries. Aſſuredly in this
they are captious : For tho' there be no ſtated point
of Eaſt or Weſt in the Globe, yet India being the
neareſt region of this Continent to that part of the
Horizon where the Sun daily firſt appears, it has,
not without reaſon, gain'd the additional Epithet of
Eaſt. And 'twas here the Macedonian Hero ſweat,
becauſe he could conquer no farther, unleſs he
would have begun a war with the Fiſh of the
Sea.

There are many other paſſages related of Alexander's temperance, moderation, juſtice, fortitude,
and ſuch like virtues, and ſomething of his vices.
But I will not tire thee with all that is ſaid of this
invincible Monarch ; nor trace him in all his
marches through Aſia. I will not trouble thee with
what they ſay of his journey into Egypt, and aſpir-
ing to be called the Son of Jupiter Ammon ; his

being

being poifon'd at Babylon, in the height of all his
triumphs; and the cantonizing his Empire among
his chief Captains. Whatfoever in thefe Hiftories
is agreeable to the holy Alcoran, I acquiefce to;
what is repugnant to that fummary of truth, I reject as a Fable.

Tell me, thou Sovereign Refolver of Doubts,
Whether on thefe terms I may not read the Writings of Infidels? Books are a relief to the mind
oppreffed with melancholy, and efpecially Hiftories,
which alfo bring profit, by rightly informing us of
the tranfactions of paft ages : So that things, which
were done thoufands of years ago, are made prefent
to us. Where then is the crime in reading thefe
Memoirs of the Ancients? Is it not confiftent with
the Faith of a Muffulman to read thefe Hiftories,
becaufe they were penn'd by Heathens? Muft we
reject all that the Pagans did or faid? Why then
are the Works of Plutarch had in fuch veneration
by the Princes of our Law? I tell thee, I not only
read Plutarch, Livy, Tacitus, Xenophon, Polybius,
with many other Hiftorians, that were Pagans, but
I improve by their Writings. Such rare examples
of virtue, fuch illuftrious patterns of juftice, fuch
folid precepts of morality as thefe authors abound
with, cannot, in my opinion, hurt any man, who
defires to fquare his life by the beft rules.

I read alfo the Poets, whofe Fables and Parables
feem to me but to veil many excellent and profitable
Maxims of human Eafe.

The Story of the birth of Typhon, his warring
with Jupiter, and his final overthrow, denotes the
monftrous rife of factions in a State, and their
ruin.

The Cyclops being employ'd by Jupiter in making thunderbolts, and killing Æfculapius, for
which they themfelves were afterwards flain by
Apollo, intimates the ufe which fovereign princes
make of cruel, covetous, and unjuft officers; who,
when they have fulfill'd the pleafure of their mafters, are abandon'd by them to the revenge of the
                                             opprefs'd

oppress'd subjects. This is commonly experienced
in all Monarchies, and especially in the mighty
Empire of the Osmans ; where the Bassa's, though
the Grand Signior, for the ends of State, connives
a while at their unjust oppression of the Mussulmans, under their government, yet in due time, to
shew his abhorrence of their villanies, consigns 'em
over to the Executioner. Thou knowest to whom
the bow-string was sent last ; I wish his Successor
may not equally merit it.

Actæon's being devour'd by his dogs, only for
seeing Diana in a Bath, might have serv'd as a
warning to Useph the Black Eunuch, who could
not restrain his tongue from babbling out the private
amours of Sultan Ibrahim. It was danger enough
to know the secret ; but to divulge it, was a sure
way to incur the revenge of the Prince.

Not much unlike was his error, who, 'tho'
he did not report it to others, yet had the pre-
sumption to check his sovereign to his face, and reproach him with luxury. Had he been acquainted
with the Fable of Endymion and the Moon, it
would perhaps have taught him, That it is not the
part of a Favourite to take notice of his Master's
stolen pleasures, but rather to invite him sometimes
from the Toils of State, and unbend his Mind with
Recreations.

There are many other profitable remarks hidden
under the fictions of the Poets ; which, tho' they
may seem mysterious at first view, yet being examin'd with a little attention, prove as easy to be
understood, as the Hieroglyphics were of old to the
Egyptians, who knew no other letters.

God the first Intellect, who imprinted his Mind
on Tablets of Marble, in Letters of Arabic, and writ
the Decalogue with a Beam of his Glory ; having also
inspired all nations with the knowledge of Letters,
grant, That whilst I read the Records of the Gentiles,
I may not forget the Precepts of the Alcoran.

Paris, 23d of the 7th Moon,
   of the Year 1646.

                L E T.

LETTER IX.

To Murat, Baſſa.

A Courier came to this city laſt night, bringing news of the taking of Courtray by the French army. This is a conſiderable town in Flanders, and commands a great part of the country. The Duke of Orleans inveſted it on the ninth of the laſt Moon, and on the eighteenth lay down before it with the whole army. The Spaniſh General haſten'd to its relief, and brought thirty thouſand men of ſix nations, to combat with the French. But they quarrel'd about precedency of poſt. High words paſſed between the Duke of Lorrain and General Lamboy. Thus, while they ſpent their time in needleſs conteſts, the French took the town : And having left a ſtrong garriſon there, part of the army commanded by the Mareſchal de Grammont, is marched to join the Hollanders, with deſign to attack Antwerp : and the reſt follow the Duke of Orleans, who, they ſay, intends to beſiege Mardyke. This is a ſea town that has nothing in it conſiderable enough to tempt a Conqueror, ſave the haven, which is of great importance in thoſe ſeas.

We have had no rains here theſe three Moons, which makes the people fear a Famine. Proviſions of all ſorts are very dear; and thoſe who have great quantities of corn will not bring it to the markets. The fruits are all blaſted, and a diſtemper rages in the city, which fills all places with death and mourning. The cattle drop down dead in the fields, and the rivers are almoſt dried up. Men languiſh and wither, as if parch'd up by ſome inward fire. Fearful Apparitions are ſeen in the air; each night brings forth new Prodigies. The people lament the preſent, and preſage greater calamities to come. While Mahmut perſeveres unmov'd, and neither moleſts himſelf nor others, about the inevitable

Decrees

Decrees and Destiny. I keep in the path of my duty, without turning to the Right hand or to the Left. I serve the Grand Signior faithfully. I pray for his health, and for the welfare of the Empire. I neither give alms to the Infidels, nor do them any injuries. In fine, if I cannot reap any profit from other mens Virtues, I take care their Vices shall do me no harm.

'Tis said there will be a Procession here shortly, whereat the King, the Queen Regent, and the whole Court will assist bare-foot, for an example of others. The body of a certain female Saint, whom they esteem the Patroness of this city, will be taken out of the Church where it lies, and will be carried with other Reliques of Saints thro' the streets of Paris, to atone the wrath of Heaven, which seems to be kindled against them.

In the mean time I pray Heaven to send down its blessings on the Ottoman Empire, and preserve the True Faithful from the three Scourges of God.

Paris, 23d of the 7th Moon,
of the Year 1646.

LETTER X.

To the Aga of the Janizaries.

I Perceive thou hast follow'd the Advice I formerly gave thee to read Histories, wherein thy letter speaks thee very conversant. Thou wilt have no reason to repent of a labour that affords so agreeable a diversion, especially to a Soldier and Statesman. They open the graves, and call forth the dead, without disturbing their repose; and present to us those Heroes living, talking and acting great things, whose bodies have lain buried in silence and obscurity many ages.

They

They introduce us into the clofets of Princes, revealing their moft fecret counfels. They make us familiar with the Intrigues of Politicians, and the Stratagems of Warriors. In fine, there is nothing public or private, in the Courts or Camps of the greateft Monarchs, to which an Hiftorian is a ftranger.

I applaud the choice thou haft made of Grecian Hiftories, and others of the Eaft; yet I counfel thee not to neglect thofe of the Weft. The ancient Roman writers are full of rare examples; and modern France, which emulates all great and glorious undertakings, takes equal care to commit to pofterity, the Lives of illuftrious perfons. I fay not this, in contempt of other countries in Europe. The Chriftians of thefe parts in general are accurate Hiftorians. They are univerfally learned, in regard there is no kingdom in Europe, where they have not Schools and Academies, where all Languages and Sciences are taught. The plough-men in the field fpeak Latin and Greek, which thou knoweft are now grown obfolete, and no where to be learn'd but in books. The Mechanics are Philofophers; and every man fets up for an Hiftorian, or an Antiquary. It was not fo in former times, when the Ecclefiaftics had engrofs'd all manner of Learning to themfelves, except fome few of the Nobility and Gentry, who had the advantage of patrimonial libraries, and leifure to apply themfelves to ftudy. For then it was difficult to purchafe Books, there being but few; and for thofe, they were obliged to the labour of the Scribe. Hence it came to pafs, that only fuch as had plenty of money, and a ftrong inclination to knowledge, monopoliz'd the chiefeft Manufcripts into their hands, and bequeath'd them as a legacy to their Off-fpring. But, fince the invention of Printing, Books are infinitely multiplied, grown cheap and common: And thofe Hiftories and Sciences, which before were fhut up in the Latin, Greek, or fome of the Oriental Languages,

Languages, are now tranflated into the vulgar Speech of every nation ; whereby the loweft fort of people, who can but read, have the privilege to become as knowing as their Superiors, and the Slave may vie for learning with his Sovereign. This makes the Nazarenes upbraid the true Faithful with ignorance and barbarifm, becaufe Printing is not fuffer'd throughout the Muffulman Empire. They confider not the bad confequences of this Art, as well as the good : And, that the Liberty of the Prefs has fill'd the world with errors and lies : Befides, they are ftrangers to the education of the Muffulmans, who are generally taught the Arabic and Perfian tongues from their childhood : In which Two languages, how many famous Hiftories have been writ ? There is no point of ufeful wifdom, which is not compriz'd in the Writings of the Eaftern Sages. And as for unprofitable treatifes and pamphlets with which the Europeans abound, they are fuperfluous and burdenfome, bringing a double lofs, both to writer and reader ; while they rob them of their time and money, and commit a rape on their underftandings. Add to this, the fatal effects which this depraved indulgence of Printing has produced in Chriftendom. What facrileges, maffacres, rebellions and impieties, have overflow'd moft parts of the Weft in this licentious age ? What hatred among Chriftians, what feditions among fubjects, diverfities in religion, contempts of all Law, both Divine, Natural, and thofe of Nations ? The vices, at which former times would have blufh'd ; nay, at the very naming of which our Fathers would have ftarted, as at a Prodigy, are in thefe days committed openly, without fhame, without contradiction ; whilft there are authors who dare publicly affert the caufe of impiety, and patronize all manner of profanations.

But thou, who haft the honour to guard the incorruptible Seat of Juftice and Virtue, the bright

Throne

2

Throne of the Ofman Emperors, who are the Shadows of God on Earth, haſt made ſuch a choice of Books, as commends thy wiſdom, and the ſincerity of thy morals. Thou wilt not ſuffer thy imagination to be tainted with thoſe enchanting Ideas of evil, which are drawn by the pens of ſome elegant Writers : All that thou ſeekeſt in Books, is to inform thy underſtanding, rectify thy judgment, and enflame thy affections with the love of virtue. To this end ſerve the divine Precepts of our holy Doctors, and other learned Sages; the Writings of Philoſophers, and the examples of renown'd Heroes. From theſe thou gathereſt ſtrength, to practiſe the four material Virtues, and all the good Qualities that ſpring from thoſe Roots.

Go on, and increaſe in the graces and accompliſhments, which ſhall render thee worthy to be made the Subject of a particular Hiſtory ; while the old ſhall recommend, and the young ſhall covet, nothing more paſſionately, than to read the Life of Caſſim Hali, Janizar Aga.

Mahmut ſalutes thee with a kiſs of affection. Reverence thyſelf, and all men will honour thee. So taught Pythagoras.

Paris, 17th of the 8th Moon,
    of the Year 1646.

LETTER XI.

To the ſame.

I Had forgot to perform in my other letter what thou commandeſt me. Yet knowing the eſteem thou haſt for Women of virtue and rare endowments, and with what pleaſure thou readeſt their Stories, I ſhould never ſend any Diſpatch to thee wherein there is not a relation of ſome Heroine.

Heroine. I will be more diligent hereafter, to observe the difpofition of my Superiors, and will endeavour to procure a collection of the Lives and Characters of all the famous Women that have been recorded in Hiftory. In the mean while, hear what the French fay of Chriftina Queen of Swedeland, of whom thou requireft a defcription.

She is the only daughter of Guftavus Adolphus, the moft victorious Prince that ever govern'd that nation, and one of the moft fuccefsful Warriors in the world. As his whole life was led in the field, fo there he received an honourable death, being flain in the battle of Lutzen : Some fay, by the treachery of Duke Albert, who had in appearance deferted the Emperor, and offer'd himfelf a volunteer to Guftavus Adolphus. I formerly mention'd this Duke, and that he was kill'd by a Swedifh Lady. If the fufpicion of the Swedes be well grounded, and that Duke Albert was really guilty of the murder of Guftavus, it may be this was the motive which brought thofe Amazons into the field, to revenge the death of their Prince. But it is impoffible to be affur'd of the truth, among fo many different opinions.

When the French fpeak of Guftavus Adolphus, they cannot reftrain their words on this fide a Panegyric. They fay he was a Prince above all praife. 'Tis certain, his very enemies admired his inimitable courage, and matchlefs fortune. I have fent thee the true Effigies of his face, where thou wilt fee a moft agreeable mixture of majefty and benignity, creating refpect and love at the fame time in the beholders. He was fo familiar with every one, as if he had forgot himfelf, as well as he was a ftranger to pride. He was a great ftudent in his youth, and made himfelf mafter of Latin, French, and Italian ; being alfo perfectly fkill'd in ancient and modern Hiftories. He had a wonderful faculty in difcovering impoftors ; a dexterous wit in time of danger and difficulty, being ready at counfel, and fwift in execution ; and as cunning at a ftratagem, as he was bold at an onfet. He was liberal to the officers, and to all men of merit; but a fevere punifher of diforders in his army. And that which crown'd all the reft of his virtues, his piety to God was fingular and worthy of remark. The French relate a memorable Saying of this King, when he was once in his camp before Werben. He had been folitary in the cabinet of his pavilion fome hours together, and none of his attendants durft interrupt him; till at length a favourite of his, having fome important matter to tell him, came foftly to the door, and looking in, beheld the King very devoutly on his knees at Prayers. Fearing to moleft him in that facred exercife, he was about to withdraw his Head, when the King fpied him, and bid him come in; faying unto him, " Thou wondereft to " fee me in this pofture, fince I have fo many " thoufands of Subjects to pray for me. But I " tell thee, that no man has more need to pray for " himfelf, than he, who being to render an ac- " count of his Actions to none but GOD, is for " that reafon more clofely affaulted by the Devil, " than all other men befide."

Guftavus was born in the Year 1594, at which time they fay, a Comet was feen in the Form of a Sword, with its point directed toward Germany; which the Aftrologers of thofe times interpreted as a prefage of that King's warlike Genius, and of his future conquefts in the Empire. He came to the government before he had feen full feventeen Winters, and was cut off in the eight and thirtieth year of his age.

It is faid, That a few days before his death, when his foldiers received him with infinite acclamations, and all the marks of an unufual and intemperate joy, he feem'd to be troubled at it, faying, " That he took that exceffive demonftra- " tion of his foldiers love, for an Omen of fome " approaching difafter: And that he was affured " GOD would, by taking him away, teach them,
" that

" that there is no confidence to be repofed in any
" Mortal."

After the death of Guftavus, the States of the
Kingdom affembling, proclaim'd Chriftina Queen,
and during her minority committed her to the
Tutelage of five principal Officers of the Kingdom,
who alfo took on them the whole care of the Commonwealth.

She is perfect in feven Languages; well vers'd
in ancient and modern Philofophy, and a complete Hiftorian. In fine, fhe has acquir'd the
Title of the moft learned Princefs of her time.

She is of a moft graceful and majeftic afpect;
has a piercing eye; wears part of her hair loofe
about her temples, and flowing down in curls
to her fhoulders; the reft braided up behind, in
form of a wreath. Thus is fhe reprefented by
her Picture, which I have feen in a gallery of
Cardinal Mazarini's palace, who profeffes a great
veneration for this Queen. Could I have purchafed this Portraiture, as I did her father's, I
would have fent it thee: But all the pencils in
Paris are hardly fufficient to fupply the clofets and
galleries of the Nobles with this admired Figure.
She is become the Idol of the French.

Many great Matches have been offer'd her, but
fhe refufes all, either for reafons of State, or diflike of the perfons, or an averfion fhe has for a
married life; or through oppofition of her Nobles;
who feem to covet to be govern'd by a Maiden
Queen. Soon after her father's death, the King
of Denmark attempted to make her his wife; but
his addrefs was abruptly rejected.

No better encouragement did the King of Poland lately meet with, who twice folicited the fame
thing for himfelf, and was as often repulfed. But
this, 'tis thought, proceeded from fome politic
reafons, he being defcended of Sigifmund, a former abdicated King of Sweden; all whofe Pofterity are for ever excluded from enjoying the Swedifh
Crown, by a law.

G 2

Th

The Englifh alfo gloried in a Virgin Queen the laft age : Her name was Elizabeth, whom thou can'ft not but have heard of. She was the daughter of Henry VIII. King of that nation. She was a Princefs of an extraordinary Genius, remarkable for her wit and learning. 'Twas one of her fubjects, who the firft of all Mortals, fail'd round the Globe : And by his fortunate fervice, fhe vanquifh'd the reputed invincible Armada of Spain. She govern'd her kingdom with fuch exquifite conduct, as made the greateft Potentates revere her wifdom. 'Tis to her Bounty the United Provinces owe the rife of their prefent grandeur and riches ; when they addrefs'd this potent Queen in a form of humble fuppliants, intitling themfelves, "the Poor Diftreffed States." But now they're High and Mighty, pufhing for an equality with Sovereign Princes.

I cannot comprize in a letter, all that may be faid of this great Queen. Befides, Hiftorians vary in her character. Thofe that fpeak moft impartially, fay, That fhe had extraordinary Virtues, yet was not free from great Vices. We muft not expect in any Mortal, a temper exempt from the common malediction ; much lefs in that Sex, whofe natural weaknefs claims our indulgence and excufe. It is admirable to fee or hear of a Female, whofe active foul can difengage itfelf from the common frailties of Women, and perform things fcarce below the power of mafculine virtue.

If thou thinkeft my letter too tedious, accufe thyfelf for commanding me to write of perfons whofe uncommon gifts and tranfcendent virtues, the moft accurate Hiftorians can but render in Epitome ; and the moft durable Records of Fame will injure it not being capable to tranfmit them to Eternity.

We ought not to contemn the excellencies of the Nazarenes ; who, although they are unhappy in not knowing the Alcoran ; yet they have

a Law

a Law engraven on their hearts ; which if they
obferve, they fhall be in the Number of the Bleffed.

I am no ftranger to thy moderation and juftice,
being fully fatisfied, that thou honoureft juftice,
even in the moft prejudiced enemy of our holy
Profeffion. Let the Furiofo's among the Muffulmans or Chriftians fay their pleafure, thou and
I fhall be conformable to our holy Law-giver in be-
lieving, " That the innocent and good of all
" religions, fhall have no reafon to tremble at
" the fecond Sound of the Trumpet."

Paris, 17th of the 8th Moon,
    of the Year 1546.

LETTER XII.

To the Selictar Aga, or Sword-Bearer to the Grand Signior.

THE Duke of Orleans is newly return'd from
the campaign in Flanders. He feems to
be either tired with his fatigues of war, or at
leaft to be fatisfy'd with his exploits this fummer.

After the conqueft of Courtray, of which thou
haft heard in the Divan, this Prince march'd
directly to Bergues, which he took after a fiege
of fix days. Thefe being join'd by the Duke of
Enguien's forces, he lay down before Mardyke.
This town had been in the Spaniards poffeffion
ever fince laft Winter. Now it held out to a
miracle ; but after a ftout refiftance, was at laft
forced to furrender. There were flain before it,
many of the chief nobility of France. The French
enter'd it on the four and twentieth of the laft
moon.

The Churches here are hung with Mourning,

and

and the Efcutcheons of the Heroes, who loft their lives in the bed of honour. The bullets which know no difference between the noble and vulgar, feem in this battle to have been directed by art or envy : As if the flower of the army had been cull'd out for marks.

In a letter to Murat Baffa, I gave an account of a grievous Drought and Mortality in thefe parts. Now Heaven feems to be pacify'd; and the Angel of Death has put up his fword. Yet the fcarcity of corn, and other neceffaries, continues ftill; only there is plenty of wine; which the poor, who have moft need of it, abftain from, left it fhould enrage their appetites, already fharpen'd with hunger, whilft they have little or nothing to eat.

Thou wilt wonder at the diet of thofe miferable wretches, whom oppreffion and poverty has forced to feed on Frogs and other Vermin; yet they extol it for a dainty difh. Both poor and rich reckon it a feaft, when they can make an addition of a few Mufhrooms, which they commonly gather themfelves. This is a Vegetable, of which the Italian Proverb fays " Mufhrooms " well pickled with fpices, may do no harm, but " can do no good."

God, who has commanded us to feparate the clean from the impure, and has taught us what we may eat without pollution, grant, that we may not, either through neceffity, or to indulge our appetites, tafte of any thing, which has in it the leaft of the feven Maledictions.

Paris, 14th of the 9th Moon, of the Year 1646.

LETTER XIII.

To Abubechir Ali, Merchant, in Aleppo.

THOU telleft me a tragical ftory of one of thy Wives, that fhe is become a fugitive, and gone away with thy Slave Lorenzo, whom I remember to have feen at thy houfe at Conftantinople. Either theu wert too unkind to them both, or gaveft them both too much liberty: Whichfoever of thefe ways thou haft exceeded, thou art in the fault. Too great an indulgence, either to a wife or a fervant, makes them prefumptuous: And too great feverity hardens them to defpair. However, fince it is fo, I advife thee to comfort thyfclf with this thought, That thou art rid of two Evils. Had they prov'd faithful, they would not have merited that Title; but now they are neither worthy of thy grief, nor thy revenge.

But if thou art refolved to purfue them, afk not my counfel or affiftance in this place, where I fhould have as much reafon to apprehend danger, as they. 'Tis true, I know thy Slave; but were I to meet him in the ftreets of this city, I fhould be very unwilling, by difcovering him, to be made known myfelf. Befides, thy paffion has made thee forget, that the Nazarenes would commend his wit, and rejoice in his fortune, who being a Slave to one whom they efteem an Infidel, has now, by his wife conduct, purchafed both his liberty, and a beautiful mate, with no fmall treafure.

I rather advife thee to apply thyfelf to Jafmir Sgire Rugial, the little Aftrologer in Aleppo, who perhaps may tell thee fome news of 'em. There is not a ftar in the eighth fphere can ftir, without his being privy to it. And he pretends to behold in their motions, whatever is done on earth.

But to be ferious, thy Slave was an ungrateful fellow, thus to abufe all thy favours. Thou hadft

made

made him in a manner mafter of all thy riches, only referving thy wives to thyfelf. And if the defire of liberty tempted him to efcape, he ought in juftice to have facrificed his luft to the regards he owed thee. But every Slave is not a Jofeph. Lorenzo's villany puts me in mind of the continence of an Italian Marquis.

This young Lord fell in love with a Duchefs of fingular Beauty, but knew not how to make her fenfible of it. At length Fortune favour'd him with an opportunity, beyond his expectation. One evening as he return'd from hawking, he pafs'd through the fields of that Duchefs, bordering on the Palace. The Duke her hufband, and fhe, were walking together, as the young Lord came by. The Duke feeing his train, and what game they had been at, afk'd him fome queftions concerning their fport; and being of an hofpitable difpofition, invited him into his palace to take a collation. Nothing could be more agreeable to the young lover. He accepted the offer, and here commenced an acquaintance, which made way in time for an affignation between the Duchefs and him. He was let into the gardens one night, and fo conducted privately to her chamber, where fhe lay ready in bed to receive him. After fome compliments, the Duchefs faid, " My " Lord, you are obliged to my hufband for this fa- " vour; who, as foon as you were gone from our " houfe, the firft time we faw you, gave you fuch " commendations as made me conceive an imme- " diate paffion for you." " Is it true, Madam?" (reply'd the young lover, already half undrefs'd) " Then far be it from me, to be fo ungrateful to " my friend." With that he put on his garments again, and took his leave.

But it cannot be expected that fo much virtue fhould be found in a Slave. I would not have thee vex thyfelf for what cannot be recover'd. Adieu.

Paris, 14th of the 5th Moon,
of the Year 1646.

L E T-

LETTER XVIII.

To Solyman Kyzlar Aga, Chief of the Black Eunuchs.

I AM juft now return'd to my chamber, from the Palace of the King. As I pafs'd along the ftreets, I faw in every face the fignatures of a profound forrow, which feems to have diffufed itfelf over their whole bodies; for both the Court and City have put on Mourning for the death of Henry Bourbon, late Prince of Conde.

He was not full fixty years of age, when he left this vifible world, to be new born in a region utterly unknown to mortals. The French, not without reafon, lament the lofs of a man, who, to fpeak the leaft of him, buoy'd up the domeftic intereft of this kingdom, which feem'd otherwife inclining to totter. He was the balance which pois'd the different paffions of the Court and City, by his prudence and juftice calming both into a peaceable mediocrity.

He was born fome Moons after his father's death, whom the moft execrable method of murdering would not fuffer to fpin out thofe years which Nature would have indulg'd him, being fnatch'd away by poifon.

Henry IV. fo long as he remained without iffue, fixed his eyes on this pofthumous young Prince, and gave him an education fuitable to one whom Fate had defign'd to be the Heir of the Crown. Yet afterwards jealoufy cool'd his affection, when the Prince had married Charlotte the Duke of Montmorency's daughter, whom Henry IV. loved to a degree of paffion.

It is dangerous to have a fovereign prince one's rival in love. That match had well nigh ruin'd the young Prince of Conde. He was forced to fly

into

into Holland with his Princeſs, and make that Province the ſanctuary of her honour. From thence he travelled through Germany, and returned not to France, till after the murder of Henry IV.

During the minority of Lewis XIII. he headed the factions, affecting to become popular. Were it not for this ambition, his life had been without blemiſh, and he might have blown out Diogenes his Mid-day Candle. But no man is free from fault. All the difference between the virtuous and vicious conſiſts in this, That one commits fewer crimes than the other, and thoſe not by intention or habit, but through the inſuperable proclivity of Nature. Every Man has his genial vices, his conſtitutional errors, and tho' he may appear as a Saint in all things elſe, yet in theſe he will ſtill be a Sinner.

He ſuffer'd five years impriſonment in the Baſtile, which is a place put to the ſame uſe, as the Caſtle of the Seven Towers in Conſtantinople. The Princeſs his wife was his companion all the time, and ſhared in his misfortunes as well as his proſperity.

During that tedious confinement, he became father of a daughter, who was afterwards married to the Duke of Longueville. And when he was ſet at liberty, he begot the Duke of Enguien, now Prince of Conde, and the Prince of Conti.

The French ſpeak well of the departed Prince. He was of a lively ſpirit, cheerful and affable in converſation, mixing daily recreations with his ſeverer buſineſs, regularly obſerving order in all his affairs. Yet they ſay he was covetous, having heaped up great treaſures by a parſimony, which none of that Blood had ever before practiſed.

On his death-bed, he recommended two things to the practice of his ſon, the Duke of Enguien,
" Never

" Never to revenge a private injury; and freely to
" hazard his life for the public good."

I chofe to tranfmit to thee the news of this
Prince's death, with this brief account of his life,
and characters of his difpofition, in regard thou
haft feen him in Germany, and I remember to
have heard thee fpeak in his praife.

Continue to love Mahmut, who is never for-
getful to oblige his friends.

Paris, 15th of the 11th Moon,
of the Year 1646.

L E T T E R   XIX.

To the Kaimacham.

THE Pofts from Catalonia came in laft night
laden with ill news from the army, which
has been found to encamp from before Lerida,
leaving the greateft part of their artillery to the
Spaniards. That place was always fatal to the
French. Yet the paffion of the Court vents itfelf on the Count de Harcourt, becaufe he could
not reverfe the Decrees of Deftiny. All his former meritorious actions feem now to be cancell'd
by this one difgrace, though it was unavoidable :
So peevifh are princes, when their expectations
are crofs'd. Some fufpect him guilty of private
correfpondence ; others·tax him with cowardice.
All this is during the heat of their refentment:
The fame perfons, it may be, will change their
cenfure when they confider, that he had lain before it feven Moons, even till the trenches of
his camp were filled with fnow, and that his
foldiers died of famine or cold : For the Winter
began to be infupportable, and the country was
barren

barren of all things neceffary to fuftain fuch an army. I cannot fee wherein this General deferves reproach; unlefs it be a crime to be a man, and to have the command of fuch as are made of flefh and blood as well as he.

In Italy, the French have taken Piombino, and Porto Longone. This latter is the moft important town in the Ifle of Elbe, yet was not able to fuftain above nineteen days fiege.

They fay, there is a fountain in this Ifland, whofe waters flow at the fun-rifing, but in the evening are dried up The fuperftitious have had conceits of this fountain relifhing of the ancient Pagan vanities; but the learned attribute it to natural caufes. So the Jews tell of a river in the Eaft, that ftands ftill on the Seventh Day of the Week. This they adduce as a confirmation of their Law, which commands them to reft from labour on the Seventh Day, becaufe on that day God refted from forming the creatures of the World. They fay alfo, That the Satyrs, and other Monfters of the Defarts, fhun the light of the fun that day, hiding themfelves in the caverns of the earth, and curfing the Sabbath, becaufe it furprized God before he had quite finifhed their Forms; for which reafon they are imperfect and monftrous to this day.

The Divine Unity, who is the root of all Numbers, and has confecrated the number Seven to many myfterious ends, grant, That neither thou nor I may forget the anfwers we muft give to the Seven queftions of the Porter of Paradife.

Paris, 7th of the 12th Moon.
of the Year 1646

LETTER XX.

To Bajazet, Baſſa of Greece.

IT appears to me by evident ſymptoms that there is ſome deep deſign afoot in this Court. The Grandees aſſemble often, and ſit late. Extraordinary Couriers are ſent out, and come in, at all hours of the night. Strange reports are induſtriouſly ſpread about the city. Trading is at a ſtand, the banquiers reſerv'd, and little money ſtirring, which makes the populace murmur. They complain of the times, as is uſual in public diſcontents: The old diſcourage and incenſe the young, by making compariſons of this age and reign, with the happy days of Henry the Great. They fill their ears with golden ſtories of former times; and inſpiring into them a love of the paſt, they equally introduce a hatred of the preſent government. Theſe are the common artifices of faction; and though none appears yet under any diſtinct name or title, yet it is eaſy to prognoſticate from theſe preludes, that ere long the maſk will be taken off, and ſedition will ſhew herſelf barefaced.

T'other day a fellow run crying through the ſtreets, "God ſave the King, but the devil take the " Italian." He was followed by a few, and thoſe of the moſt contemptible. Yet no officer or magiſtrate in this city, would cauſe him to be apprehended, or attempt to ſupprefs the mutiny he was raiſing. The citizens ſmil'd at his boldneſs, and money was brought him from unknown hands: The women bleſs'd him as a Prophet, and the virgins fell down before the Altars on his behalf: The Temples were crowded with votaries, or rather with the fautors of this new ſedition; as if they ſtrove to draw their Gods into the cabal, and would make Heaven itſelf abet their

4   tumults.

tumults. His train increas'd as he meafur'd the ftreets; till at length he was feiz'd by the Royal Guards, the rabble difpers'd, and all things reftored to quiet. That night a double Watch was kept throughout the city; the fellow was ftrictly examined, and put to the Rack, yet no confeffion could be extorted from him, fave, "That "the public good induced him to take this courfe: "That the tyranny and oppreffion which Cardinal "Mazarini exercifed were infupportable: And that "he was ready to facrifice his life for the wel- "fare of his Country." He is condemn'd to the gallies during his life. And great endeavours are ufed to find out the authors of this novelty. For he is looked on but as an inftrument fet at work by fome malecontents of higher quality, and the fore-runner of fome more formidable infurrection.

Proclamations are iffued out, to forbid all difcourfe of State matters: But the people fpare not to whifper their fentiments.

The young King is taken ill, which augments the public jealoufy: Men fhake their heads, and look dejected, as they walk along the ftreets. Some menace revenge with their furrow'd brows; others fpeak only, "That the kingdom is fold "to ftrangers." A general confternation and diforder has feiz'd all, while their fears prompt them daily to expect a change. To obviate the mifchiefs which thofe popular paffions threaten, foldiers are drawn from divers parts of the country by Mazarini's orders, and by infenfible companies quarter'd up and down Paris. Between thefe and the citizens, there happen divers quarrels, frequent murders are committed: While the night, which covers all things with darknefs, ferves to fhroud their mutual outrages, and private revenges. Thus the public calamities are cherifh'd: What will be the iffue, time will evince.

In the mean while, the affairs of Germany and Swede-

Swedeland, feem to be in a fair way of compo-
fure. Divers Treaties are on foot in order to a
general peace in Chriftendom. The Embaffadors
and Deputies of the feveral contefting Crowns,
have frequent conferences. But each party in-
fifts fo vehemently on circumftantials, that nothing but fruitlefs demurs conclude their meetings. France has a great ftroke in all thefe affairs : And 'tis grown to a Proverb, " That Car-
" dinal Mazarini carries all the Courts of Europe
" in his bofom."

The Swedes treat like Victors ; and the Germans tho' much enfeebled, yet cannot forget the
Majefty of the Imperial Sceptre. The Danes
have an Intereft to profecute, and the Poles are
not without their Pretenfions. National pride and
honour have a great Influence on thefe Crowns.
But the Hollanders, like merchants, act according
to the rules of profit. They ftand on no Punctilio's, but fuch as advance their traffic ; knowing
that money is the nerves of war. In this they are
to be efteem'd wife, their Commonwealth being
as yet but in her nonage : Her ftrength not knit,
nor fhe in a capacity to wreftle with her potent
neighbours.

England finds bufinefs enough at home, to
employ both her money, wit and arms. Nor
can fhe be at leifure to attend to foreign tranfactions.

Spain ever follows the intereft of the German
Court, it being the unalterable maxim of the
Houfe of Auftria, "to remain united, and aggran-
" dize itfelf."

Italy has various interefts ; and Venice in particular, is in ftrict friendfhip with this Court.

Portugal is ftill upon her guard, againft the
reftlefs Spaniards : And Don Juan de Braganza
makes Foreign Alliances.

The fupreme Monarch of the vifible and invifible Worlds, who fits on the Throne of Adamant,

mant, under the Covers of the Eternal Tree, grant, That the diſtractions of theſe Infidel Princes and States may continue, 'till the time appointed by Fate ſhall come, wherein the faithful Oſmans ſhall poſſeſs the Red Apple.

Paris, 25th of the 1ſt Moon,
    of the Year 1646.

LETTER XXI.

To Peſteli Hali, his Brother.

I Thought myſelf forgotten by the Son of my Mother, who has ſuffer'd ſo many Decads of Moons, to meaſure out the term of his unkind ſilence, and of my melancholy. 'Tis now three years ſince I heard from thee : But I will not complain of a fault ſo ingenuouſly expiated, though late.   Thou haſt made me ample amends, in ſending me ſuch an elaborate and ſuccinct Hiſtory of thy Travels : In reading of which, I know not whether my pleaſure or profit is greater. Thou haſt ſo interwoven delightful adventures of thy own, and pleaſant paſſages of others, with curious and ſolid obſervations, that a man improves himſelf inſenſibly, whilſt the charming language and miſcellany ſerve as a ſpur at once to rouſe and faſten his attention to points of moſt uſeful knowledge.

The Chriſtians are apt to deſpiſe the True Be- lievers, as a company of ignorant people, unac- quainted with the world, unpoliſh'd both in their underſtandings and manners, not vers'd in the liberal Sciences, nor addicted to the ſtudy of any thing but riches and honour, and how to aug- ment the Muſſulman Empire.   They conſider not at the ſame time, That God has made us rational

creatures

creatures as well as them; has endued us with
the fame natural faculties; and, That in all Nations he has infpired fome with a thirft of knowledge, furnifhing them alfo with the abilities and
means to attain it. They confider not, That if
Printing be prohibited among us, 'tis to fupprefs
the multitude of unprofitable Books, with which
Europe too much abounds: And that in their
ftead we have many thoufands of induftrious
Scribes, whofe whole employment is to tranflate
the moft excellent and learned Treatifes of the
Ancients. And, that confequently, a ftudious
Mahometan cannot be deftitute of fuch Books, as
may inftruct him in true Philofophy, found Morals,
and Hiftory of the moft memorable tranfactions
in the world. Affuredly, our Arabia may boaft
of her Avicens, Mefues, Averroes, Halis, and
Albumazars; and that fhe hath brought forth
many others who need not, in any point of Human or Divine Learning, yield the Palm to the
moft eminent Doctors, Philofophers, Orators and
Poets, among the Chriftians.

Add to this the equal benefit fome of our Belief
reap, by travelling into foreign countries, which
crowns all their ftudies with experimental knowledge and wifdom; rendering them as familiar with
the different Natures of Men, and the various
Conftitutions of Government, as before they were
with Books.

This appears evident in thy letter, which is
replenifh'd with fo many folid remarks, and fage
comments on the Laws and Cuftoms of the Regions through which thou haft pafs'd, their Religions, Strength and Riches, and whatfoever elfe
was worthy a Traveller's notice; that were this
Narrative publifh'd in Chriftendom, the Nazarenes
would forbear to fpeak fo contemptibly of the
True Believers.

But they flatter themfelves with a falfe notion,
that the Ottomans never travel beyond the limits
of their own Empire, except the public Chiaufes,

who are fent by the Grand Signior. They are ignorant, that the auguft Porte maintains private Agents in all Nations; and that there is hardly any Prince's Court in Chriftendom without a Muffulman in it one time or other. 'Tis true, we appear not in the Garb peculiar to the Eaft. Our Miffion requires a Conformity to the Fafhions of the people where we refide. But we ftill retain the interior veftments of Mahometan Purity, being in a double fenfe circumcifed. Thus we become mafters of the Chriftians fecrets, whilft they account us ftupid, ignorant, and men void of common fenfe.

Befides, had we not this advantage in thefe Weftern parts, yet the univerfal privilege of travelling and maintaining free commerce over all the Eaft, muft needs afford great opportunities of accomplifhment to fome among the Caravans of fo many thoufands as vifit Perfia, India, China, Tartary, and all places where the Faith of the Miffioner of God is profeffed.

I am extremely pleafed with thy fortunate efcape from Robbers on the road, whofe malice rarely extends farther, than to deprive a man of thofe outward Goods, which, if he be wife, he will not call his own. Much more am I delighted with thy deliverance from thofe Female Thieves, who fteal from men their hearts and reafon, which laft is our nobleft, and only proper inheritance. All Perfia and the Indies abound with Courtezans; and he had need of Ofman's chaftity, who would withftand fo many and ftrong Temptations.

Thou needeft not wonder at the effeminacy of the prefent Mogul, who fuffers himfelf and his State to be governed by Women. That fubtle, and afpiring Sex, have always fought to undermine, or over-reach our Race. They keep behind the Scenes, yet act their Parts in all the Tragedies and Revolutions of the World. The father of the prefent Indian King made an abfolute refignation of his Sovereignty to his Queen,

2 · for

for four and twenty hours. This Prince by a
ftrange affectation, called himfelf "King of the
World." His wife was the daughter of an Arabian
Captain, who had ferved him in the wars: But
having forfeited his head by fome notorious Treafon, his daughter went and threw herfelf at the
Mogul's feet to beg his life. He fell paffionately
in love with her, (for fhe had not her equal for
beauty in all the Eaft) granted her Petition, and
married her. Afterwards fhe got fuch an Empire over him, that he would do nothing without her advice and confent. At her inftigation
he made War or Peace: And to pleafe her cruel
humour, he put out the eyes of his eldeft fon.
But, not fatisfied with thefe difcoveries of his
love, and refolving to make herfelf famous by
fome extraordinary action, fhe never ceas'd foli-
citing the King with all the arts of female policy, till fhe had prevail'd on him to furrender
up his authority to her for the fpace of a day.
In which time (having prepared all things beforehand ready for her purpofe) fhe caufed two millions of Roupies, in filver and gold, to be coin'd
and ftamp'd with the twelve Signs of the Zodiack,
contrary to the fundamental Laws of the Empire, the exprefs Prohibition of our Holy Prophet, and the univerfal Practice of the Muffulmans throughout the world, who admit not the
Reprefentations of any Creatures that have Life.
This relation I had from my uncle Ufeph, who
refided in the Indian Court eleven years. He
added moreover, that during this fhort Female
Reign, fhe cut off the heads of feven Grandees
the moft zealous for the Muffulman Faith among
all the Indian Princes, and eftablifh'd as many
Idolaters in their Places: And that, if her orders
had been fully executed, fhe had quite changed
the government, confecrated the moft beautiful Mofques to the fervice of Idols, exterminated
the true Faithful, and reftored the ancient Abo-

minations

minations of the Infidels; which thou wilt not think impracticable, when thou confiderest, That the number of the Uncircumcifed in the Indies, far exceeds that of the Muffulmans, there being ten thoufand of thofe to an hundred of fuch as profefs the Unity of the Divine Nature. But however, there was Loyalty found even among thofe Pagans; and they would not fuffer a blind Zeal for the Worfhip of their Gods, to fupplant the Duty they ow'd their King.

The Defcription thou haft made of Candahar, and the method thou haft projected to take that impregnable City, difcover at once thy conduct and diligence, in procuring liberty to furvey fo narrowly, the moft important place of the Indies; and thy fkill in fortifications, with the quick-nefs of thy invention; which has fuggefted to thee that which all the Engineers of Afia have never fo much as dreamt of. This is the right ufe of travelling, when a man returns from fo-reign nations, cultivated with experimental know-ledge, and ftock'd with improvements, that may render him ferviceable to his country.

Thou condemneft the injuftice and avarice of the Indian Moguls; who, as foon as any of the Omrahs or great Men die, caufe all his eftate and goods to be feiz'd, to their own proper ufe Whereby it comes to pafs, that the widow and children of the deceafed, are reduced to the loweft condition of poverty, being many times forced to beg for fubfiftence. 'Tis true, this is an op preffion not to be juftified, efpecially in thofe who profefs to believe in one God, Creator of all Things, the incorrupt Judge of the Univerfe. But what thinkeft thou then of our Sultans, who not having patience to wait till a natural death fhall make them Heirs to the Wealth of a Baffa, generally fecure their Title, and haften their pof-feffion by a Bow-ftring? Thefe are royal vio-lences; though the Refignation of Subjects muft
not

not tax them with any crime, who are accountable to none but God.

It was however a notable piece of raillery, with which the widow of a rich Merchant reproved this unreasonable custom in the present Mogul. Her husband was an Idolater, who had heaped together an infinite treasure by trading, and usury; and when he died, left her worth two hundred thousand Roupies. Her son, some years after, coming of age, demanded of her a stock to set up with as a Merchant. Which she, either out of avarice, or for other ends, refused him; furnishing him only with such small sums as served to nourish his discontent, and tempt him to a lewd, careless life. But at length, not being able to prevail on his mother to part with so much as would answer his expectations, he complained to the Mogul, disclosing also what estate his father had left. The Mogul being informed of so much riches, sent for the young man's mother, and commanded her to send him half her Money, ordering, That the other half should be divided between herself and her son. The widow, not being at all surprized; or cast down at this unjust proposal, made the Mogul this short reply: "O King, May the Gods make "thee happy. My son has some reason to re-"quire his share of his father's estate, having "his blood running in his veins; but I desire "to know, what relation thou art to my husband, "or me, that thou claimest a share to his inheri-"tance." The Prince abash'd at so smart and bold an address, commanded her to give half her estate to her son, and so dismissed her.

I have heard some of our Chiaufes praise the Magnificence of the Mogul's Court, the infinite number of his attendants: But above all, they extol the inimitable grandeur of his Throne, which is adorn'd with so many topazes, rubies, emeralds, pearls, and diamonds, as amount to thirty millions of Roupies. But were it not

much

much better, if inſtead of all this needleſs glory, he could boaſt, That his Empire is founded in the hearts of his Subjects : He does not conſider, That ſuch prodigious heaps of envied treaſure are but ſo many glittering Snares, golden Manacles, which ſerve for no other uſe, but to chain him up from that freedom, and thoſe more innocent delights, that the meaneſt of his ſubjects enjoy.

Thou haſt, I perceive, diſcourſed with the Indian Bramins : Doſt thou not diſcover, even in theſe Idolaters, a contempt of riches ? What mean thoughts have they of the ſplendor and gayeties of the court! What a low eſteem of the long and proud Series of Titles with which the Moguls endeavour to exalt themſelves ? Whilſt they are called the Lights of the World, and Companions of the Sun ; theſe poor Philoſophers know, That in a little time they ſhall be laid in Darkneſs, and have no better Society than that of Worms. What ſignifies their Pedigree, or, That the preſent Mogul is but the tenth Deſcendant from the mighty Temurlen, who made all Aſia tremble, if he has loſt the Virtue of his glorious Anceſtor ? 'Tis that alone makes all men truly noble.

Thou telleſt me, That the Empire of the Mogul affords him more Revenues than the Dominions of any two the moſt potent Monarchs on earth. I have heard as much from others, which convinces me, that thou haſt inform'd thyſelf rightly of the preſent State of the Indies. But doſt thou therefore eſteem this Monarch the richer ? Conſider the vaſt extent of his Dominions, which are ſaid to contain more than ſix hundred leagues in length, and thou wilt find, That to maintain ſo great a tract of ground, both againſt his foreign and domeſtic enemies, he is obliged to keep in conſtant pay, ſome millions of his ſubjects and ſtrangers : For he is in the

midſt

midſt of enemes, even among his own Subjects.
There are above an hundred Sovereigns in his
Empire, who perpetually by turns moleſt his
Government, refuſing to pay Tribute, and raiſing
armies againſt him : Whereby it comes to paſs,
that he is at an infinite expence to defend himſelf, and carry on thoſe endleſs wars ; thou thyſelf having obſerv'd, That once in two Moons
there is an indiſpenſable neceſſity of paying theſe
prodigious armies : Not a Soldier throughout his
Empire having any thing to live on, ſave the
wages he receives of the King.

Conſider alſo, That this Monarch always keeps
ſome thouſands of the fineſt horſes in the world
near his perſon, ſuch as coſt him thouſands of
Roupies a-piece; beſides a thouſand elephants ;
with an incredible number of mules, camels,
and other beaſts of burden, to carry his wives,
his goods and proviſions, when he takes the
field : That whole cities, even as large as Conſtantinople, are obliged to follow the King's camp
for ſubſiſtence, their livelihood altogether depending on the army. Add to this, the immenſe
charges of his Seraglio, his caſtles and ſea-port
towns, with all the other neceſſary expences of
the State, and thou wilt conclude, That when
this Potentate comes to caſt up his accounts, he
will find himſelf a poor man.

But I ſhall cloy thee with a rehearſal of ſuch
things, as thou canſt not be a ſtranger to.

Only tell me, Whether one of the Raias or
Princes ſubject to the Mogul, be the real Deſcendent of Porus, the ancient King of India, in
the time of Alexander the Great? I have been
told by ſeveral travellers, That there is ſuch an
one, that his name is Rana, and that an hundred
of the idolatrous Princes pay homage to him, as
to their natural Sovereign.

Thou confirmeſt the truth of what has been ſo
often reported in theſe parts, That the Prince of

Java had fix fingers on each hand, and as many toes on his feet.

But that feems very ftrange which thou relateft, of a certain Language among the Indians, which is not vulgarly fpoken; but that all their Books of Theology, and Pandects of their Laws, the Records of their Nation, and the Treatifes of Human Arts and Sciences are written in it. And that this Language is taught in their Schools, Colleges, and Academies, even as Latin is among the Chriftians. I cannot enough admire at this; for, where and when was this Language fpoken? How came it to be difus'd? There feems to be a myftery in it, that none of their Brachmans can give any other account of this, fave, That it is the Language, wherein God gave, to the firft Creature he made, the four Books of the Law: Which, according to their Chronology, was above thirty millions of years ago. I tell thee, my dear brother; this news has ftarted fome odd notions in my mind: For when I confider, That this Language, as thou fay'ft, has nothing in it common with the Indian that is now fpoken, nor with any other Language of Afia, or of the world; and yet that it is a copious and regular Language, learn'd by Grammar, like the other material Languages; and that, in this obfolete Language, Books are written, wherein it is afferted, That the World is fo many millions of years old; I could almoft turn Pythagorean, and believe the World to be within a Minute of Eternal. And, where would be the abfurdity? Since God had equally the fame infinite power, wifdom and goodnefs, from all eternity, as he had five or fix thoufand Years ago. What fhould hinder him then from exerting thefe divine Attributes fooner? What fhould retard him from drawing forth this glorious Fabric earlier, from the Womb of Nothing? Suffer thy imagination to ftart backwards, as far as thou canft, even to millions

of

of ages, and yet thou canſt not conceive a time, wherein this fair unmeaſurable Expanſe was not ſtretch'd out. As if Nature herſelf had engraven on our intellects, this Record of the World's un-traceable Antiquity, in that our ſtrongeſt, ſwifteſt thoughts, are far too weak and ſlow to follow time back to its endleſs origin.

The Revolution in China ſurpaſſes the common Changes in Kingdoms and Empires. There is ſomething exceſſively tragical in the Cataſtrophe of that Royal Houſe.

Brother, in beholding that, thou haſt ſeen Hu-man Nature in a Trance: And thou art ſo thy-ſelf, if, after this, thou canſt be fond of any thing on earth. Traveller, Adieu.

Paris, 2th of the 1ſt Moon,
  of the Year 1647.

LETTER XXII.

To Afis, Baſſa.

SEveral Diſpatches have been lately ſent be-tween this Court, and that of Swedeland, con-taining rather matter of compliment, than any thing of great importance. Queen Chriſtina has been very ill, which has occaſion'd letters of con-dolance from the Queen Regent of France.

Thoſe which come from that part, ſay, That General Torſtenſon is made a Count; and the Dignity entail'd to his Poſterity, in recompence of his eminent ſervices to the Swediſh Crown.

Theſe letters add, That there have paſs'd ſome high words between Monſieur Chanut, and the Swediſh Secretary of State. And that the latter, in going out of the chamber where they diſcur-ſed, laid his hand upon his ſword, with theſe words: " Monſieur Chanut, Were it not for the

fence

" fence which the Law of Nations has rais'd
" about your perfon, I would anfwer you in ano-
" ther language." To which Monfieur Chanut
replied, " That he wore a fword to defend himfelf
" and his private honour, as well as any Swede in
" the kingdom."

The occafion of this quarrel was, The great re-
fort of Roman Catholic ftrangers to Monfieur
Chanut's chapel, which gave difguft to the Swedes,
who allow not the Exercife of the Roman Religion
within their territories. They caftrate all the
Priefts of that Communion whom they find, and
profecute the Laity with rigorous penalties. But
Monfieur Chanut pleaded the Law of Nations :
And when the Secretary told him, That the Quee i
permitted him and his family the liberty of their
Religion, but defired him not to admit any other
perfons of what Nation foever : This Minifter replied, " That he could not receive as a favour, or
" permiffion from her Majefty, the liberty of ex-
" ercifing his Religion, fince he held it only of his
" Mafter, the King of France, who had fent him
" thither, and that he would not fhut the door of
" his Chapel againft any that would come in :
" That their Law, which according to his own
" calcule, was made about two thoufand years af-
" ter the foundation of their Eftate, could not ab-
" rogate the Law of Nations, which is eternal :
" That this perpetual Law gave particular privi-
" leges to certain perfons, and efpecially to the
" Minifters of foreign Princes : That their new
" Law, fuch as it was, being only made to maintain
" the public Worfhip, refpected not what was
" done in the Houfe of a foreign Minifter, by a
" fpecial privilege, it being of no confequence to
" the State, whether fuch foreigners ferved God
" or not, or whether they worfhipped him in a
" right or wrong way : That no Swede came to
" his Chapel, but only fome French, who were —
" fojourners in the land : That they did not ufe
" the Swedifh Ambaffadors fo in France, who ad-
" m tted

" mitted whom they pleafed into their Chapels:
" That the houfe where he now dwelt, was the
" houfe of the King of France; and that therefore
" he could not by confequence refufe any Catho-
" lics an entrance into it, efpecially fuch as were
" born fubjects of his Mafter: And in fine, That
" it was very rude to oblige him to be the execu-
" tioner of this fevere law, in requiring him to
" fhut his doors upon his countrymen, againft the
" common Law of Hofpitality, the Honour of a
" public Minifter, and the Pleafure of the King
" his Sovereign."

To this the Secretary made fomething too tart a
reply. Whereupon words increafing between
them, and the French Ambaffador being refolute
to affert his privilege, the Secretary broke out into a paffion, as I have before mention'd, laying
his hand upon his fword, as he was leaving the
room.

The Swedes are naturally a rugged, furly people,
as are all the Northern Europeans. They are
ftrangers to civility, and the gentle addrefs of the
French. Yet the Queen, when fhe heard of this
paffage, was angry with her Minifter, and excufed
his rudenefs to Monfieur Chanut; telling him,
" That the Secretary was a faithful Servant,
" but had been educated among the Bears of the
" Foreft."

This puts me in mind of a Story which the
French tell of another Ambaffador, whom Lewis
XIII. fent to the Court of Spain. The Spaniards
are of haughty temper, expecting more than ordinary fubmiffions from thofe who approach the
King's prefence. This Ambaffador, on the fame
ground, was required to do fome homage, which
would not confift with the inftructions of his Mafter, and therefore he refufed to comply. The King
of Spain thinking to put him out of countenance,
faid aloud, " What! has the King of France no
" other men in his Court, that he fends me fuch
" a fool as this?" To which the Ambaffador replied,

plied, "My Mafter has many wifer men than my-
"felf about him; but to fuch a King, fuch an
"Ambaffador."

Thou wilt not perhaps approve fuch raillery as'
this to Crown'd Heads, who ought to be treated
with reverence and gravity. Yet, I believe, thou'
wilt condemn the cruelty of a Duke of Mufcovy,'
who caufed the hat of a French Ambaffador to be'
nailed to his head, for fitting cover'd before him.'
This is contrary to the Genius of the Eaft, who'
abhor to fee a man bare-headed.

But every Nation has its Mode: And I, according to the fafhion of my country, kifs the border of thy veft, in token of my fubmiffion and
refpect.

Paris, 7th of, the 2d Moon,
    of the Year 1647.

LETTER XXIII.

To the Mufti, moft venerable, and worthy of all Honour.

THE Critics, who fpend their time, and manifeft their wit, in defcanting on the Court and
the Grandees, find perpetual matter of difcourfe
concerning Cardinal Mazarini. His daily actions
furnifh them with new themes, and fometimes they
rehearfe the old. They compare him with his predeceffor Richlieu, and with Cardinal Ximenes, a
Spanifh Minifter. They term thefe three, the
Trinity of Chriftian Statefmen; thus diftinguifhing
their perfonal characters. Richlieu, they fay, was
crafty, covetous, and revengeful; Ximenes was
politic, fevere, and valiant; Mazarini is wife, merciful, and liberal.

The firft made good his character, they fay, in
heaping

heaping up fuch prodigious treafures; in raifing all thofe of his family or dependance, to the higheft honours; in occafioning the voluntary banifhment of the Queen-Mother; in ruining whomfoever he fufpected; and finally, in making himfelf fo much the mafter of all fecrets, that the King, however difgufted and averfe from him, yet could never fit fafe on his Throne without him, when living, nor venture the management of the Public to any of his creatures, when dead. Thus fpeak they of that great Minifter.

As to Cardinal Ximenes, they fay, He difcover'd the qualities which they afcribe to him, in the method he took to raife himfelf to that envied greatnefs, which was, by feeming to fhun the honours at which he fecretly aim'd. For being a devoted Dervife, or religious Friar, he appear'd to be the moft mortify'd man of the whole Order: which being taken notice of, he was made Provincial; from which Dignity, he made but one ftep more to the Purple! and growing eminent for his abilities, he was made firft Minifter in the Court of Spain.

He levy'd fixteen thoufand men at his own coft, invaded Barbary, ftorm'd their ftrongeft cities, and reduced the whole kingdom of Tripoli and Algiers to his Mafter's obedience.

Whilft he was at the head of his army, one day there happen'd a mutiny among his foldiers. A certain fellow, running up and down between the ranks, and exciting them to chufe a new General, faying, "It was a fhame to ferve a poor-fpirited "Friar:" The Cardinal perceiving this, ftepp'd to the fellow, and with one blow fever'd his head from his body. This ftruck fuch a terror into all, that, from that time, there was not the leaft tumult or diforder in his army.

They fay, he was in the end poifon'd by eating of a Fifh, of which a friend of his receiv'd intimation on the road, as he was riding to the place where the Cardinal was at dinner. But he came

too late, to prevent the effects of the poifon : For
though the Cardinal was but juft rifen from the
table, yet he began to void blood by his ears, and
the extremities of his fingers; and in a few days
drew his laft breath. He was tall, and well limb'd :
His two fore teeth of the upper jaw grew fo far out
of his mouth, that he was call'd, The Ecclefiaftical
Elephant. The futures of his fkull were fo clofely
indented, that there was no more room for tran-
fpiration of the grofler vapours, than through the
moft folid part of the bone. On this account he
was ever troubled with the head-ach, contrary to
Cardinal Richlieu, who never felt any pain in that
part, becaufe he had two little holes in his crown,
through which the fumes exhal'd.

These are the remarks which are made on Cardinal Ximenes. As to Mazarini, they fay, he fur-
paffes both thefe Minifters, in the exquifite moderation of his temper : And comes fhort of neither,
in the contrivance or fuccefs of affairs, being folid
in his counfels, fecret and fwift in their execution.
He has this alfo peculiar in his conduct, That none
are more fure of his favour, than thofe who have
done him injuries. He is magnific in his expences;
building Palaces that may vie with the moft celebrated ftructures of the ancient Romans : A curious
collector of choice paintings and fculptures; furnifhing the houfes with utenfils of cedar, ebony,
filver, gold, and other ornaments, befitting the
Palace of a King. Liberal beyond the expectation
of his friends and fervants, yet not to profufenefs.
He has a wonderful fagacity in difcovering cheats
and impoftors : And no lefs dexterity in difcerning
men of merit, though never fo much obfcur'd by
misfortune.

Not long ago he catch'd a Gentleman in a crime,
which expos'd him to the laughter and contempt
of the whole Court, but not to the Cardinal's
hatred. He had been recommended to this Minifter by a Lady of the Court, for whom he had a
great

great efteem.   On which account he had free accefs to the Cardinal's prefence, and would always
mix with his Retinue.

But his curious Patron had obferv'd fomething
in his carriage, which gave him ground of miftruft.
For he would always place himfelf as near as he
could to a certain table, in the chamber where the
Cardinal gives audience.   There is a drawer under
this table, which commonly ftands half open, it
being the place where all Petitioners throw in their
bribes or prefents ; it not being feemly for a Prince
of the Church to take money himfelf.   The Cardinal obferv'd,   That this fpark always had his eye
glancing on that drawer, as if he coveted what was
there contain'd.   However, he took no notice, but
gave him all the opportunities imaginable to do
his pleafure ; yet ftill one accident or other hinder'd the Gentleman from executing his defign,
which was, To borrow fome of the gold that lay in
that drawer.   At length it happen'd, That the
Cardinal having appointed fome curious Pageants
to be made in honour of the King's Birth-Day, he,
with feveral of the Court.ers, ftood looking out of
the windows to fee the triumphant fhows pafs by.
The Gentleman, taking this opportunity, whilft he
thought all eyes were intent on the gayeties without, flips to the table, and takes out of the drawer
a bag of gold, putting it up in his pocket, and
retiring to the window again.   He imagined that
nobody had feen him, and therefore hugg'd himfelf in the thoughts of his booty.   When the Show
was over, and the company withdrew from the
window; after a while, they all took their leave
and departed : And among the reft, this gentleman
thief was going out.   But the Cardinal defired him
to tarry, in that he had fomething to fay to him.
The Gentleman, ftung with the guilt of what he
had done, fell a trembling, and was ready to drop
down at the Cardinal's feet.   But he bid him be of
good comfort, faying thus to him ; " My friend,
" what thou haft done, is not hid from me.   If
" thou

" thou haſt not gold enough, I will double. thy
" ſum." Therewith he gave him another bag of
equal value; ſaying withal, " Go thy way, and
" ſee my face no more. I pardon, but cannot
" truſt thee."

Would'ſt thou know, by what means the Cardinal diſcover'd this theft? He always wears on
his finger a ring, in which is ſet a Jewel of ineſti-
mable value; it being a Natural Mirror, and diſcovering all things that are done in the room,
though behind a man's back. 'Twas on this ſtone
the Cardinal caſt his eye, when the Gentleman
thought he was looking out of the window. Therein
he beheld him go to the table, take out the money,
and put it in his pocket. Thou ſeeſt how curious
this Miniſter is, to ſtock himſelf with uſeful rarities.

May that great Chancellor of Heaven, the Angel
who beholds in the Divine Eſſence as in a Mirror,
whatſoever is done on earth, and records all human
actions in the Book of Judgments, never diſcern
any thing in Mahmut, which may render him worthy to be excluded the Preſence of God.

Paris, 12th of the 2d Moon,
    of the Year 1647.

LETTER XXIV.

To Danecmar Kefrou, Kadileſquier of
    Romania.

THOU, that art principal among the judges
    of high dignity, the illuſtrious ornament of.
three Empires, the ſtrong ſupport of equity, who
preſerveſt reaſon, and correcteſt vice, I congratulate
thy deſerved honour: And in doing ſo, I wiſh increaſe of joy to all the faithful Oſmans.
                                        The

'The knowledge which thou haſt acquired in the Law of Nations, and in the moſt perfect ſanctions of our auguſt Monarchy, has made thee famous through the ſeven Precincts of the Earth ; and has veſted thee with the robe of ſublime honour, the gift of the Lieutenant of God.

I made choice of this occaſion at once to perform my duty, and to acquaint thee with a national villany ; ſuch a violation of the public Faith of a Kingdom, as it will be difficult to parallel.

The Civil Wars of England are known throughout the World : And thou art no ſtranger to the particular intelligences I have ſent to the ſublime Port, concerning that Nation.

Since that time the Rebels have by degrees gain'd ground of their unhappy King, chaſing him from one place to another : 'Till at length finding, that neither by Arms or Treaties, he could reduce them to any terms of reconciliation, and being beſieged in one of his cities, which was not in a condition to hold out long, this unfortunate Monarch was forced to diſguiſe himſelf, and eſcape by night; wandering through unfrequented ways, and enduring much hardſhip. He at length threw himſelf upon the faith of the Scots, who had ſolemnly engaged themſelves upon Oath, To defend him againſt all his enemies whatſoever.

The Scottiſh army was then in England, being hired to aſſiſt the Rebels. Whence ſome take occaſion to accuſe this Prince of raſhneſs, and too much credulity, in ſeeking protection from thoſe who firſt began the Rebellion, and who had ſtain'd the Records of Scotland with the Blood of many of their Kings. But innocency is void of ſuſpicion; and therefore, becauſe his own intentions were ſincere, he knew not how to be jealous of others.

However, the Scots at firſt ſeem'd to act the parts of loyal men. And when they were threatned by the Engliſh Rebels, and their pay was ſtopp'd, with Declarations alſo iſſued out againſt

their

their proceedings, they continued to affert the juftice of their deportment, in receiving and defending their injur'd King, who had fled to them for fuccour.

They detained him thus, from the 4th of the 5th Moon, of the year 1646, to the 30th day of the 1ft Moon, of this present year. At which time, having agreed with the Englifh Parliament, for the fum of 400,000 Sequins, as the price of their Sovereign, they deliver'd him up to the Englifh Commiffioners, deputed by the rebels for that purpofe.

The French Ambaffador was at that time in the Scotch army; who having been a witnefs of their deteftable perjury, took his leave: And being attended with a Guard of Light-Horfe to the fea-port, at parting he pull'd out a piece of Englifh money, valued at Half a Crown; and afking the Captain of the Guards into how many pieces of coined filver that Half Crown might be divided, He anfwer'd, Into Thirty. "For fo much " (replied the Ambaffador) did Judas betray his " Mafter."

Thou wilt better comprehend the force of this Repartee, when thou confidereft, that according to the Chriftians Belief, this Judas was a Slave of Jefus, the Son of Mary, and that for thirty Pieces of Silver, he betray'd that Prophet to the Jews.

But thefe Infidels have found out ways to elude all engagements and promifes. They couch their Oaths, in words more ambiguous than the Oracles of Delphos. As if they thought not only to circumvent men by their equivocations, but alfo to deceive Him who formed the Tongue and the Ear; even God, who is perfect in Knowledge.

Such a Story I have read of one Hatto a German Bifhop, whofe perjury is recorded. This Prelate had a Coufin who was accufed of Treafon againft the Emperor. On which account he was clofely befieged by the Imperial forces, in a Caftle feated

on

on the top of an impregnable rock. So that the
Emperor defpairing to take him by force, had with-
drawn his army; when this Bifhop came to him,
and for a fum of money promifed to betray his
Kinfman into the Emperor's hands.

This bargain being concluded, the Bifhop went
to vifit his Coufin at the Caftle, perfuading him to
go and humble himfelf to the Emperor, and he
would engage to procure his Pardon : Binding
himfelf with a folemn Oath, That if he would
rely on him, as he carried him fafe out of the
Caftle, fo he would bring him back alive and fafe
again.

His Kinfman, deluded with thefe fair pretences,
and fecured by the Sanction of an Oath, trufts
himfelf to the conduct and fidelity of the Prelate.

· When they had rode about half a league from
the Caftle, the Bifhop pretending he had forgot
fome papers of moment, which he had left behind
him in his chamber, they return'd. back to the
Caftle ; and when they had found the papers, they
fet forward again towards the Emperor's camp.
Being arrived there, the impious wretch deliver'd
his Kinfman to the Emperor, who condemn'd him
to die. He fending for the Bifhop, reproaches him
with the Violation of his Oath. But the perfidious Bifhop fought to acquit himfelf by faying,
" He had perform'd his promife, in carrying him
" back fafe to the Caftle, when he return'd to feek
" his papers." Thus was his Kinfman betray'd by
a Quibble, and loft his head. The Bifhop acquir-
ing, for that impious deed, the odious Title of
Hatto the Traitor. And the Germans report,
That he was afterwards carried away by Devils,
and thrown alive into the hollow of Mount Ætna :
A voice being heard at the fame inftant in the air,
faying, " This is the Reward of Perjury."

The Nazarenes believe this flaming Mountain
to be one of the Mouths of Hell: The fame opinion

nion they have of Strombolo and Vefuvius. I am not curious to pry into the truth of fo coftly a fecret, but leave the experiment to the forfworn, treacherous Scots, who, by this barbarous action, deferve to follow the fate of Hatto.

Much greater was the integrity and virtue of the ancient Romans, whom thefe Infidels number among the damn'd. They efteem'd nothing more facred than the public Faith ; building Temples to its Honour, and ftamping their Money with the Figure of two Hands joined together, having this Motto, THE FAITH OF THE ROMANS. But the Scots fhew themfelves to be of Lyfander's mind, who ufed to fay, " Children muft be cir-" cumvented with words, and men with oaths."

This Monarch is now led in triumph, like a captive, by his rebellious fubjects, who have confined him to one of his country Palaces, fuffering none of his friends, or faithful fervants, to come near him, but in all things endeavouring to render his reftraint infupportable.

Thou who art accurate in interpreting the Laws of Juftice, wilt condemn thefe Infidels of horrid Treafon, yet canft not acquit the Muffulmans, who have often depofed our moft auguft Emperors.

I divide my intelligence among the Minifters of the fublime Port, and the other Grandees of the State ; praying God, to guard the Sultan from fecret machinations, and open enemies ; and to grant, That an excefs of good nature may not betray him to fuch misfortunes, as have befallen this imprifon'd Monarch.

Paris, 21ft of the 3d Moon, of the Year 164.

LETTER XXV.

To Ragel Hamet, Antiquary to the
Sultan.

THIS City is pester'd with an innumerable
multitude of Bats, and a kind of Serpents,
which they call Lizards or Newts. They breed in
the walls of their houses, and molest the inhabitants
night and day, swarming more than ordinary every
ninth year.

The Parisians give an odd reason for this Plague.
They say, That in former ages, a certain Magician
had undertaken to free this City from all venomous
Creatures; and that, accordingly, he had made
several Images of those Animals, annexing to them
Enchantments, and hiding them in obscure places
under the earth; promising also, That so long as
those Images remain'd untouch'd, Paris should not
be molested with any hurtful thing. This succeeded according to his words; 'till at a certain time,
as they were digging up the foundations of an
old Temple, the workmen found several brazen
Images, some representing a Bat, some a Li-
zard. They making small account of those magical Reliques, sold them to the next Brasier for
a piece of money: Who being ignorant also of
the hidden force of these images, melted them
down for his own use. And, ever since that
time, the city has been over-run with Bats and
Lizards.

I relate this to thee, in regard I have often heard
thee speak of the ancient Statues, that were in the
Atmidam at Constantinople, and in other parts of
the city; particularly of that Pillar, which had three
Brazen Serpents winding about it, which when
Mahomet the Great beheld, the Conqueror struck
one of them with a Battle-Axe, and smote off the

lower

lower Jaw.   Upon which a multitude of Serpents
infefted the city, but were foon exterminated, in
regard the Sultan, being warned by the citizens,
forbore to do any farther injury to thofe Images,
which were the Guardians of the city.

The Annals of the Muffulman Empire make
mention of thefe Statues, as alfo of a Horfe of
Brafs, and a Bull of the fame metal.   The one
erected as a charm againft the Peftilence;   the
other, as an oraculous fign, That the enemies of
the Grecian Monarchy fhould in that place be repulfed and driven out of the city.   Yet it proved
otherwife: For the victorious Muffulmans againft
whom the Enchantments of the Infidels could not
prevail, enter'd the Market-Place, where this
Image ftood, and drove from thence the timerous
Grecians; cutting in pieces all that made refiftance, and rendring themfelves Lords of Conftantinople, at that time the richeft city in the world.

The Romans were extremely addicted to thefe
fuperftitious vanities: believing the fafety of their
City and Empire confifted in the prefervation of
the Palladium, an Image, which they thought fell
down from Jupiter, and was tranfported from Troy
to Italy by Æneas;   being afterwards repofited
in the Temple of Vefta, but burnt in that dreadful Conflagration which happen'd in the Reign
of Nero.

They had in no lefs Veneration the Buckler,
which they were taught dropp'd down from Heaven,
into the hands of Numa Pompilius;   whereon the
Fate of Rome was engraven, in Characters which
none could read.   Fearing left this Sacred Shield
might be ftolen, they caufed eleven others of the
fame figure to be made, and all to be hung up together in the Temple of Mars.

And, to the end the Guardian Genius of the City
fhould not be enticed from them by the Enchantments of their enemies, the true Name of the city
of Rome was kept fecret, even from its own inhabitants ;

habitants; infomuch, that Valerius Soranus was put to death, for publifhing it to one of his Friends. Many have guefs'd at the hidden Name; fome faying, It was Valencia; others, That it was Velia; a third fort call it Anthufa. But there is no certainty in their conjectures. For the Pagans were above all things careful to conceal the Names of their Cities and Patron Gods; knowing, that thofe Spirits would not forfake them, till they were call'd forth by their proper Names.

They us'd alfo to chain the Images of their Gods to the Altars, left they fhould depart from them by ftealth. Thus the Tyrians, when Alexander befieged their City, and they underftood from the Priefts, That Apollo the Guardian of Tyre, was difpleas'd with 'em, they faften'd his Image with ftrong fetters of iron. So dealt the Spartans with the Image of Mars. And this was the common practice among thofe idolatrous nations.

As for us, who have received the Law clear and intelligible, and believe in the Unity of the Divine Effence: We ufe no Charms ourfelves, neither do we fear the Magic of the Uncircumcifed. All our confidence is in God, and the protection of his Prophet: We go boldly to the wars, whilft we fight in defence neither of Statues, nor fictitious Reliques, but of the Volume, replenifh'd with Truth and Light, the Book brought down from Heaven by an Angel.

Paris, 17th of the 4th Moon,
of the Year 1647.

LETTER XXVI.

To the Vizir Azem.

I AM now returned from Orleans, whither I went in obedience to thy appointments; and not without abundance of pleafure to myfelf, it being the time of year when all things confpire to make a traveller pafs his time away with delight.

Yet my return was melancholy, in regard I could not accomplifh what I aim'd at, nor be in a capacity to render thee that fatisfaction thou requireft, either in buying the Jewels, or in eftablifhing any correfpondence. Thofe who inform'd thee of the Germans inhabiting that city, were miftaken in their character, they being only a Society or Corporation of Students, and no ways concerned in traffic or merchandize.

They told thee right, in faying, There are a great number of ftrangers in Orleans: I think the Imperial city, which commands the World, cannot boaft a. greater diverfity of Languages, than are fpoken daily in the ftreets and houfes of Orleans. There are fome, almoft of all nations, refiding in that city.

Would'ft thou know the real occafion of this mighty conflux of foreigners. It is, That they may ftudy that which the Nazarenes call the Civil Law, which is there profeffed as in an Academy, erected for that purpofe by Philip the Fair, one of the Kings of France.

If thou knoweft not the meaning of the Civil Law, it is, A collection of the ancient Roman Laws, drawn from above two thoufand Books of their Scribes, by the command of the Emperor Juftinian,

Juftinian, for a Standard of Equity in thofe corrupt times, in that univerfal relaxation and decline of good government.

This is the attractive, which draws fo many
ftrangers from all parts of Europe, to that pleafant city, where, befides the opportunity of im-
proving themfelves in the moft honourable Profeffion among the Nazarenes, next to that of the
Priefthood, they enjoy a pure and ferene heaven,
a fruitful and delicious part of the earth, and the
company of the moft obliging and courteous people in all France.

'Tis for this reafon the Germans, among other
Nations, flock to Orleans; and, through the favour of the French Kings, have obtained a privilege beyond other nations; that is, To incorporate themfelves into a Society of Students.
Neither is there any fuch thing as Merchandize
known among them.

If I have not anfwer'd thy expectation, fupreme
Prince of the Baffa's, blame not Mahmut, but accufe the Germans of Orleans, for not exchanging
their Studies for Traffic; or rather blame thofe
who prefum'd to tell thee this far-fetch'd Fable.
In finifhing this letter, I bow my head to the
floor of my chamber, and kifs the paper which
fhall have the honour to be touch'd by thy illuftrious Hands.

Paris, 1ft of the 6th Moon,
    of the Year 1647.

LETTER XXVII.

To the Aga of the Janizaries.

THOU haft heard of the Affyrian, Scythian, and Roman Heroines. Thefe were all valiant leaders of armies, women of honour and renown. Now I will inform thee of a Female which France has brought upon the Stage of War.

According to the orders which I receiv'd from the Vizir Azem, I took a journey to Orleans laft Moon; where on the third day after my arrival, beholding a folemn Proceffion in the ftreets of that populous City, attended with fome uncommon ceremonies and rejoicings, my curiofity prompted me to enquire the occafion of it. Thou may'ft imagine, I did not apply myfelf for information to the multitude, who take up things on the common credit of fame, which does not always deliver the truth. I addrefs'd myfelf to thofe who were acquainted with the Records of the Town; who told me, that this Solemnity was yearly obferv'd on the eighth day of the fifth Moon, in memory of their deliverance from the Englifh, who befieged this City, and were beaten from before it by Joan d' Arc, a Maid of Lorrain, in the Reign of Charles I. This Virago feem'd to be the tutelar Angel of France: For to her valour and conduct, that Monarch ow'd the recovery of this Kingdom, almoft loft to the King of England; this being the laft place of importance which had not receiv'd Englifh garifons. After fhe had rais'd the fiege, fhe purfued the enemy, gave them feveral battles, defeated them, took the Generals captive, reduced all the cities

to

to their former obedience, and never sheath'd
her sword, 'till she saw her Master solemnly crown'd
at Rhemes. Yet at length she herself was made
a prisoner by the English, and was publicly burnt
for a Witch at Rouen.

The Inhabitants of Orleans have erected brazen
Statues in her honour. They celebrate her
praises, and esteem her a woman divinely inspired
to save her country. Yet the more intelligent
sort say, That she was neither Witch nor Pro-
phetess, but only a Maid of good wit and courage,
whom some of the Princes of the Blood Royal
had instructed to act the part of a Missionary
from Heaven ; that so, by pretending Visions and
Revelations, she might raise the courage of the
French, now almost dispirited by their many
losses ; and whom nothing less than a Miracle
could persuade to abide the field against the
victorious English. This is certain, That she
distinguish'd the King, though disguis'd like a
Peasant, and in a crowd of people : She went
boldly up to him, and saluted him by his Title,
to the astonishment of those that stood by. She
sent a messenger to bring her a sword of an-
tique workmanship, that lay hid in a tomb in
one of their famous Mosques ; (for, the Nazarenes
of the West bury their Dead in their Temples.)
This action extremely enhanced her reputation, in regard none knew of this sword but the
King himself. She was therefore look'd upon
as an extraordinary person ; and the people could
hardly be restrain'd from paying her divine honours.

When they were encamped on a certain plain
of a vast extent, where there was no water to be
found, so that the army was ready to perish through
thirst ; the King came to the Tent of the Pro-
phetess, to consult her as an Oracle in the general distress. She bad him be of good courage,
and follow her. They went out together to the
door of her Tent, where, at a little distance, there

grew

grew a knot of flowers. The admirable Maid
ſtruck her ſpear into the ground amidſt the
flowers, and incontinently there ſprung forth a
fountain of water, to which the whole army re-
paired to allay their thirſt. They ſay the place is
ſhewn to this day, with an Image of this Maid
ſtanding in an oratory, cloſe by it, a place of
refreſhment and devotion for travellers that paſs
over thoſe barren plains.

However, whether it were artifice, or that ſhe
was endued with ſome ſupernatural gift, it had a
marvellous influence on the ſoldiers, who began
to re-aſſume courage, and feared nothing under the
conduct of ſuch a general.

'Twas revenge without doubt, rather than
juſtice, that extorted that cruel Sentence from
the Engliſh, which put an end to the heroic
Actions of this illuſtrious Maid, whoſe fame will
live for ever.

It is recorded, That whilſt ſhe was bound faſt
to the ſtake with ſtrong cords, they would have
kindled the fire upon her before ſhe had ſpoke to
the ſpectators; but that ſhe ſuddenly became
looſen'd, and ſnatching a lance from one of the
ſoldiers, ſhe drove the Guards before her: Then
returning of her own accord to the ſtake, ſhe
made her laſt dying ſpeech, foretelling many things
to come, which afterwards proved true. And
having made an end of ſpeaking, ſhe bid the Executioner ſet fire to the wood; which he did accordingly, and ſhe was burnt to aſhes.

Certainly every nation may boaſt of ſome Female warrior, that at one time or other has done
remarkable ſervice to her country. And thou art
not a ſtranger to the hiſtory of the Amazons,
who excluded men from their ſociety, yet became formidable to all the regions round about
them.

Adieu, brave commander of the Muſſulman
forces, and let the memory of theſe valiant Females

males infpire thee with frefh ardours, when the Ottoman Empire is in danger.

Paris, 1ft of the 6th Moon,
of the Year 1647.

LETTER XXVIII.

To Dgnet Oglou.

THOU art the man that muft participate in all my adventures. And I fhould be a churl, in not letting thee fhare with me, the pleafure I found in a late journey to Orleans, one of the prefidary towns in France. It was by the order of the Vizir Azem I took that journey. Somebody had inform'd him, That this town was full of merchant-travellers of many Nations, but efpecially of Germany, who brought the choiceft Jewels of the Eaft, to vend in this place at ordinary rates. That Minifter gave me commands to buy certain ftones, with inftructions to treat of another affair, which it is not neceffary for thee to know. I accordingly fet out from Paris the third day of the fifth Moon; and Eliachim the Jew (of whom thou haft heard) bore me company.

I need not defcribe to thee the country through which we paffed: It exactly refembleth the Plains of St. Ifidore, not far from Palermo in Sicily. Thou and I have reafon to remember that place of our Captivity, carrying the marks of our Mafter's cruel anger yet in our bodies. Thofe Plains, thou knoweft, afford a very agreeable profpect, efpecially at this time of the year, when the verdure of the trees, mix'd with the brightnefs of the corn-fields, and the party-colour'd

I 3   mea-

meadows, tempt the eye into a controverfy of pleafure, a man neither knowing well how to take it
off, nor yet where to fix it, in fuch an orderly
confufion and medley of charming objects.

Such is the province between Paris and Orleans,
which has the advantage of thofe Sicilian Plains,
that here all the way one rides, innumerable
magnificent and beautiful palaces appear, fhooting
up their glittering turrets above the lofty groves,
which environ thofe feats of pleafure. Indeed
this is one of the pureft airs, and the moft fertile foil in all the kingdom, which invites the
Nobles and Gentry to refide here during the
Summer, and occafions much travelling on this
road.

About mid-day, we came to a town called
Chaftres, where we alighted to refrefh ourfelves.
Travellers in thefe Weftern Parts are better
accommodated with provifions than they can be
in Afia, where they muft carry their own beds
with them, and drefs their own victuals, or lie
on the naked floor fafting. This makes the
Nazarenes call the Eaft inhofpitable. They confider not at the fame time, that 'tis the nicenefs and
delicacy of the Mahometans, which occafions
this cuftom. For the Eaftern people are fearful of defiling themfelves by eating meat prepared by other hands than their own, or thofe of
their fervants: And alfo to lie on a bed, common to all paffengers.

But thefe Infidels are like the Swine, to whom
all meat is welcome, and every ditch an acceptable bed. Here are inns all along the roads,
whereinto when you enter, the Hoft provides you
both Bed, and all other neceffaries. A man muft
venture to fleep on the fame pillow, where perhaps a Leper has lain the night before, or fome
perfon infected with a worfe difeafe. The Hoft
examines none, but harbours all alike, provided
they have money to pay him. And as for victuals,
'tis

'tis the cuftom of all travellers, to eat together at one common table, where feveral difhes of meat are ferved up, and every man is free to eat what and how much he pleafes, paying a ftated price for his dinner.

Thus no fooner were we come into our inn at Chaftres, but the Hoft faluting us after the manner of the country, invited us to fit down at the Ordinary, (for fo they call their public dinner in an inn.) We were not fo fcrupulous as to refufe his offer, but follow'd him into the chamber where the dinner was prepared. There were many guefts at the table, and all bufy in feeding themfelves. We took fuch feats as we found vacant, and without much ceremony, fell to eating. The Jew trufted to the indulgence of Mofes, and I to that of Mahomet, for eating with the uncircumcifed, whofe meat is feldom free from the Pollutions of Blood. We knew, that neither God, nor his Prophets, required us to ftarve.

There was plenty of wine, and that fo delicious, as would have tempted an Hogia to tafte it, without the Mufti's difpenfation ; to avoid fingularity, I made a fhew of eating as the reft ; but the greateft part of my repaft confifted in bread, and fome fruits, with that exhilarating juice of the grape.

The honeft Jew fwore 'twas a banquet prepared by Cupid, to render him the moft miferable of all men. For, juft in the middle of our mirth, came in a French gentleman with a lady in his hand, who placed themfelves at the table exactly oppofite to us. I perceived evident fymptoms of fome diforder in Eliachim, who feem'd to read his fate in that fair creature's face ; yet had not power to check his wandering eyes, or guard them from inevitable wounds. He had almoft acted o'er the ftory of the Ægyptian wives, whom Jofeph's miftrefs had invited to

I 4   be-

behold his beauty; yet cut their fingers for their meat; whilst gazing on the charming youth : So poor Eliachim was all confusion, turn'd to a statue, whilst he look'd on this enchanting Gorgon. He had forgot to eat or drink, till I began to rouse him from his dream. I told him softly in the ear, This Lady was but the younger sister of Ixion's mistress. This brought him to his sense again, but could not restore his peace. Prudence taught him to dissemble the violent emotion of his soul, and not to expose himself in such a company; but nothing could expel the fatal poison from his breast.

When we had sufficiently reposed ourselves, we bid adieu to the inn, all joining company, and setting forward to Orleans. On the road both Eliachim and I had many opportunities of conversing with this young lady; such familiarity with women, being allow'd in France. We found her wit surprising as her beauty; and her mien and conduct such as gave advantage to them both. In a word, Eliachim was lost amidst so many perfections.

When we came to our inn at night, and were in our chamber together, he vented his passion in these words: Mahmut, "I have pass'd these "years hitherto without any other sentiments "of love, save those which in general I owe "to all our race, and some more particular "regard of friendship and duty. But, since I "saw this lovely creature, methinks my friends, "and all that ought to be belov'd on earth, "is now contracted into her. 'Tis not her "snowy skin, or matchless features, are of force "to move me; though they are such, thyself "being judge, as would have foil'd Apelles's "art to imitate : But 'tis a lustre which I can't "express! Surely 'twas lightning darted from "her eyes, those fair avenues of her brighter
                                                "soul !

" foul ! The fubtle flame glanced through my
" breaft, and in a moment fcorched my rea-
" fon up ! The lovely Bafilifk fhot death at
" every look ! Thou faweft how I fate as one
" transformed ; fo lifelefs, and without motion
" was I, whilft gazing on my ruin ! And to
" this hour a fatal numbnefs fpreads through
" all my veins, as if I had touched fome dire
" Torpedo."

Thus went he raving on, till I interrupted
him, with laughter and raillery, endeavouring to
cure him of his love-fick humour by ridiculing
it. I told him my own experience of this fool-
ifh Paffion, rehearfed my former adventures with
Daria, and how at length I got the victory of
this vain fondnefs by abfence, and the exercife of my reafon. But all that I could fay,
made no impreffion on the ftupid lover. He
grew but worfe, and fo I left him to feek repofe from fleep.

We came not to Orleans, till the next day,
where we tarried not long, having no other bufinefs as it happen'd, but to fee the rarities of
the town, and inform ourfelves of thofe things
it is convenient for travellers to know. After
which we return'd to Paris : I, with the fame
fentiments I had at my firft fetting out from
thence ; but it feems, the World was metamorphofed in poor Eliachim's opinion. To him the
trees had now loft all their greennefs ; the flowers,
and grafs, and corn, look'd wither'd ; the birds
fung mournful notes ; the winds blew hoarfe,
unwelcome founds ; and every thing in Nature feemed to him to droop, becaufe Falante
was not there (fo was the fair one call'd, as
Eliachim had learn'd of her) when we parted
from Orleans.

In this melancholy condition, the poor brain-
fick Jew has continued ever fince. When his
cure will commence, I know not.

I 5   If

If thou yet retaineſt thy native liberty, and haſt not ſacrificed it to unhappy love, learn by his misfortune to watch thy Senſes, which are the firſt Traitors to the Soul. Adieu.

Paris, 1ſt of the 6th Moon,
of the Year 1647.

L E T T E R XXIX.

To the Captain Baſſa.

THOU that haſt had thy education in Arſenals, and haſt led the reſt of thy life in Ships of War, wilt be beſt able to judge of the propoſal, which a certain bloody Sea Captain made to Cardinal Mazarini not long ago.

It being the general diſcourſe of this city, with what inſult and defiance Admiral Moroſini, with about thirty Men of War, enter'd the Helleſpont, and braved the Dardanels : This Officer told the Cardinal, That if he would furniſh him with half that number of Ships, he would engage to drive the Sultan out of his Seraglio, lay that Palace in the duſt, and beat down the Towers of all the Moſques in Conſtantinople, or loſe his life in the attempt. To which the Cardinal replied, " Monſieur, I believe 'tis im-
" poſſible, if you could finiſh your work, be-
" fore they would board your Men of War with
" an hundred Gallies and Saiques full of armed
" men."

It is ſaid, that Cardinal Richlieu had ſuch a project once, which made him propoſe the building of prodigious high ſhips, whoſe outſides ſhould be ſtuck all over with ſharp ſpikes, that
ſhould

A SPY AT PARIS. 179

ſhould render it impoſſible for gallies to board them.

By this thou may'ſt know, that ſuch an attempt is not thought impracticable by the Chriſtians. I wiſh it be not put in effectual execution by them, when the Porte may leaſt dream of it.

Chriſtina Queen of Swedeland, has cauſed a moſt magnificent veſſel to be built, with deſign to preſent it to Cardinal Mazarini. The inner work of the cabin is of cedar, curiouſly overlaid with flowers, and other imagery of gold. The extremity of the ſtern adorn'd with windows, ſtatues and galleries ; the wooden work all over-laid with the ſame metal. The roof of the cabin preſents the ſtory of Jaſon's expedition to get the Golden Flecce, painted by the beſt maſters in Swedeland. All the furniture ſpeaks the royal bounty of her that gives it. The cannon are of the pureſt braſs. The reſt of the tackle ſuch as are fitteſt to weather the wind and waves ; from which neither this Queen's ſovereignty in Swedeland, nor the Cardinal's grandeur in France, could exempt either of them, were they expoſed to ſea.

There are thoſe who whiſper on this occaſion, That the Queen of Swedeland has ſome inclinations to the Roman Catholic Religion ; and that ſhe has had ſeveral conferences with Monſieur Chanut on that ſubject, as alſo with his Prieſts ; that her Reſident in Portugal has openly embrac'd that Faith, not without the Queen's private conſent and approbation. It is not material to us, what Religion the Infidels profeſs, whilſt they aſſert Doctrines repugnant to the Divine Unity, and the Truth of the Sent of God. I behold, at this time, an evident ſign of his Unity in the Heavens ; it is the New Moon, juſt riſing from the lower Hemiſphere. At the ſight of this Planet, the Meſſenger

of

of God has commanded me to fall on my face, and adore the Eternal.

Wherefore praying, That her Influences may prove propitious to thee, whilft thou art on the Ocean, I bid thee adieu.

Paris, 23d of the 6th Moon,
   of the Year 1647.

The End of the SECOND BOOK.

LETTERS

WRIT BY

A SPY AT PARIS.

BOOK III.

LETTER I.

To Bedredin, Superior of the Convent of Dervifes, at Cogni in Natolia.

NOT more welcome are the rich Perfumes of Arabia, to a foul almoft expiring through grief and melancholy, than is thy letter to Mahmut, wherein is contain'd the Certificate of thy being yet on this fide the State of Invifibles. Methinks all Nature flourifhes, while thou art alive. And I feel a fpirit within me, prompts me to prefage, That thy death, like the fall of leaves in Autumn, will prove the Harbinger of the World's laft Winter. Whilft thou liveft, thy prayers and merits fupport the drooping Elements, which are now almoft ready to fall into their primitive Chaos and inactivity. The Angel of the Trumpet, in contemplation of thy virtue, delays to found the grand tremendous Blaft; which, at an inftant, fhall puff out the light of the fun, moon and ftars, and blow the breath out of the noftrils of all the living generations. That day fhall be a day of darknefs, horror and filence, till the hour of Tranfmigration comes: When at the

4 fecond

second Blaſt the firmament ſhall rend aſunder, like the opening of curtains; this old World ſhall fly away like a ſhadow, to the right hand and to the left. Then ſhall naked Souls hang hovering in the empty Space, 'twixt Paradiſe and Hell. · The Throne ſhall be placed, Judgment ſhall be given: And, to wind up the Myſteries of Fate, a new and immortal world ſhall at a Moment ſpring forth from the Womb of Eternity, and poſſeſs the place of the former.

I write not this to inſtruct thee, venerable Bedredin, who art a Mine of Knowledge: But to ſatiſfy thee, that though I live among Infidels, yet I conſerve inviolate the Faith of my Fathers, believing the Book brought down from the eternal Archives. Thou feareſt that I ſhall turn Chriſtian, being accuſed by ſome, of levity in my opinions; by others of profaneneſs and atheiſm; by all, of diſcovering too favourable an inclination to the Nazarenes.

Suffer me, O holy Preſident of the Servants of God, to purge myſelf of theſe falſe imputations, the product of envy and malice. Permit me to lay at thy ſacred Feet, a modeſt Apology for my Faith.

Let not that deſcription of the Chriſtian Meſſias which I ſent thee in my laſt letter, create in thee an opinion to my diſadvantage; nor prevail on thee to think, I can ever ſwerve from the profound attach, I owe to the Sent of God. I honour Jeſus, the ſon of Mary; and ſo I do all his Brethren, the Prophets in Paradiſe: This I am taught in the Alcoran. Where is then my crime? If I give virtue its due praiſe, even in the Infidels, am I therefore a Nazarene? If I ſpeak with reverence and modeſty of Chriſtian Princes, am I not therefore a Muſſulman? Or, does the Book of Glory teach us Arrogance? Surely my traducers will bluſh, when they ſhall conſider that our auguſt Emperors themſelves, (who are Sovereigns of all the Kings on earth) when they vouchſafe to write to Chriſtian Princes, dictate their letters in a ſtyle, full of affection and regard.

regard. They give them magnificent titles at the beginning, and at the conclufion, they wifh them encreafe of felicity, both here, and in Paradife. And would it become a Slave, to treat crown'd Heads with lefs refpect, than does the Mafter of the Univerfe? If I have contracted friendfhip with fome of the Chriftian Dervifes, it was to ferve the ends of the fublime Porte, and perform the rites of gratitude. I thought it no crime, to receive a kindnefs from any man, or to return it, without examining his Religion. But perhaps they fufpect the intimacies I had with Cardinal Richlieu, and ftill have with his fucceffor Mazarini. Reft affured, O holy Dervife, that my accefs to thefe Princes of the Roman Church, is fo far from being criminal, that without it I never had been capable of penetrating into the counfels of the Infidels, or of doing any effectual fervice to the Grand Signior. The countenance which my familiarity with thefe two great Minifters affords me, has all along facilitated my defigns: And, whilft under their umbrage, I am taken for a zealous Chriftian; I fecretly lay a foundation, whereon in due time, fhall be built, even in the heart of Chriftendom; triumphal arches for the victorious Muffulmans. 'Tis ftrange, methinks, that after all this, I fhould be fufpected! That notwithftanding I have patiently endured nine years confinement to an obfcure and private life; a melancholy banifhment to a ftrange country; yea, to a city for which I have a natural averfion; a city the moft unclean, noify and vain in the whole earth; to be fhut up, for the fake of avoiding difcovery, in a chamber fo narrow that Sufpicion itfelf, nay, even Thought, the Mother of that little Paffion, would fweat and be ftifled, when once circumfcribed within thefe walls; and after all this to be made a Prifoner of State, on jealoufy of being a Mahometan: To abide that punifhment fo many Moons unmov'd, uncorrupted, and at length to be releafed, to the

ad-

advantage of the Ottoman intereſt, and yet to be traduced at home, for a Traitor to God, his Prophet, and my Sovereign, has ſurely ſomething in it inconſiſtent.

What is then my crime? Or, why am I thus aſpers'd? Let my ſlanderers hereafter be ſilent. Unleſs they will lay it to my charge, That in ſome of my letters I have diſcovered a mind free from Superſtition : That I put a high value on reaſon, and have no low eſteem for ſome of the ancient Philoſophers; that I endeavour to guard my ſenſe, and will not ſuffer it to be muzzled with the impoſitions of ignorance and prejudice; that I do not think it a neceſſary qualification of a Muſſulman, to purſue with inexorable hatred, all men that differ from me in opinion. In fine, That in all my converſation, I ſtrive to comport myſelf as one who aſſerts the Unity of the Divine Eſſence, the Plurality of his Prophets, the determinate Number of the Elect; and who is reſolved and prepared, rather to die a thouſand deaths, than voluntarily to commit an Impiety againſt theſe Principles, or the Intereſts of the Grand Signior, who has a Right to command all mankind. If theſe be crimes, I muſt own myſelf culpable : If not, let my accuſers lay their hand upon their mouth. And continue thou, ſage Doctor of our Holy Law, to inſtruct me with thy counſels, to aſſiſt me with thy prayers, and to protect me with thy friendſhip. Then ſhall Mahmut perſevere a true Believer, a faithful Slave to the Oſman Emperor, and a devout admirer of thy longevity and virtue.

I ſhould fear this might be the laſt letter I ſhould have the honour to ſend thee, were I not convinced by ſome near examples, that old age was not reſtrain'd to the times before the Flood. Though thou haſt far out-paſs'd the ordinary years of men, yet there is at this time, not far from Paris, a man who has near doubled thy age. He is an

Hermit,

Hermit, living on a hill, where all things neceffary for human fuftenance feem to be wanting. The walls of his houfe are built of mud, with his own hands (a weak defence againft wind and rains.) His bed is compos'd of leaves of trees. A ftone ferves him for his pillow. His diet confifts of fuch herbs and fruits, as that mountain affords him. A neighbouring well allays his thirft. He has dwelt in this place, and in this manner, eighty-three years, after he had travelled moft parts of Europe and Afia. Afk him by what means he preferv'd his life fo long, he anfwers, By living free from care, and by being indifferent to all things. He foretells things to come, with marvellous fuccefs, as has often been obferv'd ; which makes the people efteem him a Prophet.

The French tell me of another who lived longer than he, being three hundred fixty and one years old when he died. He was called John of the Times, in regard he lived from the reign of Charles the Great, to that of the Emperor Con-rade. And being afk'd what diet he ufed, his an-fwer was, " Honey within, and Oil without."

This comforts me with the hopes of feeing thee on earth, tho' many years hence : Since no man can exceed thee in abftinence, fobriety, and the calmnefs of thy mind.

The Great Author of Life fo grant, That if I may not enjoy this felicity here, yet I may not by any enormous crimes merit to be excluded thy fo-ciety in Paradife.

Paris, 11th of the 7th Moon,
   of the Year 1647.

L E T-

LETTER II.

To Murat, Baſſa.

THE French are puffed up with the late defeat they gave the Spaniſh fleet in ſight of Naples. Their joy would know no bounds, were it not curb'd by the loſs of the Duke of Breze, who was ſlain by a cannon bullet in this naval combat.

The young Prince of Conde has been alſo forced to withdraw his army from before Lerida, that place being ever fatal to the French. This has leſſen'd the diſgrace which the Count of Harcourt received the laſt campaign, in not being able to carry that town after ſix Moons ſiege.

But the news from the Levant has elated all the Franks beyond meaſure : Yet, I hope, the relations that are ſcatter'd abroad on that ſubject, are rather an effect of their wiſhes, than of any real ſucceſs againſt rhe invincible Oſmans.

It is reported, That there have been two Seafights between our Fleets and the Venetians; that in the former we loſt two thouſand men, ſeven galleys, and a Baſſa; that in the latter, the Venetians took forty galleys, ſix Caramuſals, and fifty Saiques, laden with men and ammunition for the relief of our army in Candy.

The honour of this laſt victory, is aſcribed to the valour and conduct of Bernard Moroſini, and General Grimani; Bernard ſucceeded his brother Thomas Moroſini, who was kill'd, as they ſay, in the firſt battle.

The Chriſtians every where expreſs great joy for theſe victories. The open ſtreets are fill'd with tables, cover'd with all manner of dainties, at the public coſt. They feaſt and revel night and day. The bells ring continually, and bonfires are made, to celebrate the triumph of the Nazarenes. They presage to themselves, the conquest of the Ottoman Empire, and eternal victories.

From Dalmatia, the Posts bring daily news of our losses and disgraces. It is known here, that the Castles of Xemonido, Novigrade, Nadin, Carin, and all the Places of Strength which we had in our possession, except Clissa, are taken by the Venetians.

They laugh at our siege of Sebenico, where we lost two thousand men, and at length were forc'd to leave our camp to the Christians, our General being frighted away by a few women.

It seems strange and ominous to me, That those arms which have formerly crush'd the greatest Monarchies to pieces, and have changed the face of the whole earth, should now be foil'd by a few Desperadoes ! I dare be thus far a Prophet, that either the soldiers are disgusted, which will produce a Revolution, or the mighty Empire of the Osmans is in its decline, which God avert.

The Christians (who are not ignorant of our affairs, nor of the very secrets of the Seraglio) by an odd kind of charity, pray for the long life of Sultan Ibrahim : For, they say, our armies must needs miscarry during his reign ; most of the officers being offended at his licentious life, and cruel actions. Besides, they tax him with profuseness, in that he has not spared the private treasury of gold, which by the frugality of his predecessors, had been heaped together ; and which it was not counted lawful for them to touch, unless in the utmost peril of the Empire. They say, That by the additions which Sultan Amurath had made, this treasure was augmented to above thirty millions of Sequins : But that our present Emperor has squander'd most of it away on his pleasure. They compare him to Heliogabalus, the most effeminate Prince that ever reign'd ; praising at the same time, the magnanimity and valour of Sultan

Amurath ;

Amurath; who, they fay, was the ftouteft man on earth. They highly applaud his bravery at the Siege of Babylon, when he accepted the challenge of the Perfian foldier; and entering into a fingle combat with the unhappy Redhead, at one blow, with his Sabre, cleft him (though in armour) to the middle. In memorial whereof, thou knoweft, that armour hangs to this day in the Hazoda. In fine, They extol his juftice: Whereof he gave a remarkable inftance, in punifhing a certain Hogia, who had cheated a Pilgrim of his Jewels: Thou remembreft that paffage. And the Stone Mortar, wherein that miferable wretch was pounded alive by his own Sentence, is yet to be feen at the gate of the Divan, a monument of his villany, and the Sultan's juftice.

These things are not unknown in the Weft; for the Nazarenes have their intelligences in the Imperial City. Hence they derive occafions to cenfure or praife the actions of our auguft Emperors, who are Companions of the Sun, and Brothers of the Stars.

What I have faid, I truft to thy integrity: Whereof I have had experience. Thofe who degenerate from that virtue, may their fouls find no more reft in the other world than a Frenchman's Hat has in this, which is always in motion. Adieu.

Paris, 15th of the 8th Muon, of the Year 1647.

LETTER III.

To Mahomet Techli, Baſſa of Boſnia, at his Camp in Dalmatia.

THOU art a fit man to lead the Muſſulman armies, who durſt not hold up thy head againſt a few women : Perhaps thy mother's milk hangs yet on thy chin ; thou art not wean'd from the diſcipline of the nurſery. Was the ſtrong For-treſs of Schenico of ſo ſmall a price, that thou ſhouldſt baſely decamp from before it, becauſe a few females appear'd on the walls ? Is this the way to aggrandize thy Maſter ? What will the Chriſtians ſay to this cowardice ? Nay, what do they not ſay already ? The news of that ſiege had reach'd all parts of Europe ; the Nazarenes were big with expeǎation of the event. Now they know it, they laugh both at thee, and at all the Muſſulmans. Thou haſt brought a diſgrace on the moſt exalted Empire in the world.

What if thou didſt loſe two thouſand men be-fore the walls of that fort ? Is that a ſufficient juſtification of thy raiſing the ſiege ? Our glori-ous Sultans do not uſe to win cities and caſtles without blood. Neither do they ſpare to ſacrifice the beſt part of their army to the honour of their arms, whilſt our indefatigable ſoldiers have mount-ed on heaps of ſlaughter'd Spahi's, and ſcaled the battlements of their enemies. Whereas thou wert afraid of a' few ſtones, that the women hurl'd on thy men from the walls : Thou art more effemi-nate than Sardanapalus ! It were fitter for thee to handle the diſtaff and ſpin for thy bread, than to draw a ſword in the Field of Honour. It is a wonder thy own ſoldiers do not abandon thee, being aſham'd to ſerve under ſo weak a Com-mander.

I coun-

I counfel thee, fpeedily to recover thy loft reputation, by fome notable fervice. Let no perils affright thee; but remember, That true fortitude furmounts all difficulties; and that thou canft not pafs into the Temple of Honour, but through that of Virtue. It is not my part to project for thee: The whole country is before thee: Thou knoweft, or at leaft oughteft to know, the motions and ftrength of thy enemies. Do fomething fpeedily, that fhall fpeak thee wife and valiant. Thou hadft better lofe thy life fo, than by a Bow-ftring.

Take this advice as a mark of my friendfhip, for Mahmut ufes not fo frankly to reprove thofe whom he efteems his enemies. Adieu.

Paris, 15th of the 8th Moon,
of the Year 1647.

LETTER IV.

To Achmet Baffa.

NOT long ago arrived here a Courier from Swedeland, bringing letters from Queen Chriftina and Monfieur Chanut, the French Refident at Stockholm.

Among other matters, they give an account, That on the twenty-feventh day of the feventh Moon, that great Princefs had like to have been ftabb'd in the midft of her guards, furrounded with her Courtiers, before the Altar of her God; at an hour when all the fubjects of that kingdom were on their knees, to render Heaven propitious to her and the Public.

That day there was a Faft proclaim'd through all Swedeland; and he was efteem'd no good Subject, who did not repair to the public folemnities. The

2 Queen,

Queen, to give an example, went at the third
hour of the day to the Mofque of her Palace, attended by the great Officers of State, and a numerous train of the Nobility. When the Preacher
(as is the cuftom) had made an end of fpeaking,
all that were prefent fell on their knees, to perform the appointed Devotions. But it being the
fafhion of the Nazarenes to utter fome fecret pre-
parative Oraifons, the men cover'd their faces with
their hats, to be more recollected.

While all eyes were thus veil'd, a certain fellow fnatching the opportunity, fteps from his
place, and, without making any great noife, by
large ftrides, advances unfeen to the Rails which
enclofe the Pavement next to the Altar, where
the Queen was on her knees. But in leaping
over, he was perceived by a certain Nobleman,
who immediately cried out to the guards, "To
"ftop the affaffin." They crofs'd their partifans,
but the villain hurl'd them one againft another
with fo great violence, that while they were
ftriving to recover their entangled weapons, he
got quite through them. At which time, the
Queen alfo raifing herfelf up at the noife, pufh'd
the Captain of her guards, who kneel'd befide her.
He ftarting from his place, leap'd between the
Queen and the Murderer, who was now within
two paces of her. He feizes the wretch; and,
upon immediate fearch, they found two long
fharp-pointed knives about him, without fheaths;
one in his bofom, the other in his pocket. The
Prifon being in the Caftle or Palace of the Queen,
under her very apartment, fhe was not willing he
fhould be carried thither, but ordered him to
be re-conducted to his own chamber, which was
in the College of Stockholm, he being an Ecclefiaftic of the faid College; commanding alfo a
good guard to be fet over him, which was perform'd accordingly.

As foon as the Wretch faw himfelf in his
chamber,

chamber, he faid aloud, "That when he went "out in the morning, he little thought of ever "returning again, having undertaken an action, "in doing which he expected to lofe his life."

They ufed all diligence imaginable in difcovering the authors of this intended murder, but could learn nothing more, than that this fellow was a Lunatic, whom at certain Seafons an unaccountable fury fpurred on to many extravagancies.

Yet fome fufpect, that he was hired by the Lutheran Clergy to give this execrable blow; who were apprehenfive, That the Queen hearkening too much to the infinuations of her Tutor, who was a Calvinift, would innovate the eftablifh'd Religion of their country.

If this be a well-grounded fufpicion, it follows at the beft, that religion which ought to correct the Morals of men, and have an influence in reftraining their exorbitant paffions, is become the corrupter of their manners, and the fomenter of the moft enormous crimes. But this is common among the Chriftians, who being divided into innumerable Parties, are diftinguifh'd by as many feveral names; yet each Sect is fo fure that their Way is the only right Path to Salvation, that they fpare for neither murders, facrileges, nor treafons, to profelyte the reft to their opinion, being unwilling that any fhould live, who are not of the fame mind with them.

The King of France, and the Queen Regent, receiv'd the news of Queen Chriftina's delivery from this defign'd blow with much joy; the intereft of both Crowns being at this time clofely intermingled.

I can inform thee of nothing more remarkable at prefent, fave, that certain letters are intercepted, which the Duke of Bavaria had written to the Duke of Wirtemberg, and the Elector of Cologne: The contents of which difcover, That
the

the Duke of Bavaria is not far from a reconciliation with the Emperor; and that in the mean
time, he only waits the event of things, to direct
him in the choice of his Party.

God confirm thee in thy integrity, That thou
may'ft never waver or fwerve from the fervice and
duty thou oweft the Grand Signior.

Paris, 28th of the 9th Moon,
    of the Year 1647.

LETTER V.

To Cara Hali, a Phyfician, at Conftan-
tinople.

THOU haft heap'd many favours on me;
    yet I have never had an opportunity of
making the leaft acknowledgment. Accept now
a fmall prefent from Mahmut's hands, who being not mafter of wealth, can make no great
ones. I fend thee neither filver, gold, nor jewels,
which the infatiable avarice of mortals, has vio-
lently torn from the bowels of their common
Mother. Neither fhalt thou receive from me any
of the more familiar products of the earth, fuch
as grow on her furface. Expect no choice fruits,
or wine, or oil; nor any thing framed by the
art of man, whether for delight, or ufe. What
I fend thee is the Dew of Heaven, a certain
Quinteffence of the Element, an Æthereal Spirit, firft condens'd into a vapour, then into a
more liquid fubftance, and afterwards congealed
into a gum. It is the celebrated Manna of Calabria.

Adonai the Jew fent it to me out of Italy,
    VOL. III.   K   as

as a rarity. I knew not whom so properly to oblige with this present, as the studious of natural things, Hali, the sage Physician, and my friend.

The Philosopher Averroes, our country-man, has written much of this excellent substance. He calls it, the Food of the Airy Angels; and says, The young Ravens crying in their nests, are nourish'd by this heavenly diet, when the old ones forsake them: And that the Chamelions seek no other repast during their Lives, but the invisible Manna, that every where floats in the morning air. He holds it possible, That a man, after he has passed his great Climacter, may live without any other sustenance, save what he receives from this heavenly Distillation; that he may thus prolong his life for the space of seven years, which will compleat the appointed age of mortals. Many of the sublimely instructed among the Arabians, are of the same opinion; so are not a few of the Hebrew Rabbi's; but the Christians, who are gluttons, laugh at this doctrine as ridiculous and impracticable, forgetting at the same time what they read in their Bible, (which they pretend is the Rule of their Faith) that the Israelites had nothing else to feed on for a considerable time in the Desart, when they were almost eight hundred thousand souls, and the greatest part of them in their full strength, men of arms and inur'd to the toils of war.

Certainly, it were a desirable thing, That this divine Largess were distributed to all the regions on earth. But God sends his blessings to whom, and when he pleases. 'Tis he that directeth the clouds when they shall move through the air, and rest not till they arrive at barren and dry places, where they pour forth their water to refresh the earth, and render it fruitful. God! There is but one God, Lord of the World! These are signs of his Unity to True Believers, but the Incredulous have harden'd their hearts.

It

It is recorded, That in former times, the ground whereon this Manna defcended, belong'd to a certain Nobleman of the Country, who covetous of the unufual Bleffing, undertook to enclofe all that land within a high wall, to the end that fo rare a gift might not be made common to every one. But, as foon as the workmen had begun to lay the foundation of this enclofure, the Manna ceas'd to fall, and fo continued as long as they proceeded in that envious work. Which when the Lord of the ground was made fenfible of, he commanded the workmen to defift, faying withal, " The Almighty gives, and the Almighty " takes away. Henceforward, I will not feek to re- " ftrain the free gift of Heaven." Upon which, the Manna defcended daily, as before, and fo has continued to do ever fince. Doubtlefs, this is a fign of God's omnipotence.

If thou wilt permit me to play the Philofopher, I will tell thee my opinion, why this Manna is feen rather in the kingdom of Naples, than in any other region of the earth.

It is well known, That the earth of this country abounds with veins of fulphur, which are diffufed up and down through all parts, and heat the foil to an extraordinary degree. Hence it follows, That the lower Region of the air, in this country, muft needs acquire a greater degree of heat and drynefs alfo, being perpetually rarified by the fiery Atoms, which every where tranfpire through the pores of the earth, as from a furnace.

This being fo, it is not hard to conceive, That the vapours which are exhaled by the fun into the upper Region, in the heat of a fummer's day, and there become impregnated by the Æthereal Spirit, (which remains pure and uncloathed in thofe ferener tracts, and confequently is apt to incorporate with any proper vehicle,) naturally defcend again in the cool of the night ; but not

K 2 meeting

meeting with a congeneous body of vapours in
the lower Region, that air being over purify'd
and grown defecate, through the too near neighbourhood of the burning foil; fo that they cannot diffufe themfelves thro' the air, for the want
of a fit Medium, they confifting of homogeneous
parts, and following the natural pofition of the
Element, and the Laws of Gravity; con-
tract themfelves into little globular forms, the
lower they defcend; thus fettling on the leaves
of trees, on the grafs and herbs, on ftones, and
any part of the earth, appearing like grains of
tranfparent Gum.

Hence alfo I conceive, That the fame Manna,
(which is nothing elfe but an Æthereal Spirit,
embodied in light and dulcid vapours) abounds
in the air of moft countries, but remains invifible, rarely fo far condenfed, as to fettle in a
grofs body on the ground, becaufe the air of thofe
regions is not fo rarified as is that of Calabria,
having no fuch fubterranean fires to drink the
vapours up; but being moift and thick, the de-
fcending Manna, inftead of contracting itfelf into
globular bodies, and through its weight finking
to the earth, dilates itfelf, and incorporates with
the floating vapours: Juft as if you pour drops
of water into a veffel full of the fame element,
thofe drops do not fink to the bottom, but finding an homogeneous body, they mix with it, and
are difperfed every way; whereas, if there be nothing in the way to ftop them, they immediately
fall to the ground.

But I fhall tire thee with my Philofophy, forgetting that I fpeak to a man confummate in all
Sciences. Adonai relates many remarkable paffages of this country, too tedious for a letter.
I will only tell thee in fhort, That the Kingdom of Naples is efteemed one of the moft delectable Regions on Earth, the trees flourifhing
twice a year, and the foil abounding to prodi-
gality

gality with corn, wine, oil and fruits, and all
things neceffary for the life of man. Yet the
inhabitants have this Proverb common among
them ; " The kingdom of Naples is a paradife
" of delights, but it is inhabited with devils :"
So corrupted are the manners of the people.

Adieu, dear Hali, and think not Mahmut tedious
in his letters, who has no other way, at this diftance,
to converfe with his friends.

Paris, 19th of the 10th Moon,
of the Year 1647.

LETTER VI.

To Kerker Haffan, Baffa.

WHEN this Difpatch fhall come to thy
hands, be affured, That Mahmut thy
country-man, and Slave to the Slaves of the Grand
Signior, wifhes thee multiplicity of happinefs.
I have many reafons to honour thee, befides
the natural affection, which is, or ought to be,
between thofe who are born in the fame Region.
The many favours thou haft done me, far exceeded the obligation which arifes from the vicinity
of our birth ; though that was fo near, that a
ftrong man would have meafured the diftance with
the flight of an arrow.

The Prefent of Kopha, for which I return'd
thee thanks in my laft, has wrought wonderful
effects on me, being a perfect cure of the melancholy, to which I was before fubject. It has
freed me from many diftempers ; and I owe the
prefent eafe and cheerfulnefs I enjoy, to this generous gift.

Methinks, while I am drinking this excellent
K 3   liquor,

liquor, I am at Conftantinople, converfing with my friends. It revives in me the Genius of Afia; and fo advantageoufly transforms the Ideas of things which I fee, that the Croffes on the tops of the Chriftian Temples, appear to me as Half Moons; and my imagination prefents to me Turbants, inftead of Hats, as men walk along the ftreets of Paris.

Doubtlefs, great is the force of what we eat or drink, which has occafion'd all wife Law-givers, among other fanctions, to prefcribe certain rules for diet; and the care of our holy Prophet has been exquifite in this point, his prohibitions extending to all unclean meats and drinks, fince they deprave the conftitutions of men, and encline them to vice. But by his own example, he recommended to us the ufe of this admirable berry; impofing a new name on the Tree that bears it, when he called it, the Tree of Purification. Hence it is, That all the Muffulmans affect to partake of the fanctified benefit, it being the univerfal beverage of the Ofman Empire.

Were the virtues of it known in thefe Weftern parts, it would match, if not fupplant, the credit of their wines, fince it equally refrefhes the fpirits, without intoxicating the brain.

I know not whether thou haft feen Pefteli Hali, my brother, fince thy return from Arabia: Or, whether thou haft heard the news he brought with him out of the Eaft. He has furvey'd the Indies, Tartary, China, Tonquin, Perfia, and other Regions, whofe names are hardly known in fome parts of the Ottoman Empire. Indeed, we have formerly had but an odd Idea of thofe remote countries; but efpecially China has been hid from the greateft part of the earth.

In my earlier years, I have heard men of gravity, who would be taken for knowing perfons,

fons, fay, That China was but a tributary Province of the Tartars, a contemptible corner of Afia, and fo barren, as it could hardly afford fuftenance for its inhabitants, which is a fign it is well peopled. Affuredly our fathers were ignorant of this Country, which after the perpetual Monarchy of the Ofmans may be efteem'd the fecond Empire on Earth.

My brother fays, It contains fixteen Provinces, each as large as a Kingdom: And, That all together, they fill up a tract of ground as big as Europe, which thou knoweft, is one of the Four Quarters of the World: And that this vaft dominion contains above a hundred millions of inhabitants.

The Emperor who reign'd when Pefteli Hali was there, was call'd Zunchin, a young Prince, not above thirty years of age; in whofe veins ran the Blood of fixteen Emperors, his Progenitors.

In the year 1640, two great officers in his army, having drawn to their party an innumerable company of the foldiers, and being encouraged by fome Grandees of the Court, made a revolt. The names of thefe Rebels were Lycungz and Changien. They foon became mafters of five Provinces: But, quarrelling about their fhares, Lycungz caufed his affociate to be poifon'd; and taking on himfelf the fole command of the Rebels, was proclaim'd by them Emperor of China. After which, he march'd directly with his whole forces againft Pequin, a city where the Emperor kept his Court: Knowing that the conqueft of this place would fecure to him all the remaining Provinces of the Empire.

The Chinefe are reputed a moft ingenious people, excelling in all manner of mechanic inventions, and the boldeft Architects in the world. They build bridges from one mountain to another, to fhorten the travellers journey o'er the plain

be-

between them, and raife towers almoft up to the clouds. Some of their cities are faid to be near thirty leagues in compafs, having double walls and ditches. And my brother fays, That Pequin wants not much of this extent: And, That the Palace of the Emperor is near a league in circuit, inviron'd by three walls and as many moats, befides bulwarks, and other fortifications. He adds, That this mighty City and Palace is guarded by an hundred thoufand foldiers.

This impregnable place the Rebels took by ftratagem, which was able to have refifted all the force of Afia. Lycungz held a private correfpondence with feveral Grandees within the town and palace. By whofe connivance he fent great numbers of the ftouteft men in his army, difguifed in the habit of Merchants, who lodging themfelves in divers quarters of the city, on a day appointed, fuddenly appeared in arms; and furprizing the guards who defended the gates, flew them all, and opened the gates to the Rebels.

Who can exprefs the confufion and flaughter that fill'd all parts of the city with mourning and blood? The barbarous Conqueror facrificed all the loyal and brave to his unpardonable ambition; difarm'd thofe who efcap'd the firft maffacre; and having made himfelf abfolute Mafter of the City, lays clofe fiege to the Imperial Palace.

The Emperor now finding that he was betray'd, and that it was too late to defend himfelf from the cruel perfecution and infult of the traitors, takes advantage of the fhort refiftance which fome of his faithful fervants made, to confult his own honour, and that of the Emprefs and his daughter. He had above three thoufand wives, for whom he could not provide in that flood of calamities, all his care being employ'd to prevent

vent the laſt triumph of his enemies, in not ſuffer-
ing the Royal Blood to be ſhed by the profane
hands of thoſe villains. He entered into the Gardens of the Palace, accompanied only by his
Empreſs and daughter, with three faithful Eu-
nuchs. The young Princeſs (who was a Lady
educated in all the Chineſe learning) ſeeing the
great afflíction of her Royal Parents, the inevitable ruin of her Family, and the univerſal deſo-
lation, fell on her knees, and ſpoke to her father,
as follows :

" My Lord,

" SINCE it is the will of the immortal Gods,
" thus to extinguiſh the luſtre and majeſty of
" our ſublime Race, let their Decrees be fulfill'd.
" But let not me be a ſpectator of my Parents
" fall, or ſurvive a Tragedy, at which the earth
" itſelf muſt tremble. Have this compaſſion on
" my tender years, and let theſe eyes be clos'd, be-
" fore death ſeal up yours, from which mine bor-
" row'd all their light : Think not, becauſe I am
" young, I fear to die : I long to ſee our Kindred
" Gods, and repreſent the Fate of China, ſo as
" to provoke their ſpeedy vengeance. Surely
" our defiled Anceſtors, at my complaint, would
" gather all the Thunder in the Heavens, and
" ſhower it down upon theſe perjur'd and ungrate-
" ful Traitors. Or elſe, they'd play the Chymiſts,
" and extract the moſt envenom'd Influence of the
" ſtars, and dart the heavenly poiſon on the Re-
" bels, as they lie before theſe ſacred walls, and
" thus would put a period to their curſed Treaſon.
" Make no delay, my Royal Father, but try the
" experiment; releaſe me from theſe chains, which
" hinder my eſcape to Paradiſe : And let me be
" the Herald of ſuch news, as ne'er before ſur-
" priz'd the Bleſs'd above."

K 5   The

The Emperor, mov'd with this paffionate addrefs of his daughter, drew a dagger from his girdle,
and therewith ftabb'd her to the heart : And then,
ftruck with remorfe at fo unnatural a deed, cover'd
his face with a veil of filk. Thus acting Agamem-
non's part, when to fulfil the Oracle, he facrificed
his daughter Iphigenia.

After this, the Emprefs, overwhelm'd with fo
many forrows, retir'd into a grove, and hang'd
herfelf with a filken cord on a tree. The Emperor, feeing this mournful fpectacle, was refolved
no longer to delay his own death. Wherefore,
following her example, he defpatch'd himfelf likewife by a ftring. But he firft bit a vein, and with
his blood writ the following words.

" What is there now defirable on earth, after
" I am thus betray'd by my own Subjects ? I ac-
" cufe not the inferior people : They are innocent!
" 'Tis to the Mandarins I owe my fudden fall,
" with the ruin of this mighty Empire. Be-
" hold in me the Royal Line extinct. I am the
" laft of fixteen emperors. I, that was Lord
" of fo many fpacious Regions, Guardian of the
" Bed-Chamber of the Sun, fole Monarch of the
" Orient, Lieutenant to the Gods of the Mines,
" Poffeffor of infinite treafure, at whofe name an
" hundred millions of my fubjects touched the
" ground with their foreheads, am now ready to
" be trampled under foot by the bafeft of my
" Slaves. But I will prevent my own difgrace,
" and carry this majeftic foul inviolate to my re-
" nown'd Fathers ; whofe vengeance, join'd with
" that of all the Gods, fhall fall on the perfidious
" Mandarins, who have betray'd both me, and
" this exalted State to ruin."

A Narrative of thefe mournful paffages was
printed in the Chinefe language, fuppofed to be
done by the order of the Emperor's attendants,
who

who followed him into the garden, and were witnesses of what was said and done. A copy of which my brother procured to be translated into Arabic, by a Merchant of our nation, who understood the Chinese language, and resided in Pequin.

In fine, my brother says, That when he departed from China, he left the tyrant Lycungz in possession of the Emperor's Palace, where he found an hundred millions of ingots in gold and silver, besides an inestimable treasure of pearls and precious stones. All which wealth had been heap'd together, by the frugality of the Chinese Emperors.

By this thou may'st take an estimate of the grandeur and strength of this formidable Monarchy, of which we have had such contemptible notions. Neither shalt thou have occasion to be surprized at the monstrous rise and fortune of this Rebel, who in so short a time was lifted up to the height of human sovereignty, when thou considerest, That all things are subject to vicissitude and change.

That God, who establishes whom he pleases on the Throne of the Earth, and, at the determinated Periods of Empires, deposes such as trust in their strength and riches, defend our Sovereign from Treasons, and from the Arrows that fly in Obscurity.

Paris, 13th of the 11th Moon,
of the Year 1647.

LETTER VII.

To Darnifh Mehemet, Baffa.

WHAT obligation have I to be concern'd for the Infidels? Or, what intereſt in the Uncircumcifed? Yet Nature has tied all our Race, in fome common Bonds of Affection; and Humanity teaches us, to rejoice at the Deliverance of the oppreſſed.

The Kingdom of Naples has long groaned under the yoke of Spaniſh tyranny. The labour of the people fufficed not to pay the unreaſonable Taxes that were impoſed on them. They ſweat Blood to become yet more miſerable; whilſt their cruel maſters having fleeced them to nakedneſs, would take advantage of their poverty, to rivet their chains yet deeper, and render their ſervitude paſt redemption.

The people were fenſible of their Calamity, yet knew not how to ſhake off the yoke. It had gall'd them to the nerves and ſinews; their ſtrength was gone. Deſpair of redreſs had render'd them ſupine, and took from them the very power of meditating their recovery. But Heaven, which protects the oppreſſed, has raiſed up a Youth from among the meaneſt of the people, to aſſert the public Liberty. A Fiſherman, who has not ſeen four and twenty Winters, has undertaken to reſtore the ancient privileges of the Neapolitans. Who can penetrate into the Methods of eternal Deſtiny, which makes uſe of ſo contemptible inſtruments, to check the power of the greateſt Monarchs?

This bold Youth, inſpired with a zeal for the Public, ran one day into the ſtreets, crying with a loud voice, "Long live the King of Spain, but let "the corrupt Officers periſh." He had no other weapon,

weapon, fave a Reed in his hand, but was foon follow'd by a multitude of boys and young men, with clubs and ftaves, who went along the ftreets of that populous city, repeating the cry after him, " Long live the King of Spain, but let the corrupt " Officers perifh." At firft, the citizens laugh'd at the infant tumult, but in lefs than two hours, this Fifherman (whofe name was Maffaniello) had enrolled above two thoufand boys.

The next day his numbers encreafed, by the acceffion of all forts of lewd and idle perfons, malcontents, debtors, and fuch as were defirous of novelty. Nay, fome of the better fort of citizens fhut up their fhops, took arms, and mingled with the popular infurrection : So that ere mid-day, there were above ten thoufand men and boys, marching along the ftreets, and burning the Cuftom Houfe, with all their Books of Accompts throughout the city.

When Maffaniello beheld himfelf at the head of fo vaft a multitude, he thought it time to declare the reafon of his raifing this tumult. Wherefore, getting on an eminent place in one of the Markets, he fpoke to his followers to this effect :

" Rejoice, O ye faithful people, and fend up ac- " clamations to the God of Heaven, who hath " this day put it into your hearts and hands to be " your own redcemers. As for me, my fpirit " burneth within me, to fee the public oppreffion; " and I fet no value on my own life, when I firft " began this glorious enterprize. One of the " Princes threaten'd me with the Galleys, if I " perfifted : But here are thoufands my witneffes, " That inftead of fearing him, I fmote him on the " breaft, and fent him away joyful, that he efcaped " with his life. O ye faithful people, truft not the " Princes or Nobles : They are the men who op- " prefs you, and would enflave you. Truft in " your arms, and the juftice of your caufe. God " brought you together; let nothing feparate you " till

" 'till you have freed your country, your felves,
" your wives and children, from perpetual fervi-
" tude. Chufe you a Leader, a man of courage
" and refolution, who is willing to facrifice his
" life for the common Good. As for me, I have
" hitherto liv'd a Fifherman, and fo I intend to
" die."

The people, exceedingly moved with his Speech,
chofe him with one accord for their Leader, crying out with loud acclamations, " Long live
" Maffaniello, the Patron of the Neapolitan li-
" berties."

The firft thing he did after he was confirm'd
in this authority, was to fet open the prifons,
and lift the prifoners under the Banner of the
People.

Then he divided his confufed army into regiments and companies; and fent forth a Proclama-
tion throughout Naples, Commanding all to take
arms, on pain of having their houfes burnt. So
that in a little time he had above fifty thoufand
arm'd men at his heels.

Thus accompanied he marches directly towards
the Viceroy's Palace, vefted in Cloth of Silver,
with a naked fword in his hand. He was accompanied by a Cardinal, who undertook to be a Me-
diator between the Viceroy and the People. His
prefence reftrain'd the multitude within fome
bounds of moderation, for they reverenced him as
Father of the City. Yet they burnt above fixty
Palaces of the Nobles to the ground, with all their
furniture and goods; and it was prefent death for
any one to refcue or purloin any thing from the
flames; fo rigoroufly juft was this new Lawgiver,
this Mofes of the Neapolitans. It was in vain for
the Viceroy to oppofe force againft fo formidable an
Infurrection. He entertained the young Fifherman
with ceremonies due to a Prince: And having
concluded a Truce, gave him the Title of Chief
Tribune of the faithful People. This encreafed
the

the veneration the citizens had already conceiv'd for Maſſaniello : So that in a day or two more he ſaw himſelf at the head of an hundred and fifty thouſand arm'd men. He gave out all orders for the Republic, publiſh'd new edicts, and all commiſſions were iſſued in his name. He procured the Gabels to be for ever aboliſh'd, reſtored the people to their ancient liberty : And in fine, was murder'd by his own followers.

Let me not ſeem an Advocate for Sedition, when I tell thee there was ſomething brave and heroic in the actions of this Youth. So ſtrange a Revolution, in ſo ſhort a time, has ſcarce been heard of in the world : For a beardleſs Slave to raiſe himſelf in ſixty days to as abſolute and uncontrollable a Sovereignty, as the greateſt Monarch on earth enjoys ; to be obey'd by an infinite number of people, without the leaſt heſitation or demur, were it for life or death ; and all this, without any motive of ambition or intereſt, but only to aſſert the public liberty, is a convincing argument of his Virtue ; and ſhews, That Heaven approved his enterprize. But then again, For him to loſe all this power in four days more, to be murder'd in cold blood by his own party, by the people whoſe cauſe he had ſo ſucceſsfully vindicated; this ſhews the inſtability of human affairs, and that there is nothing permanent on this ſide the Moon.

I pray God to inſpire the Miniſters of the ſublime Port, to take ſuch meaſures as may preſerve the Muſſulman peace. Adieu.

Paris, 13th of the 11th Moon,
   of the Year 1647.

LETTER VIII.

To Solyman his Coufin, at Conſtantinople.

WHEN I cloſ'd up my laſt, the hour of the Poſt was near expired, and the meſſenger who carries my letters to him, haſten'd my Diſpatch, preventing what I had farther to ſay to thee.

I am ſolicitous for thy welfare, both as thou art a Muſſulman, and ſo near a relation. Do not forfeit thoſe titles, by degenerating from thy kindred, and from all the illuminated of God. Truth is comprized in a little room, but error is infinite. Thou makeſt a wrong inference from the moderation and charity of the true Believers, when thou concludeſt, That becauſe they believe, it ſhall go well with all honeſt men, let their opinions and ceremonies be what they will ; therefore thou ſhalt be ſafe, in retrenching the endleſs and burthenſome Waſhings (as thou termeſt them) of the Muſſulmans, ſo long as thou leadeſt a good and moral life.

Art thou ſuch a friend to idleneſs and impurity, that thou wilt by a moſt pitiful ſophiſtry, cheat thyſelf of Salvation, rather than take the pains to waſh thyſelf after the manner, and at the times appointed by the Prophet of God, and practiſed by our Fathers, and all the Faithful throughout the World? If it be allow'd, That ſuch as either out of ignorance, or hinder'd by ſome other inviſible cauſe, do not embrace our holy Law, are not circumciſed, and repair not to the Aſſemblies of the Faithful, ſhall nevertheleſs enter into Paradiſe, provided they obey the Law of Nature, imprinted on their hearts ; does it follow therefore, That one who has been bred up in the undefiled Faith, who has been circumciſed, and lifting up his right hand

hand to Heaven, has pronounced the Seven myſterious Words, which cannot be repealed ; does it follow, I ſay, That ſuch an one ſhall be regarded by God or his Prophet, any otherwiſe than as an Heretic or an Infidel, if he live not up exactly to the Graces that have been given him ? No, aſſure thyſelf, if thou art in the number of theſe, thou art an Apoſtate ; thy virtues are vices, and all thy good works are an abomination.

Remember the piety and magnanimous zeal of Aſſan Hali thy Grandfather ; who, when he was taken priſoner by the Coſſacks, was entertain'd with extreme rigour and ſeverity. Nevertheleſs, a certain Jew in the city who knew him, brought him every day, by permiſſion of the Keeper, as much water as would ſuffice to waſh him, and to quench his thirſt. But one day, as he went with his accuſtom'd load, and was entering the gate of the priſon, the Keeper, either out of malice or wantonneſs, ſpilt moſt of the water on the ground, forbidding the Jew at the ſame time, to bring any more that day.

The honeſt Hebrew went in with the remainder of the water, and deliver'd it to the priſoner ; who preſently prepared to waſh himſelf, after the accuſtom'd manner of the Muſſulmans. The Jew ſeeing that, told him, There was not water enough to quench his thirſt. And therewith related to him what the Keeper had done. " I ſee there is " but little, (reply'd the virtuous old man) but " he that drinks, or eats, before he has waſh'd " himſelf, is guilty of defiling his Soul, and is not " worthy to be number'd among the true Be- " lievers. Therefore it is better for me to die " for thirſt, than violate the Law brought down " from Heaven, and tranſgreſs the Traditions of " my Fathers." Having ſaid this, he waſh'd himſelf, being reſign'd to Providence.

Couſin, deceive not thyſelf with vain opinions, nor ſuffer Hypocrites to ſeduce thee. Imitate the

Adder,

Adder, and ftop thy ears againft the crafty infinuations of Heretics. It is reported of this little
Serpent, That by natural inftinct, being fenfible
when a Magician is about to utter words, which
being heard will enfnare it, lays one ear clofe to
the ground, and with its tail ftops the other, to the
end the Enchantment may have no effect.

Admit not any man to thy converfation, who
fhall attempt to warp thee from the fimplicity of
the Faith and Obedience which thou oweft to the
Apoftle of God. Without Water, there is no
Purity on this fide the grave. That Element
has a force in it, of which thou art not aware.
'Tis the third in the rank of living principles.
'Tis the Tabernacle of the winds; the Seraglio
of the generative fpirit; the ftage of wonders.
In fine, it is the purifier of every thing that has
breath.

Thou knoweft, That to ferve the neceffities of
the Prophet and his army, Underftanding and
Speech was given to a Fountain in Arabia, which
having promifed to follow him to the place of his
repofe, made a channel through the Defart, and
kept pace with the troops of the Faithful, 'till they
came to Medina Talnadi; that fo the fubmiffive to
the Will of Heaven, might not want that Element,
without which life itfelf would be a burden and a
curfe.

And yet thou fpeakeft contemptibly of Water,
as a very indifferent thing, whether we ufe it or not,
any other ways than to quench our thirft.

Thus, making no difference between the many
advantages we reap from that Element, and that
common ufe to which the beafts put it. In how
many places of the Alcoran does the Holy Prophet
record the Mercy of God, in giving us water
that is frefh and not falt? How does he celebrate
his wifdom and goodnefs, for directing the clouds
to barren and dry places? Thou canft not be
ignorant, That it is one of the Encomiums of Paradife,

radife, That there are gardens wherein flow many rivers : And after all this, wilt thou defpife fo holy and bleffed a gift, without which, earth and heaven, men and angels, could not be completely happy.

Go learn then of the Indian Idolaters, who have never heard of the Book of Glory : Go learn of thefe Barbarians, to prize their fanctified Creatures. They travel many hundreds of leagues to bathe themfelves in the waters of Ganges. With thofe incorruptible, and all-purging ftreams, the Brachmans fill certain veffels, and tranfport the invaluable liquor, to the utmoft parts of that wide Empire. They travel on foot, fometimes two thoufand miles together, each man with his load of that precious water, to fupply the wants of thofe who. live fo remote from the river. So that a bottle of it is many times fold to the Princes and Nobles, for two hundred Sequins, or eight hundred Roupies : And yet for all this, thofe very Princes would not die with a fafe confcience, had they not at leaft once in their lives made a Pilgrimage to this renown'd river, and bath'd themfelves in the Waves which blot out Sins.

O Coufin, let the example of thefe Infidels make thee blufh at thy impiety, and excite thee to a diligent and indifpenfable practice of Cleannefs : So fhalt thou have a found mind, in a healthy body : And the Angel of thy Nativity will not fhun thy perfon. Adieu.

Paris, 7th of the 12th Moon, of the Year 1647.

LETTER IX.

To the Kaimacham.

THE defeat of the Venetians and Morlacks in Bofna, has reach'd thefe parts. That news is not unwelcome to Mahmut. But I could wifh our General had ufed his victory with more moderation. The Chriftians term him Barbarian, Savage, Devil incarnate, and load him with execrations: For, having taken prifoner the Captain of the Morlacks, he caufed him to be flay'd alive, and afterwards to be impaled. This Captain was an Ecclefiaftic, they call him Scephano Sorich; and in honour of his zeal and fidelity, they entitle him, The good Prieft. They applaud his magnanimity and courage in battle; and no lefs do they extol his conftancy, during the torments of fo cruel and ignominious a death. But I tremble to think of the blafphemies and curfes they utter againft our holy Prophet, and all the Muffulmans! For the cruel Execution has fcandaliz'd the Nazarenes, and imbitter'd them, even to fury. Their Revenge is implacable: They would go to Hell themfelves provided the true Faithful might be damn'd for Company.

What will our divine Law-giver fay? Or what apology will our General make, when the Sent of God fhall charge him with driving fo many thoufand fouls into an irreconcileable hatred of the undefiled Faith? For they look not on this as the action of a private man, but of one who reprefents the Perfon of our auguft Sovereign, the great Protector of the Law brought down from Heaven. They fuppofe him to be honour'd with the particular inftructions of his Mafter: And therefore they fay, the Sultan has authoriz'd this unheard-of cruelty; and, That our Religion coun-

tenances

tenances tyranny, and the moſt nefandous method
of ſhedding innocent blood.

I am no advocate for Infidels; yet ſuffer me to
vindicate Nature, which is the common Parent of
us all. Suffer me to be ſolicitous for the honour
of our holy Profeſſion, which is blemiſh'd by this
inhuman murder. What offence had this unhappy
Captain given, that deſerv'd ſo dire a puniſhment?
Was it, Becauſe he fought valiantly, and perform'd
wonders in defence of his country? This is nothing but what becomes every honeſt man to do.
And, had our General been truly brave, he would
have entertain'd his priſoner with a reſpect due to
his merit.

Who was a more inveterate enemy of the Muſ-
fulmans than the renown'd Iſchenderbeg, Prince
of Albania? Who more valiant or ſuccefsful,
againſt the Ottoman armies? It is recorded of
him, That he never ſhunn'd a battle, never fled
from his enemies, never ſhrunk from perils, nor
was ever wounded but once, in all his life. And
yet he ſuſtained a continual war, from two ſuc-
ceſſive Oſman Emperors; defeated ſeven Vizirs
with their forces; took all their ammunition
and baggage, and, in ſeveral combats, ſlew with
his own hands above two thouſand Mahometans.

Our Fathers did not baſely revenge themſelves
for all this, but cheriſh'd a veneration for this
heroic enemy, and honoured the very duſt of
ſuch an extraordinary perſon. For, after his
death, having conquer'd Albania, they ſought out
his Tomb, where they perform'd their Devotions, as at the Sepulchre of a Prophet. They
open'd the Dormitory of the defunct Warrior,
and, with religious Solemnity, took up his Bones,
ſharing the honour'd Relics among them; and
wrapping them in Silk, wore them continually
at their breaſts, eſteeming them as ſacred Amulets
againſt Misfortune.

3   Surely

Surely our General would blush at an example of so great virtue. But perhaps he was incensed, because his Captive was a Priest: Mistaken zeal might prompt him to this horrid butchery. Thou, who art Justice itself, will not approve this bloody passion, when thou considerest, That the Priests of Jesus are men as well as others; and if they live in error, the fault is in their education. However, many of them are humble, chaste, sober, and lovers of virtue. If there be others, whose corrupt lives have contradicted this character, let the crime and the punishment rest on their heads. It is not reasonable that the innocent should suffer for the faults of the guilty. The Captain of the Morlacks had the reputation of a devout and just man, and a stout champion for his country: Had he been taken for a Spy, or an Assassin, the Law of Arms would have adjudg'd him to death. Yet such was the clemency of Porsenna, King of the Hetrurians; that when Mutius Scævola, a valiant Roman, came into his camp, with design to murder him, but by mistake stabb'd one of the Captains, thinking it had been Porsenna; and to revenge that miscarriage on himself, thrust his hand into the fire, 'till the flesh was consum'd to the bones. The King astonish'd at his undaunted spirit, sent him away in peace, raised the siege of Rome, and enter'd into a strict friendship with that nation: Such honour he bore to the fortitude of his enemy, and design'd murderer. But the Captain of the Morlacks was not taken under these circumstances: He lost his liberty in the heat of the battle, bravely combating at the head of his army.

Would'st thou know the grounds then of our General's cruelty? It was purely, for the sake of a Jest. There went a report, That when this Priest was born, his body was all over raw,

so

fo that the Phyficians were forced, by art, to fupply him with a fkin. Our cruel General, to fport himfelf in the poor man's mifery, commanded him to be flay'd alive; uttering at the fame time this inhuman Sarcafm; "There was "no reafon that he fhould carry a fkin out of the "world who brought none in." This is attefted by two gentlemen who were made prifoners with their Captain, heard thefe words, faw him executed, and afterwards made their efcape.

The Nazarenes vow to revenge this unparallel'd cruelty on the Muffulmans that fall into their hands, if this Butcher (as they term him) be fuffer'd to go unpunifh'd. I tell thee, fuch barbarous actions draw down the vengeance of Heaven on thofe that commit them; and excite the very Beafts of the earth to make war, and rid the world of fuch Monfters.

Thou knoweft what ufe to make of this intelligence: I will not pretend to inftruct the fecond Minifter in the Ottoman Empire.

Paris, 7th of the 12th Moon,
of the Year 1647.

LETTER X.

To the Mufti.

IF there be any truth in what the Aftrologers tell us, That the Stars have Influence on the Government of the Earth, one would think that Spain lies under fome malignant Afpect.

The fortune of that Kingdom has for a long time run retrograde. They have had nothing but loffes by fea and land. The Revolution
in

in Portugal, the Revolt of Catalonia and Rouf-
filion, the lofs of Ormus in Perfia, and the de-
fection of Goa, with other rich towns of traffic in the Indies, came one upon the back of
another.

Since which there have been many towns and
caftles taken from the Spaniards in Flanders.
The French made an Infurrection in Palermo,
breaking open the prifons, and releafing the prifoners: And grew to fuch a head, That the
Viceroy fearing they would revenge the Tragedy
of the Sicilian Vefpers, to pacify the multitude,
was forced to repeal the Edicts for Taxes, and dif-
annul them for ever; and to pafs an act of general indemnity, both to the Rabble, and to the
Prifoners, whom they had freed.

This tumultuous fpirit pafs'd from thence to
the Kingdom of Naples; and there like an in-
fection foon fpread itfelf through all parts, both
of city and country: Two hundred thoufand
men took up arms, to vindicate the Privileges
of the Neapolitans, under the conduct of a poor
young Fifherman. I have already tranfmitted
to the fublime Port, a relation of this formidable
Sedition; wherein it may be thought, I have
difcover'd too much tendernefs to the Infidels,
and feem'd to favour the violence of a Faction.
But I hope thou wilt acquit me, when thou
confidereft, That thefe Governments of the Nazarenes are not to be compared to the facred Ofman Empire, which is eftablifh'd by a Divine
Right; it having been determin'd by the Angels,
That he who fhould poffefs the glorious Dormitory of the Sent of God, fhould be intituled,
" The Sovereign of all the Kings on earth." Therefore it would be a crime of the higheft nature,
to raife a tumult or fedition, within the Territories of our auguft Emperor, whofe dominion
is confirm'd to him for ever by a Patent from
Heaven. But the cafe of the Nazarene Princes
is

is different; who being profeſſed enemies to the Meſſenger of God, have no other right to any thing, but what their ſwords purchaſe. And therefore, when they prey upon others, and by rapine and ſpoil augment their riches, it is no wonder if the great Avenger of Crimes ſtirs up ſome undaunted ſpirits, to free their country from ſlavery and ruin.

Thoſe who are curious, have remark'd many obſervable circumſtances in this Revolution at Naples: As that it was foretold by an Aſtrologer, a conſiderable time before it happen'd, who pointed out the very year wherein it ſhould come to paſs. The extraordinary eruptions alſo of Mount Veſuvius ſome years ago, were eſteem'd as preſages of ſome approaching troubles in the State: For it rain'd aſhes on the city of Naples: I ſpoke of this mountain in one of my former letters.

'Tis reported alſo, That about the ſame hour wherein Maſſaniello the Ringleader of the Seditious was murder'd, there was ſeen a man hovering in the air, over the principal Temple of Naples, with a ſword in his hand, which he was putting up in his ſcabbard: And that a voice was at the ſame time heard from on high, to utter theſe words, "His labour is finiſh'd, give "him reſt."

This is certain, That whilſt he was at the head of an hundred thouſand men, ſeven Aſſaſſins were hired by ſome of the Princes to ſhoot him: yet none of the bullets could penetrate his body, tho' unarm'd, and only cover'd with his fiſhing rags: And it was evident, that theſe bullets ſmote him in divers places, his garments being mark'd with them, and he ſtagger'd with the force of the blows.

Theſe are extraordinary occurrences, and would tempt one to believe, That this young Fiſherman was the inſtrument of Providence, and that Heaven protected Him and his Cauſe.

'Tis

'Tis true indeed, it seem'd at last, as if he were abandon'd by that Divine Power, which had carried him through so important an enterprize, in that he was slain by his own soldiers. But then it must be remember'd, That this was not done till his Work was finish'd, and he went beyond his Commission. Want of sleep, the multitude of his affairs, and much wine, had impaired his reason, and rendered him frantic; so that his actions were insupportable, and his own admirers grew weary of him. After his death, his head was cut off, and carried up and down the streets on a lance, and his body was dragg'd through the kennel. Yet the very next day, the multitude, to shew their own ficklenefs, took the dead body out of a ditch, where they had laid it all night: They wash'd and embalmed it, and having joined the head to it, carried it with great pomp and folemnity to the principal Temple of Naples, attended with drums and trumpets, and above a thousand Priests, with torches in their hands; a crown of gold was put on his head, and a sceptre in his hand.

Thus the Neapolitans honour'd that beardless Youth, who in ten days time had caused such a Revolution, as is scarce to be parallel'd; for he was an absolute Monarch, in effect, during that time. And of him it may be said, as it was once of an Emperor, That during his whole Reign there was neither Spring, nor Autumn, nor Winter: For his Royalty begun and ended in the seventh Moon.

By letters from Nathan Ben Saddi at Vienna, I perceive he is molested with scruples about his Religion, being desirous to build upon the surest Foundation. I sent him the best advice I could, without making myself an Hypocrite; which, thou knowest, is more offensive to God, than an open Sinner. I drew up an Abstract of
the

the Muſſulmans Records, and preſented him with the faithful Genealogy, from Iſmael, the Son of the Patriarch Ibrahim, down to our Holy Prophet. This I did to rectify an old inherent error of the Jews, who boaſt, That only the Sons of Iſaac were True Believers. I endeavour'd not to proſelyte him, by ſophiſtry and artifice ; but referred him for better ſatisfaction, to the Writings of the Ancients. I promiſed to furniſh him with Books of our Laws, and the Comments of our Holy Doctors. This it is impoſſible for me to perform, whilſt I am in this place; unleſs thou, who art a Guide of thoſe who ſeek the Truth, vouchſafeſt to ſecond my zeal. I addreſs to thee, ſovereign Prelate of the Faithful, in behalf of a Deſcendent from the younger Brother of Iſmael ; in behalf of one circumciſed, but not in the right way. Favour him with thy divine Inſtructions, and ſupply him with treatiſes of light and reaſon. A reaſonable application may bring this Hebrew into the number of the Muſſulmans, for he is already diſguſted at the Synagogue.

But if I have preſumed too far, in endeavouring to ſnatch a Soul from the paws of Tagot, correct me in thy wiſdom, for I am but as an Infant before thee.

Paris, 15th of the 1ſt Moon,
of the Year 1648.

LETTER XI.

The beginning of this
Letter is wanting in the
Italian tranflation, the
original paper being torn.

. . All mens hearts
are fill'd with joy, for this profperous news,
whilft I mourn for the difhonour of our arms.
Nothing but fad tidings grate my ears from thofe
parts, and more melancholy prefages pofícfs my
foul. Methinks I fee thick clouds gathering
o'er the Imperial City. My fleep is difturb'd
with fearful vifions; I ftart in my bed; and
walking lay my hand on my fword, as if fome
danger were at hand: I dream of tumults and
diforders, neighing of horfes, and clafhing of
arms in the ftreets of Conftantinople. I pray God
avert the Omen.

It is reported here, That Ali the Sangia-Bey
of Lippa, is taken prifoner; and that his fon
was tormented to death before his face, in a
manner peculiar to the invention of the moft
barbarous tyrants: For they caufed fharp thorns
to be thruft between his nails and his flefh,
which creates an intolerable anguifh: They laid
him on a bed of iron fpikes, and poured melted lead, drop by drop, on all parts of his
flefh. Then they made a fmall fire, and roafted
him flowly to death. If he chanced to groan,
or make the leaft complaint, in the midft of
thofe grievous tortures, they bid him remember
the good Prieft Sorech, who fet him an example
of conftancy and courage, in that he never fhed
a tear, or fo much as figh'd, when he was flay'd
alive.

5   Thou

Thou feeſt that revenge is ſweet, even to thoſe who having received no injury in their own per-ſons, yet are touch'd to the quick, with the violence that is done to another. This will ap-pear in the humour of the Italians, who pro-ſecute their enemies with irreconcileable hatred and malice, whole families being often engaged in executing the reſentments of two ſingle per-ſons, who firſt began the quarrel ∴ But much more forceable is this paſſion in thoſe, who have been notoriouſly hurt themſelves. And the re-venge of a certain Captain was extravagant; who being inform'd that his General had de-bauch'd his wife, took an opportunity to ſingle him out from all other company, pretending to walk in the fields. When he had him there alone, he clapp'd a piſtol to his breaſt, threat-ening to kill him forthwith if he mov'd hand or foot. Then he upbraided him with what he had done, in ſuch language, as convinced the Ge-neral, his life was in extreme danger. Wherefore he humbled himſelf, and confeſſed his crime; beg-ging of the Captain to ſpare his life, and he would prefer him forthwith to the beſt office in his army, next his own. But the furious Italian would not ſell his Honour ſo cheap. He forced him to deny God, and utter many · Blaſphemies in hopes of ſaving his life: and when he had thus done, the Captain ſaid "Now "my revenge is complete, ſince I ſhall ſend "thee body and ſoul to the devil." With that he piſtol'd him.

But leaving theſe Infidels to their diabolical paſſions, I am concern'd at the captivity of thy brother; if it be true which is related here, That he was taken in his return from Canea to Con-ſtantinople. It will coſt the Baſſa of Algiers a thouſand crowns to ranſom him.

Adieu Renarba. And, if thou art deſirous to raiſe thyſelf, take that method which I have now

pro-

propofed to thee. God be propitious to thy endeavours.

Paris, 4th of the 2d Moon,
    of the Year 1648.

LETTER XII.

To the Venerable Mufti.

THOU wilt fay, The Neapolitans are a
    reftlefs people, when thou fhalt know, that
there have been no lefs than forty general Infurrections in this kingdom, fince its firft fepara-
tion from the Grecian Empire, whereof it was
formerly a member ; and that, in the fpace of
two years, they have had five Kings, all of different Nations.

One-would have thought, that after the death
of Maffaniello, the Ringleader of the late In-
novation, the popular heats would have flack-
en'd, and the people return'd to their duty ;
but the paffionate defire of liberty caufed them
to continue in arms, till the confirmation of
their privileges fhould come from the King of
Spain.

In the mean time, Don John of Auftria, who
lay before the city with a fleet of fifty Galleons,
play'd upon them inceffanly with his cannon
by fea, and the caftles batter'd them by land.

Cardinal Mazarini, who has the earlieft intelligence of foreign tranfactions, has had a principal hand in fomenting this flame. For as foon
as the news of Maffaniello's death arrived here,
he difpatched away Couriers to Rome, with inftructions to the French Ambaffador at that Court,
requiring him to ufe all poffible means to cherifh
                                        the

the Tumults in Naples, and not neglect so fair an opportunity of reducing that kingdom under the protection of France.

It will not appear strange, That this great Genius should aim at the conquest of Naples, when we consider, That this kingdom abounds in all manner of riches, to which its fortunate situation contributes not a little ; for it lies in the most temperate part of the world : And the inhabitants are not second to any people of Europe, in material courage and bravery. This is a bait which tempts the Cardinal ; who is not ignorant how valiantly the ancestors of the present Neapolitans behaved themselves in the Wars of Cæsar and Pompey, and those between the Romans and Carthaginians. Nor are they less celebrated for the stout resistance they made against the Huns, Goths, and Vandals. So that this kingdom, were it once brought under the French Dominions, would prove a Nursery, from whence this Monarch might draw many thousands of excellent soldiers, to serve him in his wars.

Besides, it would be more commodious for him to make incursions from hence into the Pope's territories, if there should arise any difference between the two courts ; as there often do, about the rights of the Gallican Church, the Franchises of the Ambassadors of this crown in Rome, and other privileges, to which they pretend.

Therefore the French Ambassador, according to the instructions of Mazarini, sent commissioners to treat privately with the people of Naples, offering them two millions of crowns, twenty galleons, with eight and fifty gallies, and other vessels. They accepted the proposal, being weary of the Spanish government, and desirous of novelty, encourag'd also by what those commissioners represented to them, concerning the suc-

cess

cefs of the Englifh, who by ftanding on their
guard, and ufing that power which God and
Nature had given them, for the defence of their
lives and liberties, were now, in a manner, become a free people, having abolifh'd the Monarchy, and fet up a Commonwealth : And this
they told them, was alfo done by Cardinal Mazarini's counfels and affiftance. Now all the
cry in Naples, was, "Let France and the peo-
"ple of England flourifh ; and let the faithful
"Neapolitans affert their own liberty." So blind
were thefe people, as not to confider, That in
putting themfelves under the protection of the
French, they did but exchange one bondage for
another, it being impoffible for any foreign Prince
to keep this kingdom, and pay all his officers,
civil and military, together with thofe under
their commands, with much lefs charge than
the revenues amount to. And the French are
as good at inventing new Taxes, as any Court
in Europe.

However, the Neapolitans are enchanted with
the thoughts of fo much gold, and other affiftance offer'd by the French commiffioners ; and
fweeten'd with their fair words, and glorious
promifes. So that they immediately fent deputies, to entreat the Duke of Guife, who was
then at Rome, to come and protect them, in taking on him the chief command of their arms.

This Prince thinking it a generous action to
relieve the oppreffed ; and, that at the fame time
he fhould do a confiderable fervice to the King
of France, in rendering him mafter of this noble
and opulent kingdom, went to Naples : Where,
at firft, he was received with infinite applaufe,
was made their General, took an oath of fidelity to the people, did many notable fervices,
but was in the end betrayed, and fent prifoner
to Spain.

If the generofity and brave refolution of this
Prince,

Prince, has acquired commendation from fome, in attempting to refcue thofe people from the tyranny of the Governors, yet his conduct is called in queftion by others, who fay, He difcover'd but little prudence in trufting himfelf to the Neapolitans, who had already facrificed two of their Generals. (For, after the death of Maffaniello, they chofe another Captain, whom they called the Prince of Maffa : This Prince falling under their fufpicion, was beheaded by the inconftant people.)

'Tis certain, That there is little confidence to be put in the multitude, whofe paffions ebb and flow, and are more tempeftuous than the fea. Yet a brave and generous mind will fhun no dangers to ferve his Prince and his Country ; for whom it is a glorious Martyrdom to die. There is no great undertaking without hazards ; and he that is afraid to venture his liberty and life in a good caufe, is not worthy to bear arms. Had the Duke of Guife fucceeded, his conqueft of Naples had made him Viceroy of one of the largeft kingdoms in Europe. It is faid to be five hundred leagues in circuit, containing twelve ample Provinces ; twenty Archbifhoprics ; Bifhoprics, one hundred twenty-feven ; thirty Caftles ; Barons, one thoufand four hundred ; Earls, fifty-three ; forty Marquiffes ; thirty-four Dukes, and twenty Princes. The inhabitants of this kingdom are faid to be above two millions. The ordinary revenues of the King amount to three millions of crowns yearly, befides the voluntary donatives, which have been given by the fubjects of this State to their Kings, within the fpace of forty years, amounting to twenty-eight millions, and fix hundred thoufand ducats. This kingdom is water'd by an hundred and fifty rivers, befides ten lakes ftored with all manner of fifh ; among which is one called Averno, over which if any birds fly, they

imme-

immediately drop down dead. The ancient Pagans had ftrange opinions of this Lake, it being the place where they ufed to facrifice men to the infernal Gods. And, hard by, is the Cave of one of the Sibyls.

'There are thirty high mountains in this country, of which Adonai relates many ftrange and delightful paffages, (for 'tis from him I received this account of the Kingdom.) I will not trouble thee with a repetition of all that this Jew tells me, only one thing is worthy of remark.

He fays, That the bodies of the three young Hebrews, who were put into the burning oven by the Babylonian Monarch, becaufe they would not adore his Idols, are preferv'd in a Mofque on one of thefe mountains. And that on the faid hill, no eggs, flefh, or milk, will endure an hour without putrefaction, but prefently breed an infinite number of worms. He fpeaks in the praife of thefe mountains, which are cloath'd with vineyards, gardens, and woods, on the top and fides; and in their bottoms, have very rich mines of gold, filver, copper, iron, cryftal, alabafter, and adamant. In fine, Adonai, who has travelled over all this kingdom, calls it, The fertileft region of all Italy, which is efteemed the Paradife of all Europe.

Doft thou not think now, venerable Guide of the Elect, that the Duke of Guife had reafon to prefer the honour of conquering fo renown'd a kingdom, to the fafety of his perfon? Or wilt thou not rather conclude, That the reduction of this happy ftate would be an expedition worthy of the Ottoman arms? It is certain, that the riches and plenty of this region have tempted more nations to invade it, than any other kingdom on earth: It having been the prize, at which no lefs than five and twenty feveral nations have aim'd.

Car-

Cardinal Mazarini is much troubled at the Duke of Guise's captivity, and has offer'd great sums of money for his ranfom; but the King of Spain rejects all propofals of that nature. So that 'tis thought, the Cardinal will contrive fome way for the Duke's efcape, either by bribing his keepers, or by fome fecret ftratagem.

I am not much concern'd for the Infidels; but it would be no fmall joy to hear, That fome care were taken, for the redemption of Mahomet Celeber, who, thou knoweft, has not deferv'd ill of the fublime Porte. Adieu, holy Patriarch, and forget not Mahmut, in thy addrefles to Heaven.

Paris, 27th of the 3d Moon,
    of the Year 1647.

LETTER XIII.

To Abdel Melec Muli Omar, Superintendent of the College of Sciences at Fez.

THOU to whom the iffues of Paradife are revealed, and the road of the Angels when they come down and go up through the Seven Heavens! Thou that canft marfhal the Hoft of the Stars, and underftandeft the difcipline of the armies living and ftrong, the orders of the potentates encamp'd in the fields of light, the domeftic Guards of the Throne, bleffed for ever; tell me the age of the world, and declare the beginning of time. Refolve me, Whether this mighty fabric be but of yefterday, that is, of five or fix thoufand years ftanding, as the Jews and

3   Chriftians

Chriſtians ſay; or, Whether the years of its duration be not paſt a calcule.

The Viſions of thy Progenitor, the Lieutenant
to the Sent of God, are extant in the Arabic
tongue. In them it is written, " My ſoul on a
" ſudden became as though it had wings; a ſpirit
" enter'd me, and a ſubtle wind lifted me up to the
" top of Mount Uriel, where I beheld marvellous
" things. I looked behind me and ſaw the Ages
" that were paſt; and lo, they were without num-
" ber, or beginning. I beheld the four Seaſons of
" the Year ever returning at their accuſtom'd time,
" and the Sun forſook not his courſe, for a thouſand
" thouſand generations. I counted a million of
" ages, and yet there appeared not an hour, where-
" in darkneſs had poſſeſſed the Abyſs of matter, or
" wherein the endleſs Firmament was not illumi-
" nated by the Moon and Stars. Whilſt I conſi-
" dered theſe things, a liquor was given me to
" drink by an unknown hand; it was of the
" colour of Amber; when I had taſted it, I felt
" a marvellous force in my body, and my eyes
" were more piercing than an Eagle's. Another
" wind, more powerful than the former, blew
" out of a cloud, and carried me up to an ex-
" ceeding high place, far above the talleſt moun-
" tains: There I trod in the ſoft air, as on a
" pavement of marble. I was raviſh'd at theſe
" things; and the exaltation of my ſtate made
" me forget my mortality. I beheld the earth at
" a vaſt diſtance under my feet, as one that did
" not belong to it; it look'd like a ſhining globe,
" not much unlike the Moon, but far bigger.
" All the living Generations which had ſucceſſive-
" ly inhabited the earth from its nativity, paſs'd
" by me; and they appear'd in various forms.
" Firſt came a race of Centaurs, then of Satyrs,
" next of Angels, and laſt of Men. Whilſt I
" marvelled at theſe things, a voice reach'd my
" ears, as from behind me, ſaying, Theſe are the
" four

" four Ages of the World, and the four Species
" of Beings, to whom I gave the poſſeſſion of the
" earth; but for the impiety of the three former,
" I have exterminated them. And when Men ſhall
" have completed the meaſure of their ſins, I will
" cauſe the Trumpet to ſound, and all things
" ſhall retire into the Cave of Silence and Dark-
" neſs. Having heard this, I found myſelf in a
" moment on the Earth, which I had before ſeen
" afar off; then I knew that I had been in a
" Trance," &c.

I do not rehearſe this Viſion, to teach thee any
new thing, venerable Preſident of the Southern
Sages (for, I know, the Archives of thy College
are repleniſh'd with all manner of excellent treatiſes, and that thou art no ſtranger to the Writings
of the Prophets) but to crave thy interpretation of
ſo great a Myſtery, and to reaſon with thee about
the World's duration. My ſatisfaction would be
ſmall, in contemplating the various beauties of the
univerſe, the qualities of the elements, the natures
of living things, the virtues of plants and mine-
rals, with the force of the heavenly bodies, were I
aſſured that theſe things were not always ſo. That
thought would damp my greateſt enjoyments, if I
were convinced, That ſo many ſplendors, riches,
and pleaſures as this viſible Frame affords, were
not diſcloſed for millions of ages, but lay hid in
the boſom of eternity. Methinks, it is too low an
opinion of the Omnipotent goodneſs, and looks as
if the authors of it ſuſpected God of Envy: Who
when he might have made infinite myriads of creatures happy, in theſe viſible emanations of his Di-
vinity, without either beginning or ending of time;
yet, according to their doctrine, contented himſelf,
to let only a determinate number taſte of his mu-
nificence, for a few centuries of years. This is
not ſuitable to the character of that infinite Being,
the eternal Source of all Perfections.

What then is meant by thoſe Four Ages, and
the

the Four Species of Beings, which were shew'd to
the exalted of God in that holy Vision : Tell me,
great Light of Afric, Is it repugnant to Reason or
Faith, to believe, That the Earth has been inhabited from Eternity; since our holy Doctors teach us,
that it was peopled long before the Creation of
Adam ? No Mussulman, that has ever gone the
sacred Pilgrimage, but has visited Mount Araffa,
where Adam first saw Eve his Wife. Where he
has been instructed in the History of that first Father of mankind; and how that before his time the
Earth was inhabited by Angels, who being commanded to adore Adam, refused it, and were turn'd
to Devils, being expell'd from the Earth. Thou
knowest moreover, That it is in the sacred Traditions, That God gave to Adam a wife, whose name
was Alileth; but that she being of the Race of
those Devils, refused to obey Adam : Whence it
came to pass, that they lived in continual quarrels
and enmity, for the space of five hundred years;
'till at length, Alileth flew up into the air, and
abandon'd her husband. Of which, when Adam
complain'd to God, he sent three mighty Angels in
pursuit of her, commanding them to tell her, That
if she would return to her husband it should go well
with her; but if she would not, an hundred of her
children should die every day. The Angels followed her, and overtook her on the Red-Sea; where
they threaten'd to drown her, unless she would return to her husband. But she made excuses, and
told them, She was created to destroy young children. Then the Angels laid hands on her; when
she, to pacify them, swore by the Bottom of Hell,
That whensoever the Names of them three should
be written on any Schedule, that she should have
no Power to hurt the infants, they dismiss'd her.
After this, God compassionating Adam's solitude,
gave him another wife, call'd Eve.

This Tradition confirms the Vision of the Prophet; and we need not doubt, that the Earth was
in-

inhabited before Adam's time : And if that be granted, Why might it not be peopled for millions of ages, as well as for the fmalleft term that ignorance or error may affign to its duration ?

I have difcourfed with feveral of the Jewifh Rabbi's, and Chriftian Doctors, on this fubject, men of abftrufe learning and fublime thoughts ; yet I can find but a few, who are emancipated from the prejudices cf a fuperftitious education. They have been, from their infancy, prepoffefs'd with a falfe notion of the Works of God ; believing them to be finite, both in extent of Space and Time. They circumfcribe this vifible World, within I know not what flaming Circle ; and believe the firft Matter itfelf, to be but five days older than Adam, taking each of thofe days for the fpace of four and twenty hours, wherein the fun finifhes his diurnal circuit through the heavens. They confider not, that, according to their own bible, there was Light and Darknefs, and confequently Day and Night, before the Sun was created. Eut how long thofe Days and Nights were, is not determin'd by Mofes : Yet in another part of their bibie, it is faid, That a Day with God is a Thoufand Years ; and a Thoufand Years is a Day. So that, according to this interpretation, Adam was not created till above five thoufand Years after the beginning of the world : Yet when I bring this pofitive place of their own Scripture againft the Nazarene Sages, they fhuffle it off with empty evafions ; and rather than believe the indefinite Antiquity of the World, they contradict their own fenfe and reafon, invalidate the teftimony of a Prophet, deny their Faith, and appear unmafk'd Infidels.

Both They and the Jews have corrupted the truth with many errors ; and we muft feek farther, for the original fcience of Nature. The Illuminated of God have always taught, That the Earth was inhabited long before the appearance of Adam.

And

And all the Eaftern Sages believe a Series of generations to have dwelt on this Globe for indeterminate ages.

I have a brother lately come from the Indies: He relates ftrange things of certain Books, which are only in the hands of the Brachmans. They are written in a Language, which none underftand but thefe Priefts ; yet a Language as copious as any other, and taught in their colleges by rule. Thefe Books contain a Hiftory of the World, which, they fay, is above thirty millions of years old. They divide the term of its duration into four Ages ; three of which, they fay, are already paft, and a good part of the fourth. Now I would fain know, Who wrote thefe Books ; and at what time, and where this Language was fpoken ? They call it the Holy Language ; faying, That it was the firft fpoken on Earth. It is ftrange, That no Hiftory fhould mention fo Divine a Speech. We have the Chronology of the Latin and Greek ; and can give an account when and where they were fpoken, though they are now grown obfolete, and no otherwife to be learned, but in the Schools and Academies. This argues the antiquity of the Bramins Language and Books, in regard they fall not within any other Record, fave their own, which fays, They are as old as the world. For if this affertion were falfe, the impofture would have been difcover'd as foon as broach'd, and the learned Sages of the Eaft would quickly have difproved fo manifeft a lie. There feems to me fomething extraordinary in this pretenfion of thefe Indian Philofophers, and I would gladly be convinced of the truth. Methinks it is an illuftrious Idea of the Divine Perfections, when one conceives all this vaft and endlefs concatenation of Beings, to flow from the Eternal Nature, as rays from the fun ; and that they can no more be feparated from it, than thofe beams can from that vifible Fountain of Light. It will not
be

be difficult then to interpret the History of Mofes, by this Regifter of the Bramins, and reconcile the fix Days of the one, with the four Ages of the other; fince a day, in the Divine fenfe, may amount to millions of years, as well as to a thoufand. And it will be more congruous and agreeable to believe, That after the birth of the firft Matter, there elaps'd many Ages, before it was wrought into fuch an infinite variety of appearances, as we now behold; and that the five Days which Mofes computes, before the Production of Adam, might be fome Millions of Years: In which time, the Divine Architect gradually drew from the Abyfs of Matter, the fun, moon, ftars, plants, and animals, which may ferve alfo to illuftrate the Vifion of thy holy Anceftor, with which I begun this Difcourfe.

Adieu, fublime Intelligence of the Torrid Zone, and favour Mahmut with a tranfcript of thy thoughts concerning thefe things. But if thy filence fhall condemn my prefumptions and importunity, I will wait for thy anfwer, till the Platonic Year, when, according to the Doctrine of that Philofopher, we fhall all be alive again.

Paris, 19th of the 4th Moon,
　of the Year 1648.

LET-

LETTER XIV.

To the Mufti.

IN a former Difpatch to thy Sanctity, I have acquainted thee with the Infurrection in Palermo; mentioning the fear of the Viceroy, left the French in that Ifland fhould then take their opportunity to revenge the proverbial cruelty of the Sicilian Vefpers. If thou art unacquainted with that Tragedy, I will inform thee in brief.

About three hundred and threefcore years ago, there reign'd in Sicily one of the Royal Blood of France, they call him Charles of Anjou. He had French garrifons in all the cities of that kingdom: But thefe foldiers committed fo many infolencies as render'd 'em odious and infupportable to the Natives, who therefore refolv'd to exterminate them.

The French are very licentious in their Conquefts; neither fparing men in their anger, nor women in their luft. They make no difference between the Noble and the Vulgar, but facrifice all the regards of honour and civility, to their impetuous appetites.

They were guilty of innumerable rapes and violences in Sicily, among the meaner people, and fometimes extended their rudenefs to perfons of the beft quality. It was common for them to affront both virgins and matrons as they went along the ftreets, by tirufting their hands under their garments under pretence of fearching for hidden arms. Among the reft, the wife of a certain Lord in Palermo, going to pay her devotions at the Temple, was feiz'd by the command of the Captain of the Guards, and ftripp'd naked before all the foldiers, in order to difcover certain treafonable papers,
which

which they fufpected fhe carried about her; but finding none, fhe upbraided the Captain with inhumanity, in offering fo grofs an affront to a lady of her rank. He feeming to be forry for the indignity fhe had received, begg'd her pardon, and retiring with his foldiers out of the room where fhe was, left her to put on her apparel. In the mean while, he was enflam'd with a furious paffion for this lady, (fhe being very beautiful;) and having fent the foldiers away, he return'd to the room where fhe was. He addrefs'd her with much courtfhip; but finding that ineffectual, he forced her.

When this was made known to her hufband, he burn'd with defire of revenge; and ftirring up all the Sicilian Nobles and People, it was privately agreed between them, That on a certain Feftival, when the Bells fhould toll to Even-Song, all the Sicilians fhould take arms, and maffacre the French throughout the ifland. This plot was carried fo fecretly, That before the French could get the leaft intimation of it, they were all murder'd on the day appointed.

I forgot to acquaint thee in my laft, with a villany which was difcover'd in the late tumults of Naples. As they were marching up and down the ftreets, burning the Cuftom-houfes, and the habitations of thofe who had been concern'd in gathering the Taxes, they enter'd the Houfe of a certain Notary, or public Scribe of that city, who had been reprefented to them, as a promoter of thofe unreafonable Impofitions: They feized on the man, and began to carry his goods out into the ftreet, in order to be burnt: But as they were rummaging in an apartment which was towards the gardens, they heard a great fhrieking, as of women affrighted; and perceiving the voice to proceed from within a wall in the room where they were, they fearch'd about for a door to enter into that place, but finding none, they broke

through

through the wall; where they found two women with their hair hanging down to their ankles, and their nails grown like the talons of an eagle. Enquiring of them how long they had been there, and on what occasion, the eldest of the women made this answer: "The master of this house
" is my own brother, who, when my father died,
" was entrusted by him to pay me six hundred
" Ducats, which he bequeathed me as a legacy
" for my maintenance, my husband being dead:
" But my brother, instead of doing me this justice,
" immured both me and my daughter, whom you
" see here, between these walls, where we have
" lived these seventeen years, being allow'd by
" this cruel man, no other food but bread and
" water."

The people, incensed above measure at so barbarous a cruelty, hang'd up the Notary, and gave all his estate to this widow and her daughter. An exemplary piece of justice, perform'd by Mutineers, which could not have been done by the Law, the crime not reaching his life; tho' in the sense of all men he merited death. This is another argument, That Destiny had a hand in this Insurrection: and that Massaniello the Fisherman, was the Executioner of God.

I obey thee, sovereign Prelate, with an unconditional Devotion, and revere the Idea of thy Sanctity: Vouchsafe to pray for Mahmut, That whilst he condemns the barbarous cruelty of the Nazarenes, he may not render himself inexcusable, by doing any injustice himself.

Paris, 22d of the 5th Moon,
of the Year 1648.

LETTER XV.

To the Kaimacham.

THE Arabian Proverb fays, " There is more " danger to be feared from one of the Coreis " than from a thoufand Bobecks." Thou knoweft, both thefe were noble Families in Mecca, and fworn enemies of the Meffenger of God : But the latter, as their names import, were too open in their councils, to do any confiderable execution againft the Holy One : Whereas the former were always referved, and laying of fecret trains.

Such is Cardinal Mazarini, the hidden enemy of the Ottoman Empire. There feems to be an ambition in this great Genius, equal to that of his predeceffor Richlieu ; who would be efteem'd the moft eminent among men. Nothing will fatisfy this Minifter, lefs than a fubverfion of all the Monarchies on earth, which appear obftacles of that Grandeur, to which he defigns to raife his Mafter. Yet he attempts not this by open force, knowing that it is impracticable; but acts in the dark, ftriving to undermine thofe States by Intrigue, which he cannot fubdue by Arms. He has his Agents in all the Courts of Chriftendom ; and thou needeft not ftartle, if I tell thee there is ground to fufpect, he is not without his Creatures at the fublime Porte. All Europe is fenfible, That the late Revolutions in Portugal and Catalonia, the Infurrections in Sicily and Naples, and the Rebellion of the Englifh, Scots, and Irifh, are in part owing to the Policies of this Minifter : And I can tell thee more on that fubject than is known to every one.

Ofmin the Dwarf, who ftill retains his good inclinations to the fublime Porte, finds an unfufpected accefs to all the Grandees, to whom the fmallnefs

of

of his bulk and stature, affords no small divertisement. Besides, they delight to pose him with Problems, in regard there is always something so lucky, besides the wit, in his answers, as either creates admiration or laughter. But their mirth would quickly be chang'd into other passions, were they sensible that their little Buffoon is no other than a Spy upon them. For Osmin having so many opportunities, lurks in corners, like a spider, undiscover'd, and unthought of: He creeps into their bed-chambers and cabinets, where he becomes privy to their greatest secrets. If they should catch him in any of his concealments, behind the hangings, or under a bed, it would only pass for a frolic to give them diversion: And he never wants for a Repartee, or a Jest, to bring himself off.

I have taught him a Cypher, which he makes use of to transcribe any letters, or other papers of moment; with Characters for speedy Writing, which comprehend whole sentences in a dash or two of the pen.

'Tis but lately we have pitch'd on this method, and the first attempt Osmin made, was in Cardinal Mazarini's closet; into which he slipt, under the skirts of a Nobleman's cloak, who just then went in to speak with the Cardinal. This active Dwarf, taking advantage of the Nobleman's approach to the table, dextrously crept under the carpet which cover'd it, reaching down to the floor, where he lay unseen till the Cardinal was gone, and the closet lock'd up.

During the time of their conference, which was not very long, Osmin heard the Cardinal speak these words to the Lord: "One of the Slaves "of that Bassa, (says he) is an Italian, whom I "formerly entertain'd in my service, and one in "whom I confide: He was taken by the Turks "at sea; and as soon as he was sold to this "Grandee,

" Grandee, he acquainted me, in a let er, with
" his condition, imploring my affiftance towards
" his ranfom. I promis'd to redeem him, on
" the conditions I have told you ; and fince
" that, he has not fail'd to perform them ; his
" Mafter having accepted the Piftols, and en-
" tered in the Affociation : So that I hope in a
" little time, to fee that proud tyrannical Race
" exterminated, the Tartars excluded from fuc-
" ceffion, and the Empire divided by the Sword
" of Strangers. Ragotfki is the only obftacle ; that
" Prince is wavering, and we can't truft him.
" The Baffa of Aleppo, with thofe of Sidon,
" Damafcus, and Babylon, are ready to cover the
" fields of Afia with their armies. If things were
" as fecure on the fide of Europe, the Blow fhould
" foon be given."

There pafs'd fome other difcourfe between 'em
which Ofmin could not diftinguifh, in regard
they mov'd to the window, and fpoke low. But
this was enough to roufe his curiofity, and put
him on a farther inquifition.

As foon as the room was void by their abfence, he came forth from his retirement, and
fell to examining the papers which lay on the
table, hoping to difcover more of this Plot ; but
he was difappointed, and only met with a few
letters from his Agents in England : Wherein
among other matters, they gave the Cardinal
an account " That they had hunted the Lion
" into the Toils, paft all hopes of an efcape."
By which, I fuppofe, they meant the Englifh
King, whom the rebels have confined to a certain caftle in their poffeffion. Ofmin tranfcribed
fome of thefe letters, and brought them to me.
A copy of one of them, I here fend thee en-
clofed : 'Twas written from the Council of the
Irifh Rebels. By which thou may'ft fee, what
a fhare the Cardinal has in abetting thefe Traitors. Elfe how could they demand of him, the
                                         per-

performance of the Queen Regent's promise to assist them with money and men?

There is one also dated this present year, and subscribed by Monsieur Bellieure, the French ambassador in England: But Osmin had not time to transcribe that, being prevented by the Cardinal's return, which made the Dwarf snatch up his tools, and abscond under the table. Yet he remember'd some of the contents of that letter, and told them me at his next visit: The ambassador, in that letter, informs the Cardinal of a certain German Prophet, who foretold, "That there should be a great revolution in "the government of England, and that one of the "mightiest of all the Eastern Princes should be "deposed this year, and murder'd by his sub-"jects." (I pray Heaven, avert the Omen from "the Seraglio!) He acquaints this minister also, That he had succeeded in his negotiation with the officers of the rebels army. There were other obscure passages in the letter, which Osmin has forgot. But these are sufficient to demonstrate, how busy the Cardinal is, and what a hand he has in foreign affairs.

Another opportunity, I hope, will bring to light more of this minister's secrets. Adieu.

Paris, 4th of the 6th Moon,
of the Year 1648.

L E T T E R XVI.

To Peſteli Hali, his Brother.

THE oftner I peruſe the Journal of thy Travels, the more I am delighted with it. For it is evident, That the Countries through which thou haſt paſs'd, have been as ſo many Schools of Wiſdom to thee; wherein thou haſt learn'd, even from mens Vices, the way to Perfection; much more from their Virtues. Thou haſt found, That though mens natural diſpoſitions differ, as do the Climates, which afford them breath; yet they all agree in common Frailties. There are alſo Vices peculiar to certain Countries; 'twere to be wiſh'd they could be match'd with as many national Virtues. But Human Nature is a rank Soil, more fertile in Weeds, than wholeſome Products. Yet there are Gardens, as well as Deſarts: And thou haſt obſerved ſome perſons, illuſtrious for their goodneſs, and the noble endowments of their minds.

I am extremely pleaſed with that rare example of generoſity, which thou relateſt of an Indian merchant; who, not content to give alms to all that aſk'd him, or whom he knew to be poor, ſought daily occaſions to exerciſe his charity, hunted out the indigent and unfortunate: And where-ever he diſcovered the lineaments of poverty in a man's face, or traced footſteps of it in his behaviour, he could not reſt till he had reliev'd his wants, and made him happy to his very wiſhes. I tell thee, Poverty is a Hell upon Earth; and he that has this curſe, anticipates the Torments of the Damn'd. It eclipſes the brighteſt virtues, and is the very ſepulchre of brave deſigns, depriving a man of

the

the means to accomplifh, what Nature has fitted him for, and ftifling the noblest thoughts in their Embryo. How many illuftrious fouls may be faid to have been dead among the living, or buried alive in the obfcurity of their condition, whofe perfections have rendered them the Darlings of Providence, and Companions of Angels; yet the infuperable penury of all things, has rank'd them among the Caft-aways of the Earth, in the eyes of men! To fuch as thefe our divine Law-giver commands us to extend our charity, giving us certain characters and marks, by which we may diftinguifh them from the crowd of the unfortunate. And, I like the Indian's bounty the better, in that he fo exactly feems to, comply with this Precept of the Alcoran, generoufly preventing the requefts of the indigent, and by an excefs of benignity, courting them to accept of relief. In this he alfo verifies the Arabian proverb, which fays "He gives double "who gives unafk'd."

Thou commendeft the induftry of the Chinefe, the advances they have made in arts and fciences, which, thou concludeft, is to be attributed to the force of their Laws, which oblige the fon to follow his father's trade, throughout all generations. In this I muft diffent; for it feems rather a curb, than a fpur to ingenuity, to be confin'd to employments, for which a man may have an averfion. The fon not feldom abhorring thofe things, wherein his parents took delight. Or, if not fo, yet he may be caft in a finer mould, have a more fubtle invention; and confequently, be capable of making greater improvements, in any trade of his own choice: Since delight fets an edge on the mind, gives vigour to the body, and adds wings to bufinefs. Befides, I do not think this to be fo much thy own remark, as the infinuation of fome of that country, who are the moft conceited people in

5   the

the world: Ever extolling their own Policy, Laws, and Government; and impofing them as a pattern to all other nations.

One thing I grant they boaft of with a great deal of truth, that is, their antiquity and un-mix'd race. Though fince the Conqueft the Tartars have made of that country, they are like to undergo the fate of other nations, and corrupt their Genealogies with the Blood of Strangers.

Thou cameft away before that Conqueft was begun, or, perhaps, before 'twas talk'd of. And I can give thee but a very imperfect account of it. All the intelligence we have from that kingdom of late, comes in fragments: For the fhips which bring this fhatter'd news, left China in an uproar and confufion: Only they affure us, That the Tartars had paffed the celebrated Wall, which divides them from China: That they enter'd and fubdued the Northern Provin-ces, with an army of fix hundred thoufand men. That very little refiftance was made againft them, not even in Pequin itfelf, the Capital Seat of the Chinefe Empire, which the ufurper Ly-cungz had abandon'd to the Conquerors, carry-ing away with him all the ineftimable treafures of the palace, and retiring into one of the re-mote Provinces, was never heard of afterwards. Whence it was judged, that fome of his own party had murder'd him; partly for the fake of his prodigious wealth, which they fhared among them; and partly to revenge his Treafon againft the Emperor, and the innumerable calamities he had brought upon his country.

Before thofe merchants came away, the Cham of Tartary was proclaim'd in Pequin, and crown'd Emperor of China. They fay, He was not above thirteen years old at that time, which was in the 12th Moon of the year 1644. And that having fent for the chief Nobility of Tartary

to

to Pequin, he made preparations to pursue his conquests.

This is the best account we yet have of the affairs of that Empire; by which thou wilt easily be induced to be of my opinion, That the Blood of the Chinefes, will in time be mix'd with that of Strangers.

We must not feek for the originals of any people in the country where they dwell. The most renown'd Kingdoms and Empires in the World, had their first foundations laid by Vagabonds and Fugitives. Thou art not ignorant how vast an extent the ancient Roman Empire had through Afia, Africa, and Europe; yet that city, which was call'd the Miftrefs of Nations, the Governefs of the whole Earth, was first built by a handful of Banditti, people who lived by pillage and robbery, the out-laws and fcum of Italy, affembled together from divers parts, under the conduct of Romulus and Rhemus. Neither had that city proved any better than a fepulchre to them and their defigns, had they not, by a witty ftratagem, over-reach'd the Sabine women, and fo fecured to themfelves a pofterity, who fhould not only defend, but enlarge the dominions of their fathers: Yet thefe people, of fo obfcure and confufed an original, afterwards boafted of their antiquity and noble defcent of their families. No name more venerable in fucceeding ages, than that of a Roman.

To look no farther than the great and formidable empire of the Ofmans, we fhall find it took its first rife from colonies of tranfplanted Scythians; fo that he that would have the genealogy of a Turk, must not only look in the regifters of Greece, where they now live, but must carry his fearch beyond the mountain Caucafus, examine the borders of Palus Mœotis, or hunt his pedigree out in Cherfonefus. What revolutions have not happen'd in Afia and Afric, fince the affump-

affumption of the Meffenger of God into Paradife? Where fhall we now find any remains of
the ancient Saracens or Marmadukes? The mighty
Empire of the Ottomans has fwallow'd up all.
Thus one nation expels another, and, there is
fo general a mixture of foreign blood, made by
the converfion of innumerable different nations,
to the Muffulman Faith, that it is hard to know,
whether our Anceftors were Scythians or Par-
thians, Jews or Grecians, whether they were of
the mountains or the valleys, of the forefts or the
plains.

In this I will except my countrymen, the Arabians, and thofe who feem to approach neareft
them in manner of life, the Tartars; the one
dwelling in tents, the other in waggons: Both in
a moving pofture; both happy in this, That
they are not confin'd to the rigors of a cold
Winter, nor the fcorching heats of the Summer;
but change their foil and climate, as the feafon of the year varies: Thus, ever fecuring to
themfelves in all places, either a blooming flow'ry
Spring, or a moderate and fruitful Autumn.
Thefe were never fubdued, nor expell'd thofe
regions wherein they take delight, neither would
they ever mix with Strangers. But the Chinefe would excel all the World in the Purity
of their unmix'd Blood, were it not for the
incurfions of their potent and victorious neighbours.

The French fay, That thefe People had the
ufe of Guns and Printing, many hundreds of
years before they were found out in Europe: But
the Germans claim the honour of thefe Inventions
to themfelves.

Thou confirmeft the opinion of the former, in
telling me, Thou haft feen fome of the cannon belonging to the city of Pequin, on which
was engraven, in Chinefe Characters, a Regifter
of their Age, which was above two thoufand
years.

M 3

I had

I had a great deal more to fay, dear Pefteli, but the Poft calls on me to haften; befides an extreme dulnefs and languifhing of my fpirits, with which I have been perfecuted, ever fince this Moon firft fhewed her Crefcent : Now fhe is in the wane, and fo, I hope, is my malady. The influence this Planet feems to have on me, may make thee conclude me a Lunatic : We are all fo in one degree or other. There are not more apparent fymptoms, That the flux and réflux of the fea, owes its original to the neighbourhood and motion of that Planet, than that our conftitutions vary according to its Monthly Appearances.

He that created the Moon, and the Conftellations, not without refpect to Mankind, give us. Wifdom which fhall entitle us to a Dominion over the Stars.

Paris, 14th of the 8th Moon,
of the Year 1648.

LETTER XVII.

To the Aga of the Janizaries.

THE Duke of Chaftillon arrived here fix days ago, from the army in Flanders, bringing news of a fignal victory obtain'd by the young Prince of Conde, on the Plains of Lens. This battle was fought on the 20th of the laft Moon, the French having entirely routed the Spaniards, kill'd three thoufand of them on the fpot, taken fix thoufand of them prifoners, with all their artillery and baggage. And, to crown the day, they have taken Lens alfo :

But

But though Fortune thus favours their arms abroad, she has mix'd poison with their counsels at home. All things here seem to portend a Civil War : The Parliament thwart the proceedings of the Court, taking on them the power of the ancient Spartan Ephori : They will be comptrollers of the Regal authority, suppressing the King's Edicts, calling his expences to account; and, pretending to reform the Court, they play the Pedagogues with their Sovereign. On the other side, Cardinal Mazarini, the Duke of Orleans, and other Grandees, do their utmost endeavours to dissolve the meetings of this Senate. They perfuade the young King, That it is but a precarious reign, where the Sovereign must be curb'd by his subjects : Thus they instil into his tender years, those maxims by which they would have him rule, when he comes of age.

There is a man in the Parliament whom they call Monsieur Bruffels, one of their great counsellors, a bitter enemy of Cardinal Mazarini, and therefore cry'd up by the People for a Patriot : He is of a furious temper, and mean abilities ; yet his noisy zeal for the public Liberty, has fasten'd to him the vulgar : He is become the Ringleader of the seditious.

This man was seiz'd as he return'd from the chief Temple, where Te Deum was sung yesterday, for the late victory in Flanders : And some are of opinion, That 'twas this happy news which embolden'd the Court to snatch from the people their Darling, their Idol, the man from whose courage they expect a redress of all their grievances. Indeed one may say, it would seem safer for a traveller in the defarts of Arabia, to tear from a Lioness her young one : For, the Heads of the Faction waited but for such an opportunity to set all in a flame. And the ill success of the Court in this action, shews, That

It

it is dangerous to provoke the Multitude: For prefently we were all in confufion, the Burgeffes in arms, the fhops fhut up, the ftreets chain'd, and all the avenues of the palace barricado'd: The Rabble march'd up and down the ftreets, threatening deftruction to Cardinal Mazarini, and all his party. The Parliament were forced to become the Meffengers of the People, to carry their Petitions, or rather their Commands, to the Court; being threaten'd alfo, if they fail'd of fuccefs: For they protefted unanimoufly, That they would not lay down their arms, 'till the imprifon'd Counfellor was releafed.

The Queen appear'd at firft inexorable, and fent their Senators away with denial and fcoffs, wifhing them joy of their new honour in being made the Porters of the Rabble. And the young Monarch, incenfed to fee his native Royalty thus profaned by his Subjects, bent his brows; and cafting a look, divided betwixt majefty and difdain, on the Senators, utter'd thefe words, " Sirs! Shall it always be a cuftom, thus " to moleft the Minority of your Kings? Or do " you think our tender years incapable of the " common fenfe of other mortals, that you pre- " fume thus infolently to invade our rights? " Accufe not the Multitude, nor make them an " umbrage to your Sedition: I know the au- " thors of thefe tumults, and fhall find a time " to make them feel the weight of my difplea- " fure: Think not I wear this Sword only for " Ornament, [laying his hand fiercely on his hilt] " or, That the Blood of my renown'd Anceftors, " is grown degenerate, or turned to lees within " my veins. Go, tell your factious comrades, " there fits this day upon the Throne of France, " a King, who though he's young, yet has a " fpirit and memory which will out-laft his pu- " pilage." With that he commanded them out of his fight.

Yet

Yet notwithstanding this, the People threatened to bring their Darling away by force, if he were not released in two hours.

There were above a hundred thousand of them, in arms, and it might have proved a dangerous Insurrection. But, the Queen, at the second return of the Senators, hearkening to the advice of Mazarini, and the Duke of Orleans, and remembering the late dreadful effects of Massaniello's tumult in Naples, releas'd the prisoner; who was conducted home last night in triumph, by an infinite croud of people, who fill'd the air with shouts and acclamations.

It is discoursed here, that the Prince of Conde will speedily return to Paris : From whom, both the Court and the Faction, promise themselves new grounds of triumph.

During these commotions, Mahmut fails not to act his part, being at no small expence to maintain a certain number of strangers, whose whole dependence is on me : These I instruct to mix themselves with the rabble, to insinuate into them hateful notions of Cardinal Mazarini and the Court. They buz up and down the city, like flies in this hot season, and sting the multitude to fury with their stories. I spare no cost to procure the Cardinal's ruin : That pernicious Wit comes not short of his predecessor Richlieu, being as active in embroiling foreign States : witness the Revolutions of Portugal, Catalonia, England and Naples ; (in all which he had a principal hand) and is ever projecting, How to aggrandize his Master. And the universal success of the French arms in Germany, Flanders, Italy and Spain, has left nothing worth a thought, but the destruction of the Ofman Empire.

Eliachim brings me news every hour, how my Myrmidons succeed, for he acts abroad in the streets, while I keep my chamber, during

the

the tumults, being of Demofthenes's mind, who, when the Athenians were in an uproar, took Sanctuary in the Temple of Pallas, and proftrating himfelf before the altar of the Goddefs, utter'd thefe words; "O Pallas, I fly to thee "for protection: Defend me from ignorance, "envy, and inconftancy; for I love not the "fociety of the Owl, the Dragon, and the Peo- "ple."

Yet, whether in my chamber or abroad, be affured, illuftrious Prefect of the Imperial City, That Mahmut divides his time between the vows e makes, and the fervices he does for the Grand Signior.

Paris, 3d of the 9th Moon,
of the Year 1648.

LETTER XVIII.

To Achmet Beig.

THIS Court is now in Mourning for the death of Uladiſlaus, late King of Poland: whilft the Politicians are canvafing the next Election. Thofe who fide with the Houfe of Auftria favour the fucceffion of Prince Charles; but the French are for Cafimir, their former prifoner.

The Duke of Bavaria is alfo dead. They fay he died of grief to fee his country expofed to the infults of a victorious enemy; for all his forces were entirely defeated.

The Prince of Conde has taken Ipre in Flanders; and the Arch-Duke of Auftria has render'd him-

himſelf maſter of Courtray, without drawing a ſword, or firing a gun : The Mareſchal de Rantzau has made an unhappy attempt to ſurprize Oſtend, a ſea-town in Flanders. For, carrying his forces by water, as ſoon as he had landed his men, a tempeſt aroſe, and drove all his ſhips out to ſea : ſo that, being encompaſſed by a numerous army of his enemies, and having no way to eſcape, he and all his troops were made priſoners.

From the ſea we have advice, That there has been a combat between the Duke of Richlieu, commander of the naval forces ſent to aſſiſt the Neapolitan Revolters, and Don John of Auſtria, Admiral of the Spaniſh fleet on that coaſt : But the iſſue of the battle is not yet known ; tho' moſt people gueſs the victory to be on the French ſide, in regard Cardinal Mazarini had, by the advice of an Indian ſhip-wright, cauſed all the French ſhips to be plaiſter'd over with Alum, ſo that no fire-ſhips can hurt them. The Spaniards make great uſe of theſe fire-ſhips in all their ſea-fights, having learn'd to their coſt from the Engliſh, what damage theſe veſſels do, when they formerly loſt their whole Armada, which they before term'd Invincible, and with which they failed to conquer that Iſland.

From Catalonia the poſts bring news, which pleaſes the wives and friends of the ſoldiers in theſe parts : For the Mareſchal de Schomberg has cut in pieces the Spaniſh army, taken Tortoſa by aſſault, where the ſoldiers found a booty of above fifteen hundred thouſand Livres.

A courier is come from Swedeland, who brings an account of a late formidable Conſpiracy in Ruſſia, againſt the life of the Czar. The greateſt part of the Muſcovite Grandees were concern'd in this plot, deſigning to change the Form of Government, and divide that mighty Em-

Empire into feveral Principalities, whereof every one of the Confpirators fhould have a fhare; And that they fhould be all fubject to one Chief, who fhould be elected by the reft, after the manner of Germany. To this purpofe, they had made a private Treaty with the Tartars. Morofoph, the prime Minifter of State, and the Chancellor Nazari, were of the Confpiracy. Perhaps thou wilt lament the Fate of the latter, having received extraordinary civilities from him, when thou wert at that Court.

Banaanoph, fon of the Patriarch of Mofco, revealed the Plot, with the names of the Confpirators, to the grand Duke: Who fent to them next day to his palace, under divers pretences, where he commanded them all to be kill'd, and their bodies to be thrown to the dogs in the ftreets of that city.

The French report ftrange things of Sultan Ibrahim: I wifh all go well at the fublime Port. If thou haft the fame defires, reveal them to none but thy friends; for at fome times a man's beft thoughts will be interpreted for Treafon. Adieu.

Paris, 15th of the 10th Moon,
    of the Year 1648.

LETTER XIX.

To the Mufti.

THY venerable letters are come fafe to my hands, bringing light and confolation to the faithful Exile. With profound reverence I kifs'd and unfolded the papers which contain the facred inftructions of the Vicar of God. I bleffed my-felf, when I read the charge of royal enormi-ties, the exorbitant paffions of a Muffulman Em-peror, and the profanation of the Throne found-ed on Juftice. Thou haft prevented the qualms of a too fcrupulous loyalty, by affuring me, That it is a fundamental maxim of our Law, " That " all men in the world, without refpect of birth " or quality, are obliged to appear before the " juftice of God : And, that he who obeys not " the law, is no Muffulman : And, if the Em- " peror himfelf be in this number, he ought to be " depofed forthwith."

This has abundantly fatisfied my confcience, coming from the hands of him, from whofe Sen-tence there can be no Appeal on Earth. I fhall therefore readily obey thy orders ; and without demur, put in execution what thou haft command-ed me.

Who can blame the juft indignation of Sultan Morat's widow, who in defence of her chaftity, threatened to fheath her poniard in the breaft of her Sovereign ? But, incomparably more eminent was thy daughter's virtue, who not being able to refift the force of the mighty Ravifher, after fhe was polluted, would, like another Lucretia, have ftabb'd herfelf, had fhe not been prevented by the Sultan. How has he fully'd the glory of

the

the Ofman race by thefe effeminate vices : What
an indignity has he committed againft our holy
Law ! Againft the principal Patriarch of the Elect!
Much more noble was the continence of the African Scipio, who, when at the conqueft of New
Carthage, a virgin of admirable beauty was chofen
from among the captives, and prefented to him,
would by no means defile her, but reftor'd her again
without blemifh to her parents, faying withal, to
thofe who ftood near him. " Were I a private
" Man, I would gratify my paffion, by the en-
" joyment of this lovely maid; but it becomes
" not the leader of an army, to give fo bad an
" example; nor a conqueror to yield his heart
" to the charms of his captive."

But it feems, that Sultan Ibrahim was rather
ambitious of the character of Auguftus the Roman
Emperor, of whom it is faid, That he never fpared
any woman in his luft : But if he caft his eye on a
beautiful lady, though her hufband were of the
firft quality in the Empire, he would immediately
fend his officers to bring her to him by fair means,
or by force.

The Philofopher Athenodorus, who was very
intimate with this Monarch, took a pretty method
to reform this vice in his mafter. For, when the
Emperor had one day fent a clofe Sedan or Chair
for a certain Noble Woman, of the houfe of the
Camilli ; the Philofopher, fearing fome difafter
might enfue, (for that Family was very popular, and highly refpected in Rome,) goes before to the lady's palace, and acquainting her
with it, fhe complain'd to her hufband of the
indignity that was offer'd her. He boiling with
anger, threaten'd to ftab the meffengers of the Emperor when they came. But the prudent Philofopher appeas'd them both, and only defir'd a fuit of
the lady's apparel, which was granted him. He
foon put it on, and hiding his fword under his
robes, enter'd the Sedan, perfonating the lady. The
mef-

meſſengers who knew no other, carried him away to the Emperor. He heighten'd with defire, made hafte to open the Sedan himfelf, when Athenodorus, fuddenly drawing his fword, leap'd forth upon him, faying, "Thus mighteft thou have been murder'd: Wilt thou never quit the vice, which is "attended with fo much danger? Jealoufy and re-"venge might have fubftituted an Aſſaſſin thus "difguifed in my room: But I took care of thy "life. Henceforth take warning." The Emperor pleas'd with the Philofopher's ftratagem, gave him ten talents of gold, thanking him for this feafonable correction: And from that time began to reftrain unlawful pleafures, applying himfelf to a virtuous life.

Thou feeft, holy Prelate, that by perufing the Hiftories of the Ancients, a man may furnifh himfelf with ufeful examples, and proper obfervations. I always keep by me Plutarch's works, and thofe of Livy, a Roman Hiftorian; as alfo Tacitus, who has left the Annals of that formidable Empire to pofterity. It were a defirable thing, That the Muſſulman fcribes were employ'd in tranflating fuch Records as thefe, into the Arabic or Turkifh Languages: That fo the True Faithful, who are deftin'd by God to conquer the World, may not be ignorant of the memorable tranfactions of former ages. Some of our Sultans have been curious to have Plutarch's Writings render'd in the familiar fpeech of the Ottomans. There are other Memoirs, not lefs worth the labour. If it fhall enter into thy heart, to encourage fo profitable a work, the whole Empire of the Refign'd to God, will be indebted to thee. But, who am I, that prefume to direct the great Father of the Faithful? Thou art enlighten'd with all knowledge and wifdom? Peradventure thou haft reafons to divert thee from fuch an enterprize, which I cannot comprehend. Therefore I cover my mouth with duft, and acquiefce.

As

As to the late Revolution, I am not to difpute the Will of my Superiors. However, I receive the news of that Tragedy with lefs difcontent, in regard, thou thyfelf, who art the Oracle of the Muffulmans, haft thought fit to depofe Sultan Ibrahim; ufing herein the advice and confent of his own Mother, and of Mahmut Baffa; with that of the Janizar Aga, who, next to thyfelf, are two the moft knowing Sages in the Empire.

What remains, but that I fhall pray for the long life of Sultan Mahomet? Defiring alfo, That Heaven may direct his counfels, that he may never do any thing to merit the Fate of his unhappy Father.

Paris, 13th of the 11th Moon,
   of the Year 1648.

LETTER XX.

To Chiurgi Muhammel, Baffa.

AT length the Deputies of the Nazarene Princes at Munfter have concluded a Peace: They have been thefe fix years debating about Trifles and Punctilio's, as is the manner of the Chriftians, even in the moft important affairs. This Treaty was figned the 24th of the laft Moon, when all farther hoftilities ceafed on all fides, except on the parts of France and Spain, whofe quarrel could by no means be adjufted, in this general agreement of Chriftendom.

Thou haft by this time heard of the late tumults and emotions in this City; the difaffection between the Court and Parliament; with the fhort fiege of Paris. Now things feem to be compos'd,
and

and in a calm : But it may only prove a truce, while both parties take breath, to rush upon each other with the greater violence. The City is unmeasureably rich and populous, and can arm an hundred thousand men at an hour's warning. The parliament abets their quarrel : This encourages them to vie with the Court : The Merchants live like petty Kings : Abundance of gold fills them with pride and ambition. Whilst the Court, in the mean time, are close and reserv'd, projecting how to destroy the faction, and assert the regal authority. The Queen Regent is resolute and severe, yet suffers herself to be mollify'd with the milder counsels of Cardinal Mazarini, and the Duke of Orleans.

In the beginning of this Reign, I gave an account to the Ministers of the Port, of the Duke of Beaufort's imprisonment in the Castle of the Wood of Vinciennes, which is one of the King's Palaces: This Prince is now escap'd from his confinement, and come into the city. The Factious cry him up for a Patriot, and are resolv'd to protect him with their lives and fortunes.

If thou yet retainest thy health and vigour, thou art happy. As for me, I feel continual decays ; yet am not troubled, perceiving at the same time that I approach nearer to Immortality. Wherefore I neither seek restoratives, nor consult Physicians ; but suffering myself to dissolve gradually, I die with pleasure, pluming and preparing myself daily, as one ready to take wing for a more happy Region.

Paris, 24th of the 12th Moon,
   of the Year 1648.

LETTER XXI.

To Dgnet Oglou.

I AM not furpriz'd at the news of Sultan Ibrahim's being depofed and ftrangled. 'Tis but what I have for a long time fear'd: The reftlefs Janizaries will ruin the Ottoman Empire. Neither am I ftartled to hear that his Mother was acceffary to his fall, having a double motive, ambition and revenge, to induce her confent. She always affected to rule; and therefore, could not brook the Sultan's refolute management of affairs, without following her advice. Befides, fhe could not eafily forget her difgrace and confinement on the account of the Armenian lady's death.

But I am aftonifh'd and vex'd to hear, that the Mufti fhould be concern'd in fo black a Tragedy. How fhall we have the confidence hereafter, to reproach the Chriftians with their frequent Treafons and Murdering of their Kings; fince it will be eafy for them to retort, That the fupreme Patriarch of our Law has enter'd into the Secret of Rebels, confpired the death of his Sovereign, and caufed him to be depofed and ftrangled.

As for the Aga of the Janizaries, I fuppofe him rather over-aw'd into a confpiracy, by the forcible reafons and elegant parole of the Mufti, than any ways voluntarily engaging himfelf in crimes, to which he feems to have no inclination. Befides, he could not refufe to make one in the Party, after it had once been propofed to him; unlefs he were refolv'd to be the firft Victim of their jealoufy, and be murder'd himfelf, to prevent the difcovery of the reft. Yet his duty and honour ought to have fuperfeded all other confiderations: And he fhould
have

have chofen to die in his allegiance, rather than to live ftain'd with fo foul a crime.

However it be, I cannot approve their Treafon. For whatever the Vices of the Sultan were, they had no right to punifh him. He was accountable to none but God : And they invaded the Prerogative of Heaven, in dethroning him, whom the Divine Providence had invefted with the Imperial Diadem.

Much lefs can I approve their impiety, in defaming him now he is dead. Neither can I in confcience comply with the injunctions of the Mufti, who has commanded me, in a letter, to fpread an ill character of Sultan Ibrahim, among the Chriftians, that fo his own proceedings may appear juft. 'Tis true, I owe much to the authority of this fovereign Guide of true Believers ; yet I muft not, to pay this debt, turn bankrupt of my reafon: I owe fomething to myfelf, and to the diftinguifh-ing Character of a Man. I promifed him, indeed, to obey his commands in this point : But he that has given me a Difpenfation for all the lies and per-juries I fhall be guilty of in Paris, will, I hope, pardon me, if I turn my own Confeffor, and ab-folve myfelf, for not performing my word to him in this point.

I am not often guilty of afperfing the living, but I abhor to injure the dead ; left I fhould incur the Fate of him, who being at enmity with a famous Wreftler, purfued him with malice and revenge, even in his grave. For envying the honour that was due to this Wreftler's memory, in that his Statue was fet up in a public place, he went privately one night, with a defign to throw the Statue down : But after he had fpitefully disfigured it in feveral parts with a hammer, and was bufy in working its overthrow ; the Image on a fudden fell on him, and cruffi'd him to death : As if the Spirit of him whom it reprefented, had given it this fall, to revenge the malice of his adver-fary.

Cer-

Certainly, the Ancients were not ignorant what they said, when among other sage counsels they advised mortals, " Not to speak ill of the dead, " but to esteem them sacred, who are gone into " the immortal state." And Plato's Ring had this motto on it : " It is easier to provoke the dead, " than to pacify them, when once provoked." Intimating thereby, that the Souls of the Departed are sensible of the injuries that are done them by the Living.

Therefore I will shun detraction, especially of the Dead. And, if I cannot say much in praise of Sultan Ibrahim's Virtues, let his Vices be buried with him in eternal Oblivion.

I run no hazards in writing thus frankly to thee, being assured of thy fidelity. Besides, death (which is the worst punishment can be inflicted on me for what I have said, should it be known,) would not be bitter, when given by a friend. Dear Dgnet, adieu.

Paris, 20th of the 1st Moon,
of the Year 1649.

LETTER XXII.

To Danecmar Kesrou, Kadilesquer of Romania.

WHEN I informed thee how the Scots had sold their King to the English Rebels, it was easy to presage the consequence, without a Revelation. When Sovereign Monarchs become the merchandize of Factions, they commonly pay the Price with their own Blood : And there are few examples of Princes that have been imprison'd by
their

their Subjects, and yet have escaped a violent death: For those who have once advanced so far in their Treason, as to seize the Person of their Sovereign, can never retire with safety to themselves, or at least their own guilt makes them think so. The consciousness of what they have already done, prompts them to proceed in their wickedness: And their despair of saving their own lives, makes them conclude it necessary to take away his, whose violated Majesty, they fear, will never pardon so impudent an essay of Treason.

But the method which the English have taken to murder their King, has not a Precedent in history: These Infidels have out-stripp'd all former Traitors, in the contrivance and execution of their Regicide: They have even surpassed themselves, and their own first designs.

It has been usual for Traitors, to take away the life of a depos'd Monarch privately, by poison or assassin, either in respect to his royal Blood, or to avoid the possibility of a rescue, from any of his loyal friends and subjects. But, these Barbarians were resolved publicly to insult on Majesty, to brave the whole world in the execution of their villany, and make a pompous conclusion of their Treasons. For, they erected a new Divan or Court of Judicature, composed of the most infamous traitors: There they formally try'd their Sovereign, by a Law of their own making: condemn'd him as a tyrant and a traitor: And finally, caused his head to be chopt off with an axe, by an Executioner, before the gates of his own palace, in the sight of thousands of his subjects; that so they might appear, not so much to kill their King, as to destroy the Monarchy itself, and triumph in its ruin.

Hast thou, O venerable Judge of the Faithful, ever read or heard of such a daring treason? All Europe startles at the monstrous fact. And Cardinal Mazarini himself, who carried on that private

web

web of factious defign in England, whofe firft threads his Predeceffor Richlieu had fpun; yet ex- preffed an horror, at the news of this tragedy. And, I look not on this to be an artifice of policy in him to blind the world; but a real difcovery of his fen- timents: For he is too generous to approve fo bar- barous a proceeding againft a Sovereign Monarch, though his enemy.

T'other day he was heard to fay, " That in re- " venge of the King's murder, he would embarrafs " the counfels of the Englifh Rebels, more than " he had done thofe of their Sovereign."

This was not fpoken fo fecretly, but Mahmut had intelligence of it within an hour: For I have more ears in Paris, than thofe on my head, to hearken after the Intrigues of this Minifter: And it will be difficult for him hereafter to fpeak, write, or act any thing; no, not even in his private clofet, which will not be difclofed to me.

Yet, though I thus watch his motions as an enemy, and do my utmoft to render his defigns againft the Ottoman Port ineffectual, I cannot in my heart condemn this Minifter, who all the while acts but the part of a faithful Servant, and an able Statefman, in ftriving to aggrandize his Mafter.

His fupporting alfo the Factions in England, and nourifhing the difcontents of that giddy headed People, were but the refult of his zeal for his Country, and for the Church, whereof he is one of the principal Pillars: It being evident from his grief at that King's murder, That he bore no ma- lice againft him, but only fought to humble him into terms of compliance with France.

When I fay this, I fuppofe the Cardinal's forrow on that account, to be free from fiction: But who knows when the actions of Statefmen are un- difguis'd, and when not! For I am well affured, That whilft his Agents were bufy in embroiling that nation, he promifed the exiled Englifh Queen, to affift her hufband with men and money againft
thofe

thofe very Rebels, with whom he held a private correfpondence, and to whom his coffers were really open.

Moft of the European Statefmen are corrupted with the Maxims of a certain famous Writer, whom they call Machiavel. This State Cafuift has taught them, to boggle at no crimes, which may advance the ends they aim at ; every thing, in his opinion, being honeft, that is fuccefsful. Thus, Policy among the Nazarenes, is degenerated into fordid Craft : And that which was once defervedly efteem'd a Virtue neceffary to the government of the World, is now turn'd into a Vice ; of which the very out-laws, free-booters, and pirates, are afham'd.

God, who fuffer'd the earth to be inhabited by Angels, for an infinite number of ages before he created Adam, and then expelling them hence for their wickednefs, and turning them to Devils, gave this Globe for a dwelling place to Men ; grant, That the enormous crimes of Mortals may not provoke him to exterminate our human Race, and reftore the Devils to their ancient Habitations.

Paris, 12th of the 2d Moon,
    of the Year 1649.

The END of the THIRD VOLUME.